skin

EUROPEAN PERSPECTIVES

EUROPEAN PERSPECTIVES

A Series in Social Thought and Cultural Criticism

Lawrence D. Kritzman, Editor

European Perspectives presents outstanding
books by leading European thinkers.
With both classic and contemporary works,
the series aims to shape the major intellectual
controversies of our day and to facilitate the
tasks of historical understanding.

For a complete list of books in the series,
see pages 291–292

skin on the cultural border between self and the world

Claudia Benthien

Translated by Thomas Dunlap

Columbia University Press New York

Columbia University Press
Publishers Since 1893
New York
Chichester, West Sussex

Originally published under the title *Haut: Literaturgeschichte, Körperbilder, Grenzdiskurse.* Copyright © 1999 by Rowohlt Taschenbuch Verlag GmbH, Reinbek bei Hamburg.

Library of Congress Cataloging-in-Publication Data

Benthien, Claudia, 1965–
    [Haut. English]
    Skin: on the cultural border between self and the
world / Claudia Benthien; translated by Thomas
Dunlap.
        p.   cm.—(European perspectives)
    Includes bibliographical references and index.
    ISBN 0–231–12502–X (cloth)
    1. Skin—Social aspects.   2. Skin—History.
3. Human skin color.   4. Body, Human—Social
aspects.   I. Title.   II. Series.

GN191 .B4613 2002
306.4—dc21

                            2002019396

Casebound editions of Columbia University Press books
are printed on permanent and durable acid-free paper.
Printed in the United States of America
c 10 9 8 7 6 5 4 3 2 1

contents

preface
to the
american
edition

It gives me great pleasure to be writing a preface to this American edition, the first translation of my book to appear in print. It is, I believe, no coincidence that an American publisher has taken an interest in my study, for along with the Annales School in France, American scholars have been at the forefront of efforts to write a cultural history of the body. Among important recent works one might mention the three-volume *Fragments for a History of the Human Body*, edited by Michael Feher, Romana Naddaff, and Nadia Tazi; Elaine Scarry's *The Body in Pain*; Barbara Stafford's *Body Criticism*; and Sander Gilman's writings on body, race, and gender.

I see two other reasons why the theme of the present book may be of particular interest to American readers: first, the phenomenon of skin colors, the hierarchy and value judgments connected with skin complexion, is still largely taboo in American society, despite the fact that skin colors are ubiquitous and obvious (see Russell, Wilson, and Hall 1993). Second, while the fetishization of perfectly unblemished, smooth, and youthful skin, as well as the self-marking and self-stigmatization of this skin (by piercings, tattoos, brandings, henna applications, and so on), are now found throughout Western culture, these phenomena originated in the United States. The idea that the skin as the outermost sheath, the corporeal "dress" of human beings, their visible and performative surface, can be modified is profoundly American; the notion that a person is stuck in his or her skin, which invariably determines one's identity—age, race, social status, and so on—and from which one cannot escape, is diametrically opposed to the American ideal of the autonomous and self-determined person. It is therefore no coincidence that it was American culture that gave birth to cosmetic surgery and tanning salons as fixtures of daily life—phenomena that caught on in Europe much more slowly.

Around the time when this book was first published in Germany, there were a large number of events with the human skin as their theme. Symposia on architectural theory examined the "skin" of buildings, psychoanalytical conferences discussed the "skin ego," the annual meetings of dermatological associations examined "skin in the arts," ecclesiastical educational academies planned symposia on the aesthetic and cultural theory of the body surface. Many German radio and TV stations have broadcast features on skin during the last few years. And this is by no means merely a German phenomenon. In the summer of 1999 the National Museum for Western Art, in Tokyo, put on an international conference with the title "The Faces of Skin." Here, art historians compared conceptions of skin in Western and Japanese art and examined the entire topic from the perspective of media theory. In 1999 the Museum of Natural History, in New York, opened an exhibition entitled "Body Art: Masks of Identity." The Kulturwissenschaftliche Institut, in Vienna, is currently preparing a large symposium on the myth of the flaying of Marsyas, where the violent removal of the skin will be discussed as a paradigm of artistic creation. Many other recent events could be mentioned. In addition, the popular media is increasingly discovering and taking seriously the constructive dimension in the perception of the body. Even science magazines have interviewed cultural historians, ethnologists, philologists, and art historians on this topic. It was therefore no surprise that the first review of this book appeared in a professional journal of dermatology. Perhaps skin, as the boundary between body and culture, could become the interface where the humanities and the sciences enter into an exemplary—and long overdue—discourse.

The reason this topic is now emerging with such urgency may have something to do with the fact that skin is understood less and less as a given. Instead, it is seen increasingly as a dress—something that is worn, something a person carries around. Skin is the place were boundary negotiations take place. From the Renaissance onward it has been considered the mirror of the soul and the projecting surface of the invisible inside. But the history of Western culture reveals that the relationship between the internal and the external has become increasingly problematic and confusing over the centuries. As a reflection of the inside, a canvas of psychological, emotional, or cognitive processes, the skin has for some time now been in a crisis. To be sure, our awareness of the unknowability of the other, of the potential divergence between the inner and the outer, between reality and appearance, has had little impact (so far) on the semantics of the skin: we still believe that something is true if it is naked, the absence of makeup is still seen as a mode of authenticity, and nakedness is still the ideal of the natural. "Only skin deep" connotes superficiality, and only that which gets under one's skin can truly touch or arouse a person. But the interplay of the visible and the invisible, of surface and depth, reveals itself by no means as natural. Rather, it is a relationship subject to a great many strategies of interpretation and staging. Nakedness is therefore not an ontological category but rather a relationship that always relates to something else. Consequently, what we define as skin is also profoundly shaped by history and culture—and this, precisely, is the topic of the present book.

One consequence of the current challenge to the "naturalness" of the skin is that "natural" hierarchies have become problematic—for example, the notion that people with light skin are "unmarked" because they stand outside the discourses on skin color. Especially in the United States, numerous studies over the last years have brought "whiteness" out of its invisibility and analyzed the constructive nature of what is considered "one's own." Similarly, in gender studies, "masculinity" has (at long last) become the focus of a good deal of research—as another one of those stubborn constructs that present themselves as neutral and against which the other (the female, the foreign, the asocial) stands out as marked, stigmatized, or deficient.

I hope that my approach to this topic, which moves back and forth between historical anthropology and cultural constructivism, will appeal to American readers. Many of the works that dominate the field of body history, especially in the United States, are broad in conception and rather theoretical in orientation. By contrast, in this book I am concerned with something very concrete: a close reading of central metaphors, topoi, and mental images that have shaped the Western relationship to one's own skin and the skin of others. Instead of large, abstract theses, I prefer a method that proceeds from the singular and takes great care in generalizing the insights it derives. It is my hope that my book will be followed by further work in this field, for many aspects that I examine only cursorily deserve comprehensive studies of their own. My brief analyses of works of art and literary texts are also limited to the concrete questions I raise, and it would surely be interesting to examine what my findings and observations could mean within the larger context of the work of these artists and writers. It could also be revealing to probe into the changes in our present culture in particular, which is taking an obsessive interest in the body's integument: are we, in the age of cyberspace and genetic technology, now in the process of finally shedding our old skins? Or will the epidermis remain the last bastion of authentic being, our only shelter, our hide? Andy Warhol was once asked what his problem was. He answered: "Skin." Can we go on living with this problem?

Many of the sources examined in this book are American. As a literary scholar I studied German as well as American literature, both in Germany and the United States, and my familiarity with American texts is reflected here. A research grant to Columbia University in 1996 helped me to deepen my insight into the issue of skin color in American culture. I am grateful to Mark Anderson, Robert O'Meally, Dorothea von Mücke, Richard Newman, Avital Ronell, and Leo Steinberg for their intellectual support and stimulating discussions during that period. The grant came from the Studienstiftung des deutschen Volkes, which also generously supported my Ph.D. studies. In Berlin, Hartmut Böhme and Inge Stephan supervised my project with great skill and friendship. I am indebted to Jennifer Crewe of Columbia University Press for being a most cooperative and considerate editor. I feel deeply honored that my book is being published by the press of the very institution I will always remember as an outstanding and unique place of higher learning, where I had the great pleasure of spending a semester as a visiting scholar. A special thank you goes to Thomas Dunlap for his careful and sensitive translation.

skin

1 the depth of the surface

Introduction

This book examines the relationship among self-consciousness, subjectivity, and skin in literature, art, and science from the eighteenth century to the present. It deals with skin as the symbolic surface between the self and the world, a surface whose status has been undergoing a striking change over the last centuries. My central thesis is that the integument of the body has become an increasingly rigid boundary in spite of the fact that medicine has penetrated the skin and exposed the interior of the body. In the twentieth century, at the latest, skin—the place "where the ego is decided" (Serres 1985, 17)—became the central metaphor of separateness. It is only at this boundary that subjects can encounter each other.

This book seeks out fragments of historical evidence and scientific moments that have shaped the emergence of this kind of collective body image. It examines the conceptions and rhetorical patterns that see skin as boundary and contact surface, probes into the practices and phantasms of penetrating and removing the skin, and investigates the question of the body surface as the place where identity is formed and assigned. The book analyzes an array of images and fantasies: armored or stigmatized skin, skin color that rubs off, people shedding their own skin, the image of a tattered or transparent epidermis, flaying, and extraction. These topoi, all of which revolve around allegories of the relationship between the self and the world, are examined with respect to their historicity, gender images, and racist subtexts. In this way the present study seeks to broaden literary studies by taking an interdisciplinary and cultural studies approach, one in which literature is not examined as a disconnected, separate phenomenon but seen—in the sense of a poetics of culture—as embedded in a multitude of diverse discourses. I approach language, literature, art, and science as archives of historical body perceptions, as sources and documents of a knowledge that is no longer directly accessible or extant.

Skin is in, a fact reflected in numerous popular science books and journalistic pieces, documentaries, and essays that deal with "Western" skin and even more frequently with the richly decorated skin of the other. Today, Europeans and Americans are spending more money than ever on tattoos, piercing, branding, skin-lifts, liposuction, tanning sessions, and antiwrinkle creams. At the same time, the incidence of skin cancer, neurodermatitis, psoriasis, and shingles—diseases that manifest themselves visibly on the surface of the body—has never been higher. It has been a long established fact in popular science that there is a connection between the growing fetishization of smooth and immaculate skin—which also influences unconscious collective body images—and the condition of being stigmatized by (largely) "psychic" skin diseases.[1]

Since the 1970s, a large number of artists, especially women, have been preoccupied with skin. Their works and performances deal quite concretely with skin as a place of encounter; in the process these artists have expanded the genre of self-portrait to encompass their own bodies, bodies, moreover, no longer merely represented as likenesses but whose very surfaces become a canvas. The contemporary French performance artist Orlan, for example, undergoes continual surgery to shape her face to the ideal of beauty found in classic Renaissance painting (e.g., Botticelli's Venus or Leonardo's Mona Lisa), all the while documenting this bloody metamorphosis of the self transformed into the image. The Viennese artist Valie Export was already showing slides of a "garter belt tattooed onto the body-canvas" in the seventies (Export 1995, 468). The locus of this work of art was the artist's skin, her left thigh, which was tattooed to establish the theme of the body as the site of cultural inscriptions. Performances such as Export's

"Body-Sign-Action" question the traditional status of "woman as image" (Eiblmayr 1993) within the figurative arts. The media artist Alba d'Urbano recently fashioned a second skin of herself (figure 1), which she traced from her body with computer-generated patterns and sewed from a leatherlike material. In her installation *Projekt "Hautnah,"** the lifeless shell is draped on a hanger like a dress and could theoretically be worn by another person.

Unquestionably one of the most spectacular actions to date is the *Lustmord-Zyklus* (Sex murder cycle, 1993) by the American artist Jenny Holzer. This cycle of thirty color photographs (figure 2) about rape and gruesome murders in the former Yugoslavia gives voice to three different groups: the perpetrators, the victims, and the victims' families. The shift from one group to another is sudden, with the result that the viewer alternately identifies with or recoils from the images, although the emotions often merge in a frightening way. The texts were written on flat sections of skin with a felt-tip pen and then photographed and enlarged. Because the skin fills the entire visual space and its individual characteristics—hair, pores, impurities, pigmental spots, and scars—stand out starkly, these physical-fleshly canvases come menacingly close to the viewer. On one level, the texts deal with body fluids, excrement, and the forceful penetration into the body of another person; on another level, they also deal with hairs or nipples that protrude from the skin. Holzer conjures the theme of skin as a boundary, a fragile parchment unable to protect against violence.[2]

In contemporary art, the surface of the body is defined as a projection surface and a fetish, a place of wounds and stigmatization, an individual dress or a cover to be modified. The display of female skin, in particular, often involves violence or self-inflicted wounds, cuts, and burns, as in the body performances of the artists Gina Pane and Marina Abramoviç. In his radical "Suspension Performances" (1976–1988), the Australian body artist Stelarc repeatedly suspended himself by his own skin, which he perforated with large hooks. Here, the closed body vessel is involuntarily and forcefully penetrated and opened up by means of its own gravity.

In 1983 the FrauenMuseum (Women's museum) in Bonn hosted a large exhibit entitled "Haut" (Skin), in which numerous women artists and

---

* A wonderful play on words in German that cannot be reproduced in English, *Hautnah* literally means "close as skin," but as an idiomatic expression it can mean "immediate" or "very close," as in contact between individuals. When referring to a piece of writing, it can mean "dramatic, gripping, vivid."—Trans.

figure 1
Alba d'Urbano, *Projekt "Hautnah"* (1995)

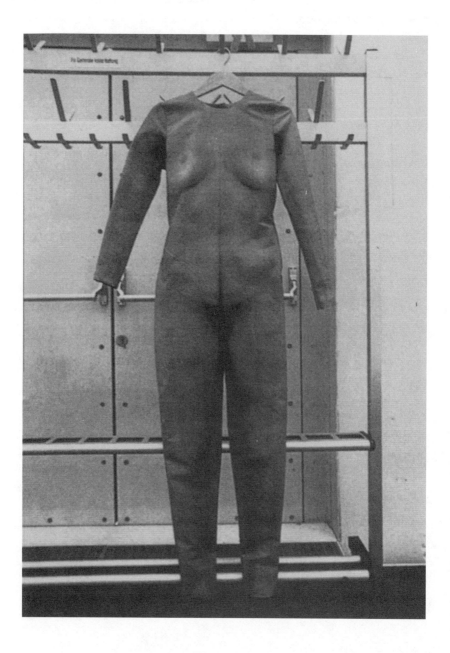

figure 2
Jenny Holzer, *Lustmord-Zyklus* (1993)

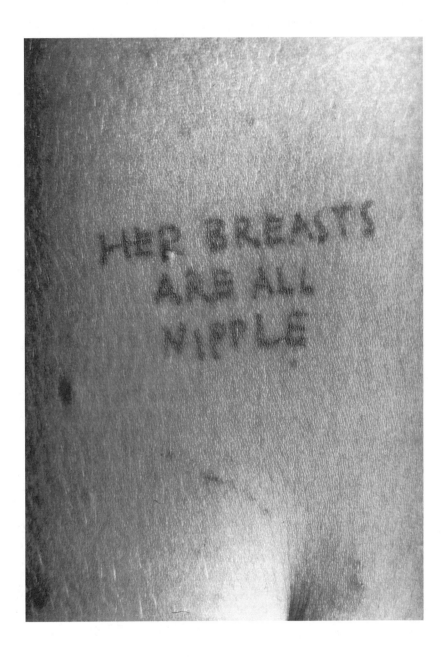

writers approached the theme in a highly subjective way. In 1995 the Bonner Kunst- und Ausstellungshalle organized an international congress on the theme of touch under the motto "The Future of the Senses." Participants discussed the significance of tactile perception for cultural processes and aesthetic experiences. In 1997 the Hochschule für Bildende Künste in Hamburg hosted a symposium entitled "Hautlabor" (Skin laboratory), which explored new strategies in the boundary region between architecture and art. In fact, for some years now there has been a lively discussion about skin in architectural theory, with architects striving to make "intelligent facades": walls responsive to the environment and capable of regulating interior climate on their own.

Skin has also become a theme in new media. New media of the future will go beyond simple visual and acoustic simulation: increasingly the goal is to incorporate the entire sensory body into virtual reality with the help of data suits. The epidermis, the largest human organ in terms of surface area, is being discovered as an interface. The controversy triggered by this utopia of skin-to-skin contact across physical distances has been exhaustively debated in the media under the catchword "cybersex." Another important level of meaning exists in discussions about the penetration and discarding of skin in cyberspace. The media critic Derrick de Kerckhove argued that the human being at the end of the twentieth century was, at long last, no longer tied to his or her own skin, for skin was now the "earthly atmosphere rendered sensory by virtue of its satellites" (1996a, 122). This kind of rhetoric about transcending the skin is one of the central topoi I will investigate in this book.

The increasing frequency of these kinds of events and themes is no coincidence. It points to a much-needed engagement with a topic that has been neglected and repressed far too long. Yet the present study does not concern itself primarily with the kinds of contemporary phenomena I have briefly sketched. Rather, it will search out the collective origins of these developments, which began to take shape during the European Enlightenment and raised the issue of the body surface as a boundary or articulated the theme of the skin as a canvas. What we are dealing with is the immense significance of skin as a symbolic form for cultural processes as a whole and its importance to the individuation and self-becoming of the human being, in particular.

"That which is most profound in the human being is the skin. . . . The marrow, the brain, all these things we require in order to feel, suffer, think

. . . to be profound . . . are inventions of the skin! . . . We burrow down in vain, doctor, we are . . . ectoderm."[3] In this dialogue, Paul Valéry conceptualized the human being as an "ectoderm" whose real profundity, paradoxically, is his skin. This idea is foreign to the modern notion of subjectivity, for the self tends to be understood rather as hidden on the inside of its body house, invisible and immaterial.

The psychologist Didier Anzieu has argued that Western thought since the Renaissance has been dominated by the fundamental notion that knowledge of what is essential means breaking through shells and walls in order to reach the core that lies in the innermost depths. But this notion is proving increasingly unsatisfactory or even false. Neurophysiology has had to come to terms with the paradox that even the brain is a rind—in other words, the human "center" is actually situated at the periphery (Anzieu 1989, 9). Valéry refers to this insight when he says that the "doctor" can burrow down all he wants; he will never actually find the essence in the depths. In much the same way, François Dagognet asserts that we can no longer rely blindly on the anatomical paradigm of penetration and uncovering that was established in the sixteenth century by Andreas Vesalius. Instead, what we need now is an "anti-vésalisme" (1993, 15) that will focus on the insights and knowledge of surfaces.

In the embryo, the skin and the brain are formed from the same membrane, the ectoderm; both are, in essence, surfaces. A substantial part of embryonal perception in the womb occurs through the skin. Touch is the first of the senses to develop, appearing when the embryo is less than three centimeters long. And numerous studies with newborns have shown that after birth as well tactile perception is primary, followed by auditory perception and only then by visual perception (Montagu 1971, 169). For the newborn (as well as the unborn), the skin is the most important organ of communication and contact. It is through the skin that the newborn learns where she begins and ends, where the boundaries of her self are. Here, she learns the first feelings of pleasure and displeasure. These primary experiences establish close connections between skin sensations and emotional states, connections that persist for life and are reflected in the figurative uses of verbs such as "feel" and "be touched," words whose etymology points to tactile origins.

Psychoanalytical theory, starting from Freud's thesis that the ego is "first and foremost a bodily ego" (1961, 26), has developed the notion of the body ego. The children's analyst Margaret Mahler has noted that a major step in early child development is "the shift of predominantly proprioceptive-enteroceptive [inner] cathexis* toward sensoriperceptive cathexis of the periphery." It represents "an essential prerequisite of body-ego formation." The first playful abandonment of the original symbiosis with the mother leads the infant, at the age of about six months, to a series of motoric experimentations with individuation. For example, the child will strain its body away from the mother in order to have a better look at her, to scan her and the environment, to get a better look at her entire figure and its external boundaries. Or it begins to probe its environment and caretakers with its hands as a way of experiencing the boundaries of its own and foreign bodies (Mahler, Pine, and Bergman 1975, 46–47, 54). Initially the infant develops the fantasy of a common skin with the mother, based on the sensations in the womb. The next stage sees a gradual suppression of this imagined common skin and the recognition by the child that it has a skin of its own, discrete and autonomous, "a recognition which does not come about without resistance and pain" (Anzieu 1989, 63).

With his conception of the skin ego, modeled on the notion of the body ego, Anzieu has developed the first systematics of psychological and largely unconscious cathexes of the skin that take shape in a child's early development and interactions. His study is fundamental to the present book. By skin ego Anzieu means "a mental image of which the Ego of the child makes use during the early phases of its development to represent itself as an Ego containing psychical contents, on the basis of its experience of the surface of the body" (1989, 40). The human skin is thus both an organic and an imaginary reality. At birth, the skin ego is still a "structure that is potentially present," realized only "as the relationship between the baby and its primary environment unfolds" (102). Freud had already explicitly called consciousness the "*surface* of the mental apparatus" and described the ego, correspondingly, as a "surface entity" (1961, 19 and 26).[4]

Anzieu defines the skin ego "as a containing, unifying envelope for the Self; as a protective barrier for the psyche; and as a filter of exchanges and a surface of inscription for the first traces" (1989, 98). In keeping with Freudian principles, the psychic functions of the skin ego rest on corresponding bodily functions, that is to say, on concrete physiological tasks performed by the skin, such as protecting against stimulation, supporting

* In psychoanalysis, "cathexis" is defined as "the investment of an object or idea with psychic energy."—Trans.

and containing the body, interconnecting various sense organs, and supporting sexual excitation.[5] Two extreme phantasms strike me as important: the masochistic phantasm of the flayed body and the narcissistic phantasm of the doubled skin. Both disorders are connected to the early childhood fantasy of a common skin with the mother. Many of the literary and artistic images that I will discuss touch on these phantasms. Notions about the psychic protection and integrity of the self find enduring symbolic representation through the skin. It would appear that contemporary concepts of the self are necessarily linked to images of envelopment, of coherence, and, at times, of something skinlike. What remains problematic within psychoanalysis is the thesis that body images have always been and will always be like this. The present study will show that this notion is, of course, false: body images and self-conceptions are products of history, subject to continuous change and cultural interpretation.

Language has always preserved the close relationship among identity, self-consciousness, and one's own skin, as reflected in countless idiomatic expressions, sayings, and metaphors. When someone says, for instance, that she is "jumping out of her skin," "is trying to save her own skin," or "is getting under someone's skin," that person is speaking most intimately about herself. These kinds of colloquial expressions are well known from everyday language, but we rarely reflect on them. Moreover, the fact that they are an important element in the shaping of poetic texts has also been overlooked until now. Speech about one's own skin is speech about oneself as body. This insight is by no means self-evident in European culture, which, beginning with Greek enlightenment, through the Cartesian division into mind and body, and on to modern subject theories, has stood in the tradition of subjectivism. But the last few years have seen signs of a change in thinking about the body in critical theory. For example, historical anthropology and an emerging cultural history of the body have raised questions about traces of the body in the present and in human history. This book will attempt a "reading of a scar text" (Kamper and Wulf 1989, 1 ff.), a reading of the overlapping layers of traces, sections, and markings of the human body. And when it comes to skin, this is to be taken quite literally!

It is revealing that during recent years I have often met with puzzled looks when I speak about my work on skin; after all, so the universal observation goes, I am not a dermatologist. David B. Morris, in his book *The Culture of Pain* (1991, 9), noted that the "greatest surprise I encountered in discussing this topic over the past ten years was the consistency with which

I was asked a single unvarying question: Are you writing about physical pain or mental pain?" In the nineteenth century, knowledge was divided into the humanities and the sciences, and the body was unquestioningly classified as part of nature, to be studied by the sciences. The time has now come to reverse this split and to ask about the dimensions that have been excluded by the purely physiological view of the body.

For a long time, only phenomena that took place on the outside of the body or were externally manipulated on the body were considered to be subject to historical change: dress, hairstyles, tattoos, makeup, dietary or surgical modifications to body shapes, corporeal measurements, or skin tones. Until now, corporeal self-perception—and thus also skin and touch—was considered to be a purely physiological matter, outside the realm of history. But the human skin is not always present in the same way, as medicine claims. Instead, it, too, is subject to cultural notions that make it appear in a constantly shifting light. According to the historian Barbara Duden, one of the most "tenacious mental habits" to this day is the implicit differentiation and separation of biology as "an immutable sphere of life" from the other realms of culture and society that are "variable and change-able over time." In this scheme the body, while seen as a "vehicle" of so-cial and cultural activities, is itself "always thought of as a physiologically stable entity" (Duden 1991a, vii).

In his introduction to *Fragments for a History of the Human Body*, Michael Feher aptly noted that "the history of the human body is not so much the history of its representations as of its modes of construction" (1989, 11), for the notion of representation always proceeds implicitly from a "real" body that lies concealed behind changing conceptions. By contrast, if one looks at representations of the body as themselves manifestations of the body, one ceases to posit the unspoken assumption that there is a real body beyond the realm of culture.

The eighteenth century witnessed a fundamental change in body per-ception and with it a change in the notion of the skin as the boundary of the individual body. With the emergence of clinical-anatomical medicine, the realm under the skin was made visible. In the premodern era, the skin still constituted a structurally impenetrable boundary to the invisible and mysterious inside, a boundary whose visual and haptic surface was of such great importance not least because it demanded some kind of interpretative art from physicians and healers seeking to render a diagnosis. By the late eighteenth century, however, skin had already become simply a place of passage to the inside. The dissection of the body in anatomy created a model of knowledge based on dismemberment, extraction, and disembodiment. A mechanizing view of the body gradually took hold. Today it finds its logical continuation in transplantation medicine, the final conquest of the inner corporeal space, what Virilio has called, for now, the "final political form of domestication" (1994, 108–109). The implantation of human organs and eventually also of technological devices leads to a forceful abolition of the classical distinction between internal and external, a distinction traditionally marked by the skin. But the many literary and historical documents I examine in this study reveal that in terms of the history of mentalities, this development has by no means rendered the notion of skin as a boundary superfluous in the collective imagination—on the contrary, that notion has taken on even greater significance.

Culturally, the perception of the skin was increasingly turned into a perception of distance as a consequence of being reduced to the visual impression of the bodily surface. This development has had far-reaching consequences: only as the observed skin of the other with whom I come face to face does skin become a sign, only through this separation can the other truly become a recognizable and classifiable object. The skin is constantly interpreted, read, invested with or emptied of semantic meaning, recoded, neutralized, and stylized. To give just one example, as late as the nineteenth century, people in the Western cultural orbit still considered a pale complexion refined and noble, while today there is a tendency to see such coloring as unhealthy and nonathletic (the dangers of skin cancer notwithstanding).

Other aspects that have been or are invested with a specific code are such disparate phenomena as tattoos, makeup, scars, blushing, pigment disorders, birthmarks, moles, and skin diseases. An examination of these kinds of projections invariably raises the question of skin color. The discourse about race is based on an outdated semiotic model constructed on the physiognomic ideas of the eighteenth century: phenomena that are external and visually perceived and categorized become, in a very deterministic manner, the basis for inferences about specific human types; classifications are created based solely on the surface of the body, which is thus turned into a supposedly reliable system of signs. One of the central themes in a cultural history of the skin is that it is continually read and interpreted in all social situations, that human beings have understood and misunderstood it as an expression of depth, of soul, of inner character. Human contact depends unavoidably on the skin: it is the manifest place of the other that is accessible to sight and touch.

If the repeated, strenuous efforts at fashioning a visual semiotics of the skin are one side of the coin, the other side is the tactile experience of one's own skin and that of others, which largely escapes external categorization and attribution. The body is not only a cultural sign but also an entity with sensation and perception. We must therefore preserve a tension between cultural construction and prelinguistic aisthesis (sense perception) to avoid reducing the skin from the outset to a projection surface and the bearer of signs. This book deals with the continual interplay between "being a body" and "having a body" (Joraschky 1986, 34). In doing so it picks up the current debate in which "there is disagreement down to the level of the processes of perception over whether the body provides model testimony for a 'natural' language or a 'historical' text" (Kamper and Wulf 1984, 10). With respect to the skin, this also requires that we continually walk a fine line between constructivism and the claim to authenticity made by bodily phenomena.

The last few decades have seen a wide-ranging debate in philology and literary studies about the relationship between body and text. Deconstructionist or semiotic theories claim that skin, too, is a text. In my own view, however, this is reductionist. The fact that the concept of text is today conceived as universal is a simplification related to the specific Western tradition of knowledge—derived from medieval theology, in which, not by coincidence, it was precisely the metaphor of the world as book that became paradigmatic. Textuality implies meaning and is tied to (implied) intent. But the skin in and of itself has no intent, even if it may very well express intention. One can communicate with the skin, and one can communicate about the skin—this is a qualitative and epistemological difference. Naturally, this study refers to sources and is to that extent largely dependent on linguistic material. But whether skin is a text or whether a text deals with skin is a profound difference.

Skin is not only coded in language; it is also an image, for example, and this posits different parameters. Perceptions in general, unlike linguistic signs, are not conventionalized and coded. Their productive ambiguity is reflected precisely in the literary perceptions of skin I will examine in this study. If speaking—as Julia Kristeva has said about love (1987, 3)—is always something that is after the fact, this might also apply to skin, which likewise is accessible to discursive treatment only after the fact and, moreover, inadequately so.

The present study on skin blends theoretical and primary texts in an unconventional way. First, it does so by confronting concrete theoretical approaches with literary texts, paintings, and similar artifacts. Second, it deliberately juxtaposes fictional, artistic sources with scientific ones. Not only does this combining of sources create interesting possibilities of comparison with respect to the various ways of depicting and understanding skin, but the documents at times also shed light on one another—for example, in terms of medical and cultural discourses about skin color. A stark juxtaposition of the two genres, the factual and the fictional, has now been cast aside in the humanities as an artificial construct; one example of this is the recognition of the constructive element in writings on foreign cultures. In conjunction with demands that we deprivilege literary texts, expand the range of sources, and give up the notion of cultures as definable and homogeneous entities, insights derived from the "crisis of representation" in ethnography (within the so-called writing culture debate) have been brought to bear in a fruitful way on the humanities (Berg and Fuchs 1993; Bachmann-Medick 1996; Böhme and Scherpe 1996). The present study, using a hitherto nearly unexplored phenomenon, seeks to set an example in heeding these demands, all of which are aimed at reforming the humanities from a cultural history perspective.

The book does not structure its complex topic historically, nor is it guided by particular mediums or disciplines. Instead, it suggests a configurative organization, one that groups individual aspects into thematic clusters without positing a consistently linear structure. The resulting principle of resonance, echo, and reflections is the goal of writing cultural poetics. It would take a large research team many years to write a literary and cultural history of the skin that would even come close to capturing all essential facets. Perhaps it is a risky venture to endeavor here to capture as many aspects as possible. But such a venture seems to be necessary, since the facets are too closely intertwined to allow for meaningful treatment of them in isolation.

The chapter "Boundary Metaphors" begins by drawing on idiomatic expressions and images of the skin. On the one hand, skin is used as a stand-in for "person," "spirit," "body," or "life," as a *pars pro toto* of the entire human being. On the other hand, and this is what makes skin so singular, it functions simultaneously as the other of the self, as its enclosure, prison, or mask. The analogy between the house and the human body has a long tradition. On closer inspection, the notion of living in the body always turns out to be a discourse about hollow space: the imaginary room created by one's own skin. This change of skin within the history of mentalities from a porous, tissuelike membrane to an impenetrable wall of separation is explored in the chapter entitled "Penetrations." There, I trace the complex of questions concerning the skin as boundary by analyzing the history of how it was penetrated and eliminated. I will show the extent to which skin, as late as the seventeenth and early eighteenth centuries, was still understood as a porous, nonclosed surface, a notion that began to change only in the eighteenth century with the creation of the bourgeois body. The practice of dermatological illustrations reveals the displacement potential of this new collective body image.

The chapter "Flayings" inquires into cultural images relating to the removal and peeling off of the skin. Flaying encodes a number of contradictory processes in art, philosophy, and medicine. For example, as a means of torture and killing it stands, on the one hand, for the most extreme inscription of power and as such must be read in direct connection with the history of anatomy. On the other hand, it is also understood as an allegory of self-liberation or change.

The chapter "Mirror of the Soul" begins by investigating why the skin is considered an identity and projection surface, the representation of the soul. The consciousness of nudity defines the human being as a creature that is naked without clothing or masking. A close look at Balzac's novel *A Woman of Thirty* reveals a literary procedure that was perfected in the nineteenth century and uses the skin as a screen on which both momentary sensations as well as continuous states of being can be read. This procedure, still a functioning semiology in Balzac's novel, becomes brittle in the twentieth century, as revealed by the facial and cutaneous descriptions in the work of Kafka and Sylvia Plath, the topic of the chapter entitled "Mystification." Through a narrowly focused fixation on various aspects of the facial surface, the person disappears as a human counterpart and becomes a foreign body, a merely objectified thing. The skin is conceptualized as something that is worn, an inescapable garment. The following chapter, "Armored Skin and Birthmarks," introduces two imagines* that encapsulate sexual body images.

---

* In psychoanalysis, an imago (pl. imagines) is defined as "a subjective image of someone which a person has subconsciously formed and which continues to influence his attitudes and behavior" (Oxford English Dictionary).—Trans.

The chapters "Different Skin" and "Blackness" deal with the question of ethnic difference, which is established by the construction of skin color. The focus is on "white" and "black" skin: as the history of the science of skin color between the seventeenth and nineteenth centuries reveals, this juxtaposition has historically produced the sharpest efforts at demarcation. Out of that discussion arises the semantic field of skin that is nontransparent, dirty, leathery, and from which color rubs off. In "Different Skin," I confront this semantic field through two literary texts. The chapter entitled "Blackness" examines the problem of skin colors from the perspective of African-American theory and literature (Ralph Ellison, John Edgar Wideman, Toni Morrison).

In the chapters "Hand and Skin" and "Touchings," the central focus is on the body surface as an organ of perception. First, I look at the anthropology of touch in science and aesthetics, which early on split the so-called fifth sense into two parts. This is followed by a discussion of the inseparability of sensual and psychological skin perceptions based on literary texts by Robert Musil and Michael Ondaatje. The concluding chapter, "Teletactility," which deals with the conception of the skin in new media, reveals the efforts at authenticating the genuineness of virtual realities by integrating and activating the so-called lower senses. Compelling historical reasons explain why it is precisely the skin that is currently emerging as the new guiding sense, and this book will show what these reasons are.

2 boundary metaphors

Skin in Language

An examination of older and contemporary idiomatic expressions involving skin in German and
other European languages reveals two levels of
meaning that point to very different conceptions of
subject and body. First, there is the idea that the skin
encloses the self: skin is imagined as a protective and
sheltering cover but in some expressions also as a
concealing and deceptive one. What is authentic lies
beneath the skin, is hidden inside the body. It escapes our gaze, and its decipherment requires skills
of reading and interpretation. Here, skin is conceived of as something other than the self and thus
as something foreign and external to it.

A second group of sayings equates the skin with
the subject, the person: here the essence does not lie
beneath the skin, hidden inside. Rather, it is the
skin itself, which stands metonymically for the
whole human being. The discussion that follows
will assemble both word fields, their metaphors and
images, and examine their connected meanings.
This approach takes language seriously as a historical
medium for the production of conceptions of the
self and treats it as a source that documents changing body images.

What has been lost over the centuries, in particular, are expressions in which skin is used as a metonymic description for the subject, that is to say, expressions from the second group. For example, Grimm's *Deutsches Wörter-büch* (1877) still contains a good many adjectives used to characterize a person, who is described as "skin": in a derogatory way one could speak of someone as a *verwegene* (reckless), *böse* (evil), *lose* (roguish), *feige* (cowardly), *frevelnde* (blasphemous), *schäbige* (shabby), and *unbedeutende* (worthless) skin; on the positive side the dictionary offers *gefällige* (pleasant), *lustige* (merry), *gute* (good), *brave* (decent), *ehrliche* (honest), and *gutmütige* (good-natured) skin. Descriptions with a somewhat more subtle or ambivalent meaning are *dicke* (thick), *bloße* (bare), *alte* (old), *unglückliche* (unhappy), *arme* (poor), and *wunderliche* (strange) skin (Grimm and Grimm 1984, 10:cols. 708–709; Röhrich 1992, 683).[1] Comparable usages can also be found in English: "nasty skin," "decent skin," "good skin" (*OED*, 15:610).

These kinds of sayings are forms of individualization in which one says "skin" instead of "person"—a way of speaking that sounds strange to our ears. Although bodies were much more extensively covered up in previous centuries than they are today, the language evidently had an aspect that was closer to the body. In particular, it would seem that language played a role as the bearer of individuality and history. In Schiller's *Wallenstein* trilogy there is an exemplary description of the self as "skin": "That's why I sold the Emperor my hide / So I'd have no more worries and cares to abide" (Schiller 1958, 16). This metaphor of selling oneself is also found in other languages, for example, in Italian: "vendere la pelle di qualcuno," which usually has a sexual connotation.[2] There is a corresponding saying in French: "se lever la peau pour quelqu'un" means to sacrifice oneself for someone else. As late as the nineteenth century, the German "Seine Haut selbst zu Markte tragen" (to take one's own skin to market) still meant doing something at one's own risk (Ersch and Gruber 1828, 203). In these sayings the surface of the body is understood as the most essential part of a person.

"Ursin is annoying and gets under my skin [lit. in German, gets on my skin], so that I have recently taken away from him my book, Phaedon," Gotthold Ephraim Lessing wrote in a letter (quoted in Grimm and Grimm 1984, 10:col. 703). Here, skin stands for something especially fragile, irritable—thus representing precisely what we today would tend to call "spirit" or "nerves." This is an exemplary illustration of the change to a less embodied conception of the subject.

Another group of sayings within this field of meaning uses "skin" as *pars pro toto* for a person's body: "If you tell callow youths what they dislike to hear, / unvarnished truth which afterwards / they learn from years of hard experience / applies to their own persons, in their conceit / they then believe it sprang from their own heads and still assert their teacher was dull-witted" (Goethe 1984, 173). Goethe's original German, "Das alles derb an eigner Haut erfahren," which Stuart Atkins rendered as "learn from years of hard experience," literally reads "which they experience harshly on their own skin." Instead of the phrase "experience on one's own skin," as used here in Goethe's *Faust* (1808), a usage that hints at a real history of skin and its painful sensations, Germans today would tend to use "am eigenen Leib erfahren" (experience with one's own body). In this shift in meaning the phrase has lost some of its pictorial vividness and the specification of precisely where the experience occurs. In older German, formulations such as "jemandem die Haut voll schlagen" (give someone a sound thrashing) and in so doing "ihm recht auf die Haut greifen" (really lay into his skin) (Ersch and Gruber 1828, 203) are much more precise than modern-day language in marking the site of the painful experience. While the actual experience "on one's own skin" was entirely possible, radical expressions that describe the destruction of a person's integrity indicate that it was probably not usually the case. Older German sayings such as "jemandem die Haut über die Ohren ziehen" (pull the skin over someone's ears), "die Haut schinden und abziehen" (flay and pull off the skin), or "aus fremder Haut ist gut Riemen schneiden" (it is easy to cut straps from someone else's skin) (203) contain traces of violent inscription. This is also found in English, for example, in the phrase, "to give a person a good hiding."

As a synecdoche of the body, skin is also used together with other body parts. Such a combination is then given the connotation of "complete and utterly," as for example in the saying "mit Haut und Haar" (with skin and hair). This paired formula arose in medieval legal language and referred to all nonmutilating corporal punishments. These were carried out by means of scourging and the cutting of the hair, that is to say, through a penal practice aimed at the surface of the body without destroying the body's integrity and basic functions. The phrase "nur noch Haut und Knochen," which is also found in English—"only skin and bones"—was and is commonly used to describe extreme bodily emaciation.

In older German, "skin" was also used as a stand-in for "life": for example, in the sayings "es gilt Haut um Haut" (it is skin for skin), "die Haut

fürchten" (fear for one's skin), "sich seiner Haut erwehren" and "seine Haut
verteidigen" (defend one's skin), "seine Haut retten" (save one's skin), "mit
der Haut zahlen" (pay with one's skin), and "die Haut für etwas geben" (give
the skin for something) (Grimm and Grimm 1984, 10:cols. 701 ff.; Ersch and
Gruber 1828, 203). French has "de se faire la peau," which means simply to
lose one's life, just as the Italian "lasciarci la pelle." The Italian "fare la pelle
a qualcuno" means to kill someone, and "vendere cara la propria pelle"
means to sell one's skin dearly.

The equating of skin and life is also common in French as "vouloir la
peau," to take someone's life, or in English and Italian as "to lose one's skin,"
"to save one's skin," and "salvare la pelle" (to save one's life). The multitude
of these kinds of formulations, which cannot be exhaustively presented here,
points to a consciousness of the existential significance of skin of undamaged
integrity, the loss of which marks the end of life. Goethe pointedly expresses this very duality of life and body in his *Götz von Berlichingen* (1773): "And
to escape with our skins we must risk our skins" (Goethe 1988a, 55).

Next to these idiomatic expressions, some in use since the Middle Ages,
in which skin in one form or another represents the self—with the self thus
characterized as a "surface entity" (Freud 1961, 26)—a second field of
meaning emerges. Here, skin becomes an insensitive and insignificant covering of the important self hidden inside. A number of sayings refer to the
imagined sheltering quality of the skin, for example, in the observation that
someone feels "ganz wohl in seiner Haut" (quite comfortable in his skin).
The function of the intact skin in creating space and providing a home is
also expressed in other languages: the English expressions "to sleep in a
whole skin" and "to come out of something unscathed" correspond to the
German "mit heiler Haut davonkommen." The French "être bien dans sa
peau" is analogous to the German "sich in seiner Haut wohl fühlen" and
the English "to feel comfortable in one's skin," while "mourir dans sa
peau" means to die in one's own skin (i.e., to die peacefully). In English,
"hide" is another word for skin or pelt and is used in figurative speech to
describe a person, while "to hide" means something quite different, of
course, namely to conceal or cover up.

Yet the state of being inside one's skin—"wrapped in flesh" (Musil 1957,
316)—has not always been imagined as sheltering within a protective space,
as suggested by these sayings, but often also as being trapped in an inescapable prison (Klauser et al. 1976, cols. 315 ff.). This is reflected in such
expressions as "nicht in der Haut eines anderen stecken wollen" (not want

to be in someone's else's skin). The fatalistic aspect of being tied to individual bodily existence is also indicated in the still common saying that someone is feeling "nicht wohl in seiner Haut" (not comfortable in his skin) and in the somewhat old-fashioned phrase "in keiner guten Haut stecken" (stuck in a not so good a skin). A similar notion of the captivity of character, which is irrevocably shaped in the body, is expressed in the Italian saying "avere il diavolo nella pelle" (to have the devil in one's skin) and in the older German expression that someone is "ein Schelm" or "ein Schalk in der Haut" (an imp/rogue in his skin).[3]

The sayings "aus der Haut fahren" and "aus der Haut springen" (to jump out of one's skin), which were originally used not only for feelings of joy or anger (as they still are today) but also to denote jealousy, ire, despair, or fear (Grimm and Grimm 1984, 10:cols. 705 ff.; Ersch/Gruber 1828, 203), project a body cover that can be cast off in situations of extreme emotions. The self transcends its own boundaries: a person "jumps out of his skin" or is "beside himself."

Literary texts devise ever new images for the problem of being stuck inside a skin that inescapably binds a person in his or her identity and character. In Friedrich Hebbel's *Maria Magdalene* (1844), for example, a protagonist says this about himself and his father: "We don't get along together, that's clear! He cannot have things tight enough around him. He would like to close his hand into a fist and crawl into it. I should like to shed my skin, like the frock I wore as a little boy, if only I could!" (1963, 1:377)

The son's skin is described metaphorically as "too tight," as a garment that is no longer comfortable but binds him inescapably. While Hebbel attributes to the father the desire for as tight an embrace as possible—symbolic of bourgeois-domestic stuffiness—the son wants to leave this crushing and suffocating environment. The father, however, once again using a skin analogy, remarks that he was not born into the world as an unfriendly, "bristly hedgehog" (which is how people were experiencing him today) but forced by his original vulnerability to turn his bristles toward the outside world: "At first all the quills were turned inward. They pinched and pressed my smooth, yielding skin, and others rejoiced over my suffering as the tips tore into my heart and insides. But I didn't like that; I turned my skin inside out. Now the quills pricked their fingers, and I had my peace" (345).

In his play *Die Schwärmer* (The visionaries, 1921), Robert Musil, picking up on Hebbel's image of the skin as a form of self-protection, creates this description of shame: "You pull your own skin tighter and tighter over your head, like a dark hood with a few eye slits and breathing holes" (1957, 307). Elsewhere in the play we read that "one hides behind one's hide" (400). These passages point to the skin's symbolic function of providing covering and shelter: the fragile inside beneath the skin is protected against invasive glances that destroy the shamed person. The shame or embarrassment that appears on the skin as blushing becomes a kind of impermeable, concealing protective armor or mask (Wurmser 1981, 18). A person who blocks out the potentially hurtful sensory impressions of the others—looks, gestures, words—can no longer be penetrated; he experiences himself as armored. In this context Nietzsche developed the metaphor of the "skin of the soul," which protectively envelops the real, raw sensations: "Just as the bones, flesh, intestines, and blood vessels are enclosed in a skin that makes the sight of man endurable, so the agitations and passions of the soul are enveloped in vanity: it is the skin of the soul" (1986, 47–48). From a sense of shame, all emotions, desires, and wishes manifest themselves only in a veiled, muted, and moderated way. Vanity functions as self-protection, shielding a person from being utterly denuded and exposed to the world. In describing the inner withdrawal, the refusal to out oneself, Musil, using a similar imagery, paints the picture of an enveloping layer of skin that shuts out sensory impressions: "I can close the eyes, the ears, close the hatches, to the point where what I know is engulfed in utter darkness" (1957, 326–327).

Yet there are many idiomatic expressions that denounce the body surface as a deceptive, illusionary integument, a false dress beneath which the inner character remains hidden—exemplified, for example, in the English saying "beauty is only skin deep." This noncongruence between external appearance and inner character is often linked to gender structure, in that a male speaker finds himself lead astray by a beautiful appearance. One exemplary illustration comes from the seventeenth-century epigrammatic poem *Zweifelhafte Keuschheit* (Dubious chastity) by Friedrich von Logau: "An upright woman in countenance, a bag of rot inside the skin / Such are many; lasciviousness lies hidden, piety is put on display" (1872, 2:103). Such an implied strategy of concealment by means of a beautiful body can also be found in the popular imagination, where women have several skins, in each of which a "quality" or a "piece of roguishness" is hidden.[4]

In the end, though, the skin cannot protect against deception by the other or against self-deception, as Goethe points out in a verse: "He who looks inside his own bosom will not feel good in his own skin" (1988e, 655). In Musil the opposite image, of inner purity and innocence, is juxtaposed to an external condition of stigmatization and guilt: "Inside you can be as holy as the horses of the sun god, but on the outside it's what you have in your files," one female protagonist says to a detective on her trail (1957, 337). Or, in another passage, "Under the skin you are more beautiful than anybody, right?" (372). The difference between surface and what lies beneath sets in motion a fluctuating interplay between being and appearance that, in the end, leaves open the question of whether truth is hidden inside or reveals itself on the outermost layer of the body (Mattenklott 1982, 14ff.).

Correspondingly, being attracted by the skin of another person is unmasked as mere superficiality. For example, in Italian, contact "fra [or "tra"] pelle e pelle" (between skin and skin) means that two people have a merely external, superficial encounter. By contrast, "entrare nella pelle di qualcuno" (get into someone's skin) refers to a passionate and inner connection. The saying "avoir quelqu'un dans la peau" in French and the similar English expression "to have got someone under one's skin" mean that one possesses the loved one fully if one has him or her in one's skin, if the loved one has utterly relinquished himself or herself.

The same assessment also lies behind the fact that only that which gets under the skin or at least is experienced up close (*hautnah*) can truly touch a person. The person who feels too strongly has a thin skin, the person who lacks feeling is described as having a thick skin or thick hide (Italian has the identical phrase: "avere la pelle dura"). Provoking someone is called "mettere in pelle," which means something like "to get under one's skin" or, in German, "einen Stachel unter die Haut setzen" (to put a thorn under the skin). In order to put oneself empathically in someone else's place, a German would say that it is necessary "sich in die Haut des anderen zu versetzen" (to put oneself in the other person's skin). In all these expressions the feeling self is located inside the skin, which, though it does offer protection, actually seems to get in the way of true feeling.

To sum up, skin holds a peculiar place within figurative speech. As perhaps no other part of the human body, it serves both as a representation of the whole and as that which conceals it. On the one hand, skin, in the idioms, sayings, and metaphors just examined, is a stand-in for "person," "spirit," "body," or "life"; that is to say, it is a synecdoche for the human being. Yet at the same time, and this is what makes it so singular, skin functions as the other of the self, by representing its cover, its prison or mask, its medium of communication with the world. These two contrary conceptual formulas—

the self as skin and the self as in the skin, both of which have developed on the basis of the historical semantics of the skin—represent the framework that will structure my inquiries in the subsequent chapters.

Following this introduction to my topic, a look at the place of skin in language, I shall first examine a second complex of subconscious ideas: ideas of "living in" and "being imprisoned in" the body, which are hinted at in the image of the skin as a wall. This requires an exploration of the traditions these imagines call forth. Primarily, however, I am interested in the question of what we can learn about the historical anthropology of the skin by turning to the models that have been used as analogies of it, chiefly the garment and the house.

It was only during the last two centuries that the model of the body as house replaced that of the body as dress. To be sure, both body images were already known from antiquity and Christianity as spatial ideas about the in-dwelling of the soul, which means that these two models, strictly speaking, did not arise in succession. Yet the porous dress is a model in which the body surface is conceived of much more closely in relationship to its phys-iological characteristics than is the case in the house model. Central to the clothing metaphor is the process of putting on and taking off the bodily garment. Biblical language, for instance, has the expressions "to put on flesh" and "to put on a body" but also "to put on the human being," which de-scribes the assumption of human form or, as in the last phrase, a change of attitude (Klauser 1978, 10:col. 983). The bodily garment, as the garment of the soul given by God, must remain unstained; should it become soiled, it must be cleansed by penance (col. 978).

The dress metaphor is an old comparison not only in relationship to the body. A "dress principle" exists also for dwellings, as Gottfried Semper has elucidated in his writings on architectural theory (Harather 1995, 9). Karin Harather, who wrote the first study on this relationship of clothing and house, as a matter of course also equates clothing and skin within this chain of analogy by describing the walls of a house as an "architectural skin" (21). Here, she is referring to a topos that was already developed in the fifteenth century by Leon Battista Alberti in his *Della Architettura*, which notes that the body of a building must be covered with a skin of multiple layers of plas-tering (Zaera 1995, 98). Architectural theory, according to Harather, made a rigid separation between construction and the "skin of the building" right up to the twentieth century. Architecture thus considered the elaboration of facades, which varies stylistically from period to period, as representation: the house is given a dress that corresponds to its individual social position.

At the beginning of the twentieth century, this conception underwent a radical change. Theorists were now calling for the complete removal of all decorative facades in favor of an exposure of the building's frame, the "open container" (Harather 1995, 39). What became visible now, instead of the encasement that strikes the viewer as soft, was the naked, smooth wall—speaking with the metaphor of the body, the skin beneath the clothes.

For some years now the transfer of body metaphors back into architectural theory has been commonplace; it is nothing out of the ordinary to hear contemporary architectural theory speak of the "skin" of a building, and the positive characteristics of the body surface have been adopted: suppleness, an organic quality, adaptability to the environment, and so forth (Zaera 1995; Taylor 1995a and 1995b; Zardini 1994). Whether stone and steel architecture can in fact embody these qualities remains questionable. Incidentally, dermatologists have also borrowed from architecture, referring, for example, to the "surface architecture" (Fritsch 1985, 566) and "surface relief" (Wollina and Wollina 1990, 521) of the skin.

The analogy between the house and the human body has a long iconographic and metaphorical tradition. In the language of Hans Blumenberg, the house is the "absolute metaphor" of the body, since it can be considered (at least in Western thought) as universal and self-referential. Absolute metaphors, according to Blumenberg, answer "those supposedly naive, essentially unanswerable questions whose relevance lies quite simply in the fact that they cannot be gotten rid of, because we do not *pose* them but rather find them *posed* at the foundation of existence."[5] These metaphors are orientational guides in the world and provide structure, in so far as they represent "the totality of reality which can never be experienced and never fully grasped" (1960, 19). Blumenberg shows the existence of "transferences that cannot be brought back to the real, into logicality" and should therefore be described as a "*basic stock* of philosophical language" (20). I shall explore the extent to which the absolute metaphor of the body as house in actuality always refers only to its skin. Body and house are vertical entities that should be conceived of simultaneously in their "unity and . . . complexity" (Bachelard 1964, 3, 17). The proportions of the house were transferred to those of the human being at an early stage, just as the facade of the house was anthropomorphized by being compared to the physiognomy of the face or the measurements of the body.[6] In the Western cultural sphere this is evident in the architectural designs of the Middle Ages and the Renaissance, which were based on the principles of proportionality and the body-house analogies of the Roman architect Vitruvius (Reudenbach

1980).[7] But to my mind it is not only these kinds of proportional and visual comparisons between buildings and bodies in their external form that are important in this regard. Special significance attaches to the parallelism between the stony house and the fleshly body as solid, enveloping, and concealing forms, as rooms in which life happens.

Until now, scholarship has failed to consider that the metaphor of the body as house presupposes a specific architectural-spatial form which is not that of the material body.[8] In the house metaphor, the body becomes a hollow, vessel-like space. This hollowed, empty form is conceivable only with reference to the tentlike, imaginary hide created by the skin. And the skin is not imagined as sacklike and soft (as, for example, in some depictions of flaying scenes) but as static and solid, as though it were either impregnated and tanned or a self-contained balloon filled with air.

Dream analysis interprets house dreams as being about the dreamer's own body. In fact, "the one typical—that is regular—representation of the human figure as a whole is a house." In this context Freud also establishes an analogy to the female genitals and to the womb, insofar as they share the characteristic of "enclosing a hollow space" (Freud 1963, 153). Consequently, all hollow shapes such as boxes, trunks, hollows, pockets, chests, and rooms become "symbols of the genital orifice" in dream analysis (156). The key that opens such a room or chest "is a decidedly male symbol" (158). Freud elaborates further: "In later Hebrew literature it is very common to find a woman represented by a house, whose door stands for the sexual orifice. A man complains, for instance, in a case of lost virginity, that he has 'found the door open' " (162).

The house as a metaphor for the womb, rare in antiquity, became popular only with Christianity, which saw the incarnation of the Son of Man in God's entry into Mary's virginal womb and birth as both God and man (Klauser et al. 1986, cols. 971 ff.). Similar to the way in which the woman's womb is understood as a hollow within a hollow, as a house in the house, in the early Christian mental world the heart, in particular, as well as the stomach and the head form doubled buildings, inner temples or fortresses (cols. 977 ff.). The house with its hollow spaces is thus commonly used as a metaphor for the female body, which can be penetrated and envelops the growing embryo, as well as for the nongendered body, which is conceived of as inhabited by a self. What explains this duplication in the metaphorical field is the fact that, in cultural history, woman was—and is—repeatedly analogized with the body.

These kinds of metaphorical notions of a body-house that can be exited is also known from Christian iconography, for example, in numerous medieval depictions of the soul departing the body space through the mouth at the moment of death. The body-soul dualism on which these ideas are based, which goes back to classical and postclassical traditions, has exerted a lasting influence even on present-day self-conceptions. The notion of the body as house, as lodging or dwelling, and the metaphor of residence or limited tenancy—for example, in Paracelsus (col. 966)—were originally models of consolation, constructs to overcome the fear of the finiteness of life; already in Plato, the earthly house of the body is conceived of as merely a transitory dwelling that we inhabit before entering into the eternal, heavenly house. And while death destroys the body, the inner soul is not affected by this dissolution.[9]

In the Christian conception—for example, in Augustine—the house of the body possesses sensory windows and doors through which perceptions pass to the inside (col. 962). The entry of these perceptions is judged to be either positive, as a gain of knowledge, or negative, as a threat to the soul from temptation. In anatomy, "the orifices of the body are in so many words termed *Leibespforten* [lit., portals of the body]" (Freud 1963, 159). Here, once again, is a metaphorical field with two levels: on one level, the windows of the body are understood to be exclusively the insular sensory organs concentrated on the skin (mouth, eyes, nose, ears). In this case, the opening is a selective membrane with respect to the specific sensory perception. On the second level, the circulatory exchange, with its acts of incorporation and excretion, is understood as entrance and exit movements in and out of the body-house, and the body orifices connected with this exchange are conceptualized as doors or gateways. The question is, what kind of notion of subject and body underlies such a conception, which thinks of the body (i.e., the skin) as hollow, inhabitable space and in so doing creates the following implications:

- the possibility of leaving, changing, and modifying the body-house, which in turn is thought of as rather immovable and static;
- the ability of intentionally opening and closing the openings of the skin-walls and with it the fundamental possibility of excluding all sensory perceptions;
- a fundamental impermeability of the skin-walls as a boundary;

- an unresolvable discrepancy between the subject in the body-house and the environment, a discrepancy that expresses itself in all processes of perception and contact;

- the notion of the skin-wall as a boundary marker between intimacy and the outside world, in which the doors and windows mediate between the private world of the individual and his or her environment?

The sensory organs are thus "glazed windows that cannot be opened under any circumstances" (Hauskeller 1995, 111). This kind of house model of sensory perception takes its cues—as is so often the case with constructs of human perception—first of all from the principle of vision, which is conceptualized as distance perception through a window, from behind a windowpane (the eyelids as the window shutters allow the subject to completely block out all impressions). This notion of the eyes as the windows to the soul is not the only supertemporal model of vision, which was originally understood as a perception of contact, as the inflow and outflow of the ray or stream of vision.[10] Moreover, the possibility of closure to sensations does not exist for the other senses (hearing, smell), which, to stay with the image, have no shutters. The notion of the skin as a house and the senses as windows implies the claim that human beings have the ability to determine, through an exercise of will, what they perceive; it ignores the fundamental penetrability of the skin, the exposure to an interaction with the world and its substances with all the senses, through odors, vapors, sounds, light, temperature, vibrations, and much more.

In the conception of the body as a house, not only are the other senses seen as locked gates or windows capable of being closed, but the skin itself becomes a stony wall, a static and impermeable boundary between the self and the world. This conception ignores the sensory perceptions of the skin, the experience of cold, heat, pressure, pain, and pleasure; the only aspects that are considered, to use Anzieu's language, are the functions of the skin in providing maintenance, acting as a container, offering protection against stimuli, and allowing for intersensoriality: "The house, without water and wind, without cold and fog, sun and night, at one time also without noise, the house offers protection, just as the belly of a ship separates us from the coldness of the sea. A second skin, which expands our sensorium. Still box and already eye. Hearing and ear conch. The house looks at the apple tree through the window. The house/skull calmly looks at the tree through the window/eye" (Serres 1985, 155). Here, Serres establishes an analogy between the house and the head; looking and hearing through the window thus become purely distance perceptions, something we already know as the model of the sense window from Christian tradition. The mediating function of the house is forgotten, and as a result it merely offers protection but at the same time separation and distance, since it "mitigates the given" (156). Serres's justified critique of this unalloyed thinking becomes clear when he interprets the epistemological situation of the classical philosopher, who wrestles with the world around him, as situated in a house in much the same way: "The philosopher forgets that this house, which is built around him, transforms an olive grove into a painting by Max Ernst" (156). The house is understood as a second skin that humankind put on "when it lost its coat of hair." In polemical language Serres speaks of how the house creates "an orthopedic sensorium around us," which transforms the given like a filter (157). Even if Serres is talking explicitly about the house, the wall-like imagined skin is implied: "Soft as we are, we build boxes that make us harder" (154).

As will become clear in the course of this book, the conception of the skin as a wall crystallizes into the canonical body image only in the wake of the processes of rationalization and objectification during the century of the Enlightenment. Norbert Elias has argued that in our culture the picture of the individual human being as a *Homo clausus*—"a little world in himself who ultimately exists quite independently of the great world outside"— determines the image of the human being in general. The core, the essence, the real self appears as something closed off by an invisible wall against everything that is outside (1978, 249). Elias makes clear that this experience of inside and outside, although it strikes us as eminently plausible, is not the basic experience of all human beings in all cultures but instead a specifically modern type of self-experience (p. 253 ff.). In the eighteenth and nineteenth centuries, the growing feeling of the unrecognizability of sensations and of the authentic inner character of the other led to a number of unveiling techniques, such as physiognomy, pathognomy, criminalistics, and, finally, psychoanalysis. What emerges is the ideal of a glassy, unveiled human being, whose authentic self is immediately visible to the observer. This idea of transparency found literary expression in Christian Heinrich Spieß's story "Der gläserne Ökonom" (The glass economist, 1795). Around the same time, in philosophy, Immanuel Kant referred to the ancient notion of a transparent breast that laid bare the authentic feelings (1978, 688). Technologically, the ideal was artificially realized in 1930 at the Dresdner Hygienemuseum with the creation of the life-size *Man of Glass* (figure 3)—the first

figure 3

Man of Glass (1930)

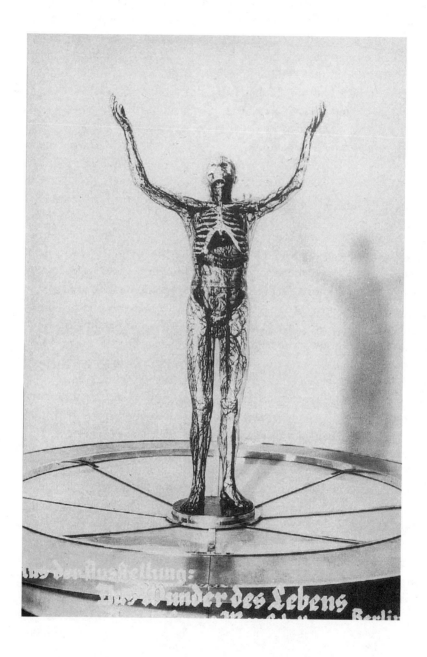

of its kind—whose subcutaneous physiology is visible while the integrity of the form is preserved (Beier and Roth 1990).

The more intense the need to veil the innermost parts, the greater the fears that develop about being involuntarily exposed. In more recent psychoanalytical theory, fears related to the boundary of the body—for example, the fear of unbearable penetration and of the psychic defenselessness it entails—have consequently become just as much a topic of research as phantasmatical notions of a perforated or excessively thin body surface or of a character armor. Contemporary art offers powerful depictions of this problem of the skin-armor. In the last few years, for example, a number of artists working with digital photography have created naked bodies or faces with completely closed skins devoid of orifices or sensory organs. Works of art like those by the duo of Anthony Aziz and Sammy Cucher (figure 4) or Inez van Lampsverde (figure 5) thus represent body images that are symptomatic of the late twentieth century, images composed only of a facade—and only of skin. That this psychohistorical process of the symbolic smoothing of the body and the hardening of its external boundaries is painful is also apparent in the literature of the nineteenth and twentieth centuries, which increasingly wrestled with the problem of armoring and reification. In 1835 Georg Büchner put these words into the mouth of Danton in his drama of the same name: "How do I know? We know little about each other. We're all thick-skinned [*Dickhäuter*], we reach for each other, but it's all in vain, we just rub the rough leather off. . . . We are very lonely" (Büchner 1986, 59).

In this passage Büchner is describing the loneliness that the isolated subject suffers in his or her bodily boundaries, which are experienced as an impenetrable armor, as a thick leathery skin like that of the elephant (*Dickhäuter* [lit., thick-skinned animal] is a figurative word for this animal in German; compare the English word "pachyderm," which means the same thing). Genuine contact with another person seems impossible. Almost a hundred years later, Musil expanded on this problem of being sewn into a concealing skin by adding the aspect of emotional loneliness: "Masses of fat, skeletons; sewn into a skin that is a sack of leather impervious to emotion" (1957, 317).

In Hans Henny Jahnn's trilogy *Fluß ohne Ufer* (River without banks, 1951) and in the fragment *Perrudja* (1929), the narrator describes the desire for intimacy with the other person: "I was so earnest and fulfilled that I wanted to reach out for his heart. And he kept such solemn and saintly silence that I thought he was reaching for my heart. But it was only the skin

figure 4
Anthony Aziz and Sammy Cucher,
Chris (1993)

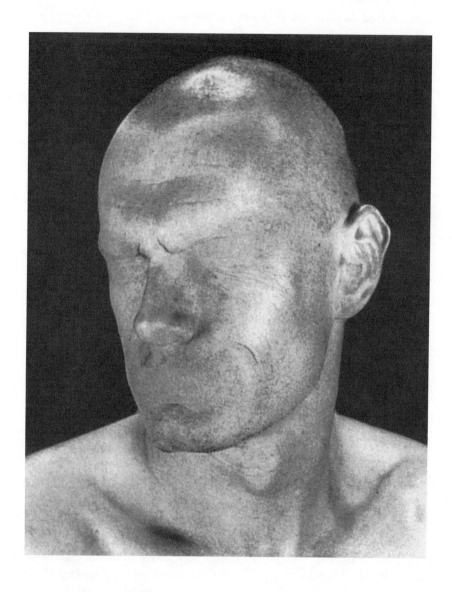

figure 5
Inez van Lampsverde, *Joan*, from the series
Thank You Tightmaster (1993)

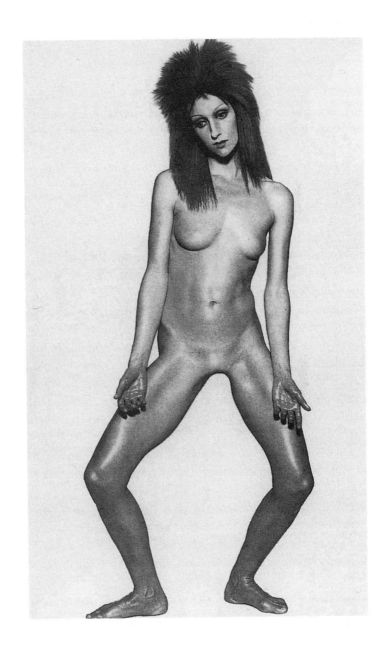

that we touched, groping it until it was sore" (1986a, 353); "All I could do was look at him. And all I ever saw was the boundary of his skin. At most, a silky abyss would shine forth from the glass of his eyes" (395); "Nobody knew the other. If there were a glass held before the eyes, one looks through it as deeply as one desires. The clothes off. The skin off. The muscles off. The bones remain. Or the heart. The soul. This something, which, unadorned, does not lie" (1985, 710).

These examples features many of the elements of classic body-soul dualism. The body becomes, as Jahnn explicitly stated, the "body prison" (771), the skin a barrier.[11] This skin-wall prevents both knowledge of the other and emotional connection. Underneath the skin, in the place to which one cannot penetrate, is the "heart" or the "soul" of the other. The eyes are the only windows into the hidden inside; they must bear witness to everything that goes on invisibly and beyond reach. Given a substitute function, the skin becomes a medium: instead of the essence, it is the skin that is looked at and touched, because it alone is accessible. Kafka, in a diary entry from 1920, captures the paradox that a boundary both separates and protects in the oxymoronic phrase "My prison cell—my fortress" (1990, 859). Elsewhere in the diary he writes: "What is it that binds you more intimately to these impenetrable, talking, eye-blinking bodies than to any other thing, the penholder in your hand, for example? Because you belong to the same species? But you don't belong to the same species, that's the very reason why you raised this question. The impenetrable outline of human bodies is horrible" (1976, 847). The isolated bodies, perceived as objectlike things similar to a writing implement, bodies of whose hidden inner life only the eye-windows bear witness, are something foreign, incomprehensibly other, eternally unattainable: "We are all buried alive and entombed like kings in triple or quadruple coffins—under the sky, in our houses, in our coats and shirts. / For fifty years we scratch on the lid of the coffin" (Büchner 1986, 108). Danton, in whose mouth Büchner has placed these despairing words, uses the coffin metaphor to make the body-house into a multitude of enveloping layers that prevent any aliveness. Where exactly the self conceals itself—whether behind the veils or on their opaque surface—becomes an open question. And so the outcry in *Danton's Death* that one must finally tear off the masks draws Danton's response that "the faces will come off with them" (20). The mask becomes the true self, which no longer hides invisibly inside but can be found only in the shell, the wall, the mask. That which conceals becomes the identity. The wall of the house shuts in the inside, but in the final analysis one can no longer say anything about the inside's absence, presence, or topography. In Jahnn's expressionistic early work *Pastor Ephraim Magnus* (1919), a deranged "seeker" kills and dismembers a woman. In court he states that he eventually "peeled the skin off the face" because he believed that "a face had to be hidden behind this mask." But to his disappointment he found "only raw, bloody flesh" (1988, 98).

Jahnn's drama *Straßenecke* (Street corner, 1931) wrestles with the problem that a person needs "neighborly, pleasant flesh" because one is "locked in" (1993, 33); in *Fluß ohne Ufer*, the human being is correspondingly defined as a "fortress of suffering" (1986a, 363). In his drama *Die Krönung Richards III.* (The coronation of Richard III, 1921), Jahnn puts the following words into the mouth of one of his characters: "For what we human beings know of one another is no more than what we can make out with our hands from the body of the other. And our hands are full of calluses, and our eyes stop at the external, and our ears hear only the words" (1988, 405). The idealized, homoerotic love that Gustav Anias Horn and Alfred Tutein live out in *Fluß ohne Ufer* prompts Tutein to fashion a picture of his friend in the nude. When the latter sees it, he reads the caption: "Anias, how I saw him and how my thoughts see him inwardly, and how he is dear to me in spite of it." Horn notes in amazement: "Tutein had quite obviously rendered my skin as transparent as glass and exposed my inside" (1986a, 715). The transparent skin becomes the mark of a love that experiences itself in a state of isolation, captive in an opaque body.

In literature, the penetration of the boundary of the body—in the form of the transcending of the "everyday reality of separated sacks" (Tibon-Cornillot 1979, 35)—is increasingly described as violent. We encounter the desire to injure the armored body and to penetrate into the body of the other frequently in Jahnn, occasionally in Kafka, and in many other (primarily male) authors of the twentieth century (Theweleit 1993, vol. 1). Apart from the ardent desire to return into the maternal body, which ends in death for the object of that desire, this destructive urge expresses the phantasmatical hope of finding something primal and authentic inside the hidden fortress of the body. Every means is employed in the vain search for a soul in the interior space of the other body, a soul that supposedly inhabits this thoroughly locked-up house. There is a possible—though not necessary—link between this and the constellation of the genders. Thus, while both male and female writers deal with the theme of being locked into one's own skin, the self-reference is often different. In Sylvia Plath, for example, we read repeatedly that the narrator "feels the wall of her skin" or that she is imprisoned in the "cage of her body." The experience of one's own skin is described as passive captivity, as a depressing but largely self-inflicted condition. Liberation from this "prison" is self-destructive and leads to a lesser degree to desires for external destruction or for penetration into other bodies.[12]

The skin marks not only an actual but also a profoundly symbolic boundary that is subject to cultural and historical change. The analysis of the semantic field involving the skin at the beginning of this chapter revealed a duality of thinking about skin as a phenomenon of cultural history: the skin as covering as distinct from the skin as self. These two modes of looking at the skin represent two models of the so-called body-soul relationship that still predominate today.

The conception of the skin as a house, as an enveloping layer in which the subject lies hidden, is diametrically opposed to the perception of skin as a felt boundary that can be experienced through the sensory perceptions of pain and pleasure and thus forms, in the early childhood process of individuation, the precondition for all object relationships later in life. For the discovery of the world by way of the skin constitutes a great metaphorical source for experience of every kind—for example, the characterization of people or places as cold or warm, irrespective of actual conditions. Elasticity as a quality of the skin and the self—on the one hand, defying resistance and, on the other hand, being permeable and supple—is also a common transference of skin qualities to the psychological realm. And while the skin has now been rehabilitated (in the sciences and the arts) as an organ of perception, the notion of the body as house still persists: we encounter it every time a differentiation is made—in the sense of the anthropological dualism—between a body and a subject that possesses it, lives in it, and has a specific relationship with it.

3 penetrations

*Body Boundaries and the Production of Knowledge
in Medicine and Cultural Practices*

The previous chapter discussed the extent to which
we can uncover, in idiomatic expressions and poetic formulations from the last few centuries, a conception that imagines the body as closed and hollow inside. The skin did not always constitute such
a linear boundary, for this conception was the result
of long-term processes that began in the Renaissance. Crucial to this transformation was the history of human anatomy since the sixteenth century as
the history of a literal transcending of the skin and
the rise of dermatology around 1800. Another important factor was the change in mentality that sub-
stituted the perception of the body as porous, open,
and at the same time interwoven with the world in
a grotesque way with one that viewed it as an indi-
viduated, monadic, and bourgeois vessel that the
subject was considered to inhabit. This chapter will
therefore identify epistemological moments and
cultural practices that led to the symbolic recoding
of the skin as a final body boundary. I will deal,
first, with collective moments when individuality
was restructured, then with medical and hygienic
procedures, and, finally, with the relationship between the production of knowledge and artistic
representation in anatomy and dermatology. Since

this transformation is subject to the *longue durée*, it is impossible to grasp it in its entirety. All I can do here is to collect central aspects of the genesis of the modern notion of skin as a closure and boundary surface.

Michael Bakhtin has traced the process by which the body notion that dominated European popular culture from the Middle Ages to the Baroque gradually disappeared. Eventually a new bodily canon emerged, one that conceived of "an entirely finished, completed, strictly limited body, which is shown from the outside as something individual. That which protrudes, bulges, sprouts, or branches off (when a body transgresses its limits and a new one begins) is eliminated, hidden, or moderated. All orifices of the body are closed" (1984, 319–320). This new conception of the body stands in contrast to that of the grotesque body, which displays a notion of corporeal wholeness and its boundaries that is foreign to us. In the grotesque body, the boundaries between body and world and those between individual bodies are much less differentiated and more open than they are in the new body canon: the very boundary of the grotesque body reveals the intermingling with the world in that protruding body parts (the nose or stomach, for example) are understood as projecting into the world, and the inside of the body comes out and mingles with the world. The main events in the existence of this grotesque body thus happen through other bodies and substances; Bakhtin lists eating, drinking, defecation, copulation, pregnancy, sickness, death, and decomposition as the kinds of "acts of the bodily drama" that occur at the "confines of the body and the outer world."[1]

The artistic logic of the grotesque ignores the closed, regular, and smooth regions of the body surface. Instead, it concentrates on its excrescences and orifices, only on "that which leads beyond the body's limited space or into the body's depths. Mountains and abysses, such is the relief of the grotesque body; or speaking in architectural terms, towers and subterranean passages" (318). Bakhtin speaks of a "boundless ocean" of grotesque body motifs that "extends to all languages, all literatures, and the entire system of gesticulation" and can be found across cultures in rituals, religious and popular ecstasies, and carnival. By contrast, the new body canon of art, literature, and polite conversation in the modern period is merely a "tiny island" (319) in this ocean. It is an island of profound consequence, however, for the bourgeois body is a singular one that no longer possesses any signs of duality. This body is a strictly demarcated entity with an impenetrable, smooth facade. The surface of this closed body is thus marked by two-dimensionality, whereas the baroque corporeal surface of the grotesque body, with its protrusions and recesses, was far more three-dimensional. Only when the collective imagination came to look on skin as such a two-dimensional and linear boundary surface was it possible to read the body for its individual physiognomy, its attributed race, and its spontaneous sensations and sensory expressions, as well as its diseases.

Barbara Duden has noted that the conditions that shaped the modern body perception did not emerge until the second half of the eighteenth century (1991a, 1). Using as her source the journals of a women's doctor in Eisenach around the year 1730, she shows that even as late as the early eighteenth century, the body surface was invested with a meaning very different from the one it has today. The skin was understood as a porous layer with a multitude of possible openings, many of which would no longer be seen as such today. Here, the surface of the body is a place of permeability and mysterious metamorphoses. "Fluxes" that are in constant motion in the body and can continually change their form exit the body as blood, pus, urine, phlegm, or sperm. Body fluids such as sperm or menstrual blood are by no means always understood as indicative of gender (the menses and the "golden vein"—the term used for hemorrhoids at the time—were still interpreted as equivalent therapeutic evacuations of the body as late as the early eighteenth century) (116ff.).[2] All these "fluxes" have a functional resemblance. Accordingly, doctors did not distinguish between normal and pathological excretions but only between their various degrees of efficacy for the body. Therapeutic intervention on the part of the physician consisted primarily in clearing a path to the surface for the flows that were making the inside sick in order to achieve a purifying effect. The physician prescribed medicines, baths, and unguents to set this healing excretion in motion. If the body did not open on its own, an exit was created through bleeding or a blistering dressing. As becomes clear from this account, wounds and bloody discharges from the skin, which today are regarded as pathological, something to be stopped if possible, were seen as quite the opposite until the early eighteenth century.

In this pre-Enlightenment conceptual world, there are many more body openings than we would recognize: eyes, ears, nose, mouth, breasts, navel, anus, urinary passage, and vulva (120). These "orifices" are primarily exits whose intentional direction points from the inside to the outside. The body surface itself is everywhere a potential exit, because it can open or be induced to open anywhere. Wounds, bulges, or tears in the skin are channels from which something flows that would otherwise choose a different route.[3] Duden notes: "The skin was fragile and it was a boundary, but it was not meant to demarcate the body against the outside world. It was above all a surface on which the inside revealed itself" (123). The inside of the body is conceived as an unstructured, osmotic space whose processes remain invisible. Speculations about this inside are possible only through signs that appear on the skin or through significant discharging "fluxes."

What is important in this context is that body orifices and skin pores were still thought of as structurally analogous at this time. For example, Zedler's *Universal-Lexikon* (1753) has this to say about the skin: "It also has large and small holes, large ones being mouth, nose, ears, and so on, where the skin can be said to be thinned rather than perforated, and small holes, generally sweat holes, which are larger and smaller for passage through, which comes in the form of hair, vapors, and sweat" (1961, 12:col. 925). If the pores of the skin and the "large" body orifices are seen as functionally equivalent and different only in size, this indicates that the skin was understood less as a wall in which closable windows and doors were embedded and more as a kind of porous tissue that could potentially have an opening anywhere.

Walter Schönfeld, a historian of medicine, compiled the medical practices that were applied to the skin over the centuries for the purpose of "treatment, prevention, and the identification of ailments at some distant location." He showed that a conception of the skin as a "therapeutic organ" (1943, 71) did not fully cease until the middle of the nineteenth century. Right up to the nineteenth century, a plethora of methods "for conduction through the skin" were practiced, some of which go back as far as Hippocratic medicine. In accordance with the doctrine of humoral pathology, manifestations on the skin were not regarded as independent illnesses but as signs and indications of internal disturbances (44). Numerous therapeutic methods for drawing off diseases were developed. The principle they share is that some injury or stimulus was inflicted on the skin as a way of exerting a positive influence on internal ailments.

Such practices include, for example, the application of a cautery to the skin, the creation of a "fontanel" (a small, artificially produced sore maintained by an irritant), the insertion of a "seton" (a wick or a strip of linen that was pulled through a wound for several days to produce pus), the use of natural and chemical skin irritants, and the application of leeches. These kinds of therapeutic procedures for bringing about *morbi auxiliares* (helpful ailments) were applied either in proximity to the presumed internal disease or at delicate and soft areas of the skin. Into the nineteenth century, a lotion known as "pox ointment" was also frequently used as a therapeutic: it caused vigorous pustules and was considered an effective agent that triggered in the skin itself a disease process that altered the structure of the skin deep below the epidermis (59). The nineteenth century also still saw the use of a therapy called "life awakener" (*Lebenwecker*), a club studded with needles that caused superficial injuries and bleeding and was used together with irritating skin oil and "skin-conducting" tea (60–61). Scarification, the scratching or cutting of the skin for the same purpose, was another therapy in use as late as the nineteenth century.

These kinds of practices, which a modern perspective is more likely to associate with torture and scourging than with medical methods, destroyed the smooth surface of the skin. It would seem that the flawlessness of the epidermis was not the primary good it became in the twentieth century, a good that had to be preserved at any price. Instead, the skin was actively damaged in order to affect the inside. Of the many medical therapies, some of which I have briefly indicated here, the only one that has survived is the hygienic, bloodless, and nonscarring practice of acupuncture. At some point, then, a radical shift eliminated the skin as a therapeutic organ. This development was based on a fundamentally changed picture of the body. Practices whose goal was to open the skin sack in order to let pathogenic agents exit the body have been replaced with methods that leave the body-vessel closed: oral (or anal or venous) medicines that are introduced into the body, medicines that must engage in invisible battle with the pathogenic agents on the inside. Only when medication fails is the body anesthetized, disinfected, and cut open; the wounds and scars produced in this process are unavoidable side effects but not sites capable of taking on semiotic meaning. Moreover, the purpose of opening the body is no longer to allow harmful substances to flow out but primarily to produce knowledge or repair injuries or infections. Michel de Certeau consequently speaks of how the conception of medical treatment as the removal of something harmful is replaced by the notion of treatment as the introduction of something that is missing.[4]

The fundamental restructuring of medical diagnosis and treatment to deal directly with the inside, without applying treatments on and in the skin, could not fail to influence the collective body image. A conception of the skin as closure and a necessary boundary layer could arise only after these multifarious practices of drawing off substances through the skin and opening the epidermis were dismissed as prescientific and replaced by intracorporeal medication or surgical intervention (which opened the body but afterward neatly closed it up again). Moreover, from a historical perspective, the body had to be individually demarcated and fundamentally demystified before the anatomist could cut it open as matter that had ceased to embody symbolic meaning. The links between the inside of the body as microcosm and its relationship to the macrocosm surrounding it, which were deeply embedded in culture, had to be cast aside along with the belief in the kind of living exchange between the inside and the outside that Bakhtin has highlighted for the grotesque body of popular culture. In terms of cultural history, this paradoxical process did not end until around 1800, when the body as a meaning-bearing, communicating entity was finally silenced and isolated, so that subsequently it could be "objectively" opened again (by the anatomist and later the clinical surgeon).

Another indication that the skin in older body conceptions was still thought of as open comes from the gradual shift of the dirt boundary from the inside to the outside: although the fluxes surging from the body were, of course, treated increasingly as a problem, controlled, and banned, henceforth it was the threat of external things that posed a potential threat to the body. The skin interface thus became the primary danger zone of possible penetration and infection. A new concept of hygiene slowly began to spread, starting in the eighteenth century, one that saw first miasma and later germs as the cause of disease. Until then, medical thinking had still been based on humoral pathology, according to which a disease was essentially an imbalance of inner fluids. This model was only now displaced by the notion that health was protected by shuttering it against potential external dangers of infection. This explains why even the medieval plague and later syphilis did not cause people to keep their distance from each other, for disease was understood as a process triggered in the individual himself (Böhme 1989, 55).

Up to the nineteenth century, contact with water remained problematic and anxiety-ridden—and not merely out of fear of germs but because the skin was still seen as not closed off. Cleansing the body with water was strictly measured so as not to attack what was understood to be the exceedingly fragile protective layer of the skin, for into the eighteenth century, it was assumed that water could penetrate into the body and influence the internal organs. People believed that water settled in the "interstices" of the interior—between the organs and the blood vessels—and disturbed the body through mechanical effects (Vigarello 1988, 95). Only toward the end of the eighteenth century did the habit arise of washing with warm water, though afterward the pores were closed with sticky substances to strengthen and protect the body. This treatment of the corporeal openings with rose or huckleberry oil was considered a necessity, for the body was forti-fied and invigorated only by "closing" the pores, "stopping them up"; in this way an "alien hand worked on the skin, hardened it, and managed it" (127–128). It was a very slow process that gave rise to this "aggressive hy-gienic and corporeal policy" that, on the one hand, demanded the daily cleansing of the body with water and soap and, on the other hand, "creat-ed spatial and protective zones between the subject and his own body and the bodies of others" (Barthel 1989, 144).

The foundational text of modern anatomy appeared with Andreas Vesalius's *De humani corporis fabrica* (1543). Here, the anatomist for the first time stepped down from his lectern and took over the handiwork of dissection himself. Until then, medical instructional dissection was still characterized by a trinity that is clearly visible in contemporary illustrations: the scholar who, from an elevated position, lectures from an anatomical tractate; the *demonstrator* who performs the actual dissection; and the *ostentator* who points out the relevant points (Sawday 1990, 118). By contrast, Vesalius was the first to portray himself, on the title page of the *Fabrica*, on the same level with the corpse, which he himself—and this is the critical point—also dis-sected in person: the scholar and his object now confront each other di-rectly. Experimental, practical exploration and the discovering gaze com-peted with traditional book learning, which, right up to the Middle Ages, was still largely based on the ancient writings of Galen and his analogies be-tween animal and human anatomy. Beginning with Vesalius, the human body came into view as the sole locus of knowledge and understanding. The removal of the skin is the emblematic act of this production of knowl-edge, which is why numerous anatomical title page engravings from the baroque period show the skin detached from the body, whether held up by a figure or in lieu of the traditional title page drapery (Herrlinger 1968, 474ff.). What follows are two examples from the rich, abstruse iconogra-phy to illustrate the extent to which the skin was given a highly symbolic place in modern anatomy.

On the frontispiece of Alexander Read's *Manuall of the Anatomy or dis-section of the body of Man* (1638), the table of the anatomist, traditionally shown in the lower half of the image, is found in the upper half (figure 6). The title page drapery, which usually hangs from the upper edge of the image, is here moved to the lower half. Closer inspection reveals that this is not a cloth at all but a human skin. Robert Herrlinger has described it as

figure 6
Frontispiece, Alexander Read, *Manuall of the
Anatomy or dissection of the body of Man* (1638)

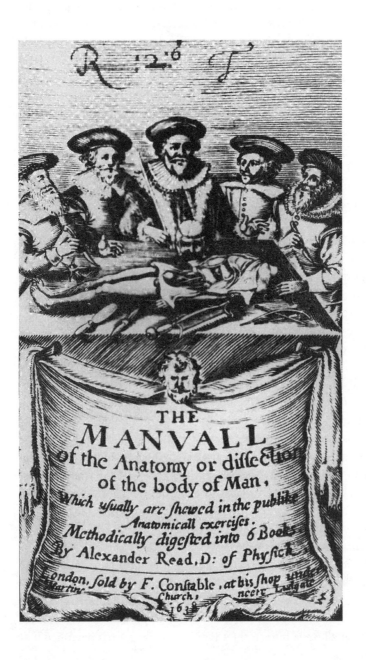

the earliest example of the motif of the "skin as frontispiece" in the history of medical illustration (478).

Thomas Bartholin, on the title page of his 1651 work *Anatomia reformata* (figure 7), "boldly casts overboard the entire emblematic ballast that weighed on the graphic design of baroque title pages" (478): all that is left is the human skin hanging from two nails. The cast-off cutaneous garment, assuming the macabre pose of the crucified, is nailed to a frame that opens into the depth behind. The skin has become an entrance curtain in front of a mysterious world, nothing of which is yet revealed on the title page. Opening up the tractate thus becomes tantamount to peeling the body out of its skin. The secrets below the skin are hidden inside the weighty book-body. And the fact that the title itself (as in the work of Read) was printed directly on the skin turns the latter into a kind of trophy, with the act of taking possession of it marked discursively.

The Florentine Academy of Arts was the first institution to introduce anatomy as a required subject for artists in the sixteenth century, thus initiating the close connection between art and medicine that persisted far into the nineteenth century. At the same time, again in Florence, the first wax and wooden sculptures of *écorchés* were presented to the public. And the earliest, at first still sporadic, public dissections were also taking place (Lemire 1993, 73). For that very purpose, so-called anatomical theaters were designed, where the dismemberment of a corpse was publicly staged as a theatrical act. Old churches and chapels were often used for such spectacles, and in these spaces the dissection then took place on the altar—an admonitory reminder of perverted ancient sacrifices (Mollenhauer 1989, 182). The anatomical theater became highly popular in the seventeenth century, as a result of which the "anatomical idea" (Putscher 1972, 59) was implanted in the consciousness over wide social strata. Only the pathological dissection of the eighteenth and nineteenth centuries was once again seen as a purely medical, private affair and moved into closed chambers.

Initially, the opening of corpses was still subject to religious and philosophical taboos and possible at all only under special ritualized conditions. There was also a constant shortage of bodies. As early as the sixteenth century, substitutes for real organs were therefore fashioned for educational purposes from various materials (wood, wax, ebony, papier-mâché, plaster, and resin). Compared to illustrations in books, these models had the advantage that they were three-dimensional and the various parts could be taken apart in the way a dissection would progress (Lemire 1993, 72 ff.). Especially wax

figure 7
Frontispiece, Thomas Bartholin, *Anatomia
reformata* (1651)

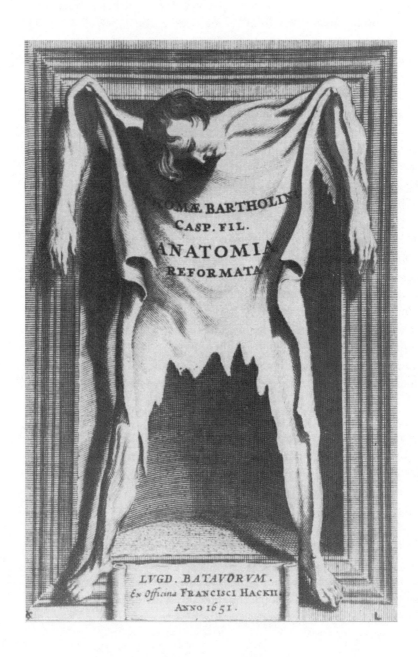

models, which were produced from the seventeenth century on in increasing quantities, were often more realistic than real preserved specimens,[5] since they permanently captured the form and color of fresh organs and muscle layers, did not suffer from dessication or age, and possessed an opaque surface sheen that readily became moist and therefore corresponded especially well to the thin, transparent inner skins and membranes.

Italy had a long tradition in the art of wax modeling to fashion relic and votive images. Although the subject matter and use of the sculptures underwent a fundamental change, the reliclike aura of the objects was initially still preserved: what took place, in the words of Michel Lemire, was a "sacralization of the body" (79). The anatomical wax sculptures were presented in special rooms on custom-made pedestals, resting on precious silk pillows and lace drapes inside glass cabinets. Large anatomical collections were assembled toward the end of the eighteenth century in the newly established court-financed museums of natural history in Florence, Bologna, and Paris and later in the new medical military academy in Vienna. The eighteenth century also saw a number of private cabinets of wealthy noblemen who devoted themselves to physics, optics, natural history, and the like; here, too, anatomical sculptures were a popular collector's item (Lemire 1990, 104).

The *anatomia plastica* (a term Goethe coined after visiting the collection in Florence) was fashioned from original specimens. Except for life-size whole body models, which were presculpted in clay,[6] these models were directly cast in plaster from the specimen—the dissected body; this cast then served as the mold for the wax moulage. The depiction of an opened, dismembered, or flayed body was thus always based on direct physical contact with the corpse. The anatomical wax sculptures of the eighteenth century still reveal the need to beautify artistically what is really an unattractive, unpleasant object. This mode of presentation changed in the nineteenth century. The objects no longer served the secular contemplation of an elite. They ceased to be precious objects and became instead indispensable tools of medical training; the naturalism of their appearance was henceforth the sole artistic criterion that mattered (92). The aesthetic effect and artful presentation of the objects was no longer a concern.

In the eighteenth century, not only individual organs were fashioned but often life-size bodies with open abdomens and removable internal organs. On many sculptures, the skin has not been pulled off but merely opened and flipped back, exposing the underlying muscle fibers or the intervening network of veins. Especially poignant are head sculptures where one half shows the exposed muscular structure while the other half retains is covering of skin, with the object gazing intently at the observer (figure 8). The incisions that the anatomists had to perform in order to separate the skin from its underlying fat tissue are documented by having the skin hang over or frame the exposed flesh like a curtain with folds that has been pushed aside. In the process, the cross section through the epidermis and the dermis is also shown: while the skin is lifted off, it is reproduced with great care.

Women, when they are depicted as whole bodies, wear handsome makeup, their hair is styled, and they are softly bedded on purple satin pillows (figure 9). The famous life-size figure commonly called the Medici Venus in Vienna's Josephinum Museum (figure 10), which looks at the observer with alert, sensual eyes, also wears a double strand of pearls that inscribes a boundary line on the body: on one side is the living, made-up face with its porcelainlike skin tone, on the other side is the opened, dissected trunk with its removable organs. The skin of women's bodies is rosy white, devoid of hair or blemishes, and as though faintly powdered—an idealized skin that contrasts sharply with the hygienic conditions at the time and is reminiscent of classical marble sculptures. The incisions in the body are shown to be emphatically clean and smooth; they highlight the artificial moment of the sculpture, the gesture of the virtual; they show an imaginary view under the skin that eliminates the bloodiness. This practice of using opened-eyed humans as illustrative objects, apparently alive, in spite of their opened or skinned bodies, judging from their facial expressions or posture and gesture (one impressive example is a wax *écorché* by André-Pierre Pinson; figure 11), anticipates something only twentieth-century medicine was able to achieve with the help of radiology, electrocardiography, and ultrasound: observing the processes under the skin in a living body (Stafford 1993, 283). Only then did it become possible to dispense with the ear and the hand as "temporary, substitute organs" (Foucault 1973, 165) in rendering diagnoses.

Initially, the uncovering of the topography of the interior of the body in the seventeenth and eighteenth centuries produced a fascination with the mechanical-physical connections between organs and channels, which, like some ingenious machine, together created functional units and chains: tubular connections, pumping systems, leverage mechanics. Life and mechanical movement were equated (Sonntag 1989, 90). It is not until around 1800 that the network of sensations—the nerves—was discovered,

figure 8

Francesco Calenzuoli, *Myologie de la face
et du cou*

figure 9

Clemente Susini, *Circulation artérielle,*
veineuse et lymphatique de l'intestin

figure 10
Clemente Susini, so-called Medici Venus
(ca. 1775)

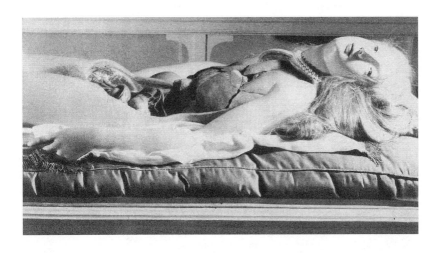

figure 11
André-Pierre Pinson, *Le grand Ecorché* (1773)

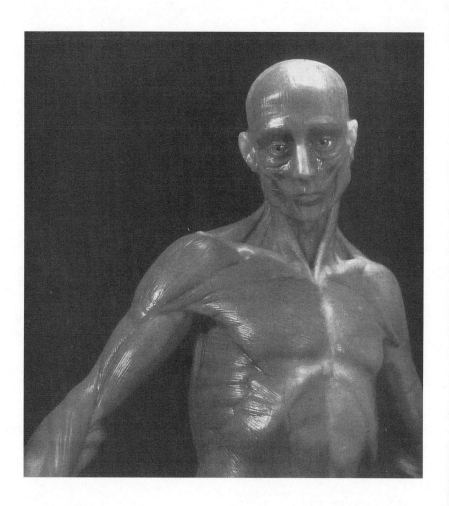

a discovery that overthrew this mechanistic-hydraulic conception of the body. A new field arose for medical illustration: the exploration of the lymphatic and neural network directly below the skin, between the layers of the skin and the muscle tissue (wax, so pliable, was particularly well suited as material for this task). After years of searching in the depths of the body there now began an examination close to the surface, which recognized the skin itself as an independent organ. Observers believed they had finally discovered a manifestation of the soul in this web of nerves, this "new medium or 'atmospheric' third world of fleeting emotions and fluid instincts coursing beneath the skin" (Stafford 1993, 38). The history of anatomy can thus also be read as reverse archaeology, a paradoxical uncovering of layers in which the deepest strata were conquered first and the gaze returned only gradually to the surface, where a more refined analysis revealed that the material that was initially flipped aside unnoticed was significant. The quest for "l'âme au corps,"[7] for a manifestation of the soul in the body, also led back epistemologically to its integument, to the place where the boundary to the world and its sensitivity begins.

It was only toward the end of the eighteenth century, when the entire corporeal space had been modeled in all its nuances, that sculptural anatomy began to focus on the pathological body. (The epistemological change in some sense leads to the creation of the normal body in the first place, in that the abnormal creates the norm as its own counterpart). Interest in visible pathologies gave birth to dermatological illustrations and models. A healthy skin offers no new insights, since it is visible and accessible; only when it departs from the norm does it become the object of medical interest. Just as anatomical cartography of the body began deep inside the body and returned from there to the surface, dermatology as such is a very young discipline within medicine and asserted itself as a separate specialty only in the nineteenth century. At all times, however, dermatologists, who were immediately given the unpopular field of venereology as a subfield when the discipline was formed (and this remains the case today), were marginalized by their professional colleagues. Dealing with skin diseases and suffering resulting from sexual activity was and is considered an inferior occupation, as compared, for example, with internal surgery, which has to this day preserved its symbolic state of "mystification" (Goffman 1959, 67) because of the persistent strangeness of its object.[8]

The systematization of dermatological and venereal diseases did not begin until the end of the eighteenth century. This, too, indicates that the skin became an object of science only as a two-dimensional surface, as the skin of an individual person. Robert Willan's *Description and Treatment of Cutaneous Diseases* (1798) was the first work on dermatology that contained color illustrations (colored copperplate engravings). Classification was done according to local characteristics (Pusey 1933, 64). Just as the diagnosis of skin diseases at the time was still based primarily on visible manifestations, their representation in textbooks required illustration. The descriptive text increasingly took second place, whereas in the work of Willan, an early representative of dermatological systematics, the discursive description was still seen as equal to its visual counterpart, the two forms complementing each other.

The situation is different in Jean-Louis Alibert's *Clinique de l'Hôpital Saint-Louis* (Clinic of the hospital of Saint Louis, 1833). This color atlas by the French dermatologist who was the director of the clinic consisted almost entirely and literally of portraits of individual diseases (figure 12), which are embodied by individuals who at times are depicted in what are virtually classic portrait poses. The dermatosis sits on the skin like an externally applied blemish (figure 13). The patients that are portrayed, often young, lovely women, meet the ideal of beauty of the time: oval faces, clear eyes, and pale, smooth complexions with slightly blushed cheeks. The disease is seen as an external rash that afflicts the individual from the outside and sticks to the skin as a stigma. As late as the nineteenth century, skin diseases were understood as external rather than internal conditions, as we see them today (Buchborn 1988, 350). And since the disease was portrayed as a blemish from an external affliction, treatment was likewise external and local.

The textual element clearly takes a back seat to the visual element in these presentations, as is clear from the lavishness of the illustrations in relationship to the comparatively short text. Furthermore, the family tree of dermatoses that Alibert developed in his *Nosologie naturelle; ou, Les maladies du corps humain distribués par familles* (Paris, 1817) shows that skin diseases were classified exclusively according to their visual equivalences.[9] Stafford attributes this tendency toward visual presentation in the atlases to the epistemological change in the eighteenth century "from a text-based culture to a visually dependent culture" (Stafford 1993, xviii). This led to a continuing devaluation of the other senses and an increasingly abstract understanding of visual perception itself, a trend that was further reinforced by the interposition of new optical instruments.

figure 12

Scarlatine normale, from Jean-Louis Alibert,
Clinique de l'Hôpital Saint Louis (1830)

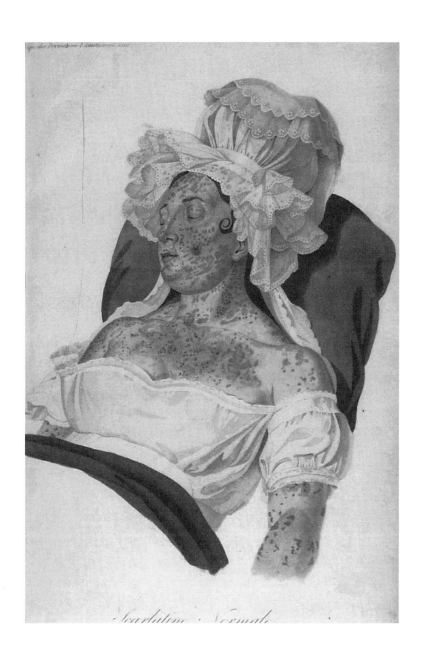

figure 13

Varielle pustuleuse, from Jean-Louis Alibert
Clinique de l'Hôpital Saint-Louis (1830)

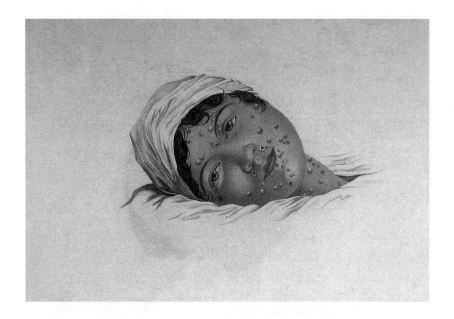

The illustrations in Ferdinand Hebra's *Atlas der Hautkrankheiten* (Atlas of skin diseases, 1856–1876) a few decades later are very different. Compared to those in Alibert, the coloration of the pathological lesions is much more muted and restrained, which can be attributed to the new technique of chromolithography (Klimpel 1980, 3). Moreover, the theatrical moment of the presentation has largely receded: the patients are no longer depicted in individual poses, their physiognomy and facial expressions are less conspicuous, and the illustrations have no discernible overall artistic composition. The most critical change from Alibert, however, lies in the fact that this work, like that of Willan, depicts mostly body fragments (figure 14). But in the spirit of a progressing naturalism, the illustrations now capture the site of the actual infection and not, as in Willan, the least shameful and therefore most neutral skin areas. Now, the focus is especially on the buttocks and genital region. The diseased areas are presented isolated by white sheeting, a method that points to a growing abstraction of the seat of the disease. The pathological fact is fixed more precisely and reproduced in a more realistic manner.[10] Moreover, the note "Painted from nature" on the title pages of all ten volumes points to the real-life basis for the illustrations. It is no longer the bearers of a disease who are individualized (as persons), as was still the case in Alibert, but only the dermatoses themselves. Ethical and moral taboos increasingly take a back seat to the all-embracing desire for enlightenment.

Dermatological illustration eventually reached a high point in the wax moulages fashioned by Jules Baretta and his successors for the Hôpital Saint-Louis in Paris beginning in 1878: in their work, propriety and modesty yield to the desire for knowledge.[11] The museum in the world's first skin clinic (founded by Alibert), which houses more than four thousand moulages of every conceivable skin disease and is still open to the public, looks at first glance like a cabinet of horrors. But there are no monsters on display—those would be individuals, after all—only monstrosities. The moulages are displayed in glass cases in white drapings against black velvet backgrounds, similar to the fragmented body segments in Hebra's atlas. In the right-hand corner of each object can be found the signature of the artist and the year of execution. The frames and isolation freeze the objects into artificial pictures that, in spite of their seeming realism, display a high degree of abstraction (figure 15). The three-dimensionality and surface quality of the wax (often furnished with real hair, nails, and special varnishes) renders the skin sculptures strikingly real—but dissected. For

figure 14
Scabies, from Ferdinand Hebra,
Atlas der Hautkrankheiten (1865)

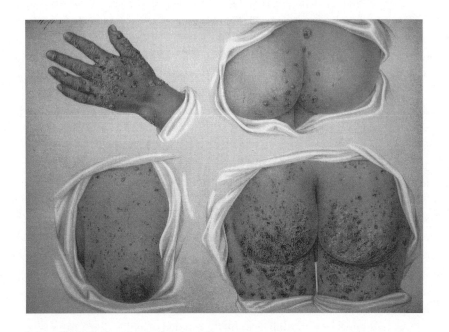

below the frame of white cloth, the volume diminishes drastically, which invariably creates the impression of incisions that are concealed but should be imagined by the observer. The relieflike projection of the objects from the surface produces a twofold aesthetic effect: first, the protruding lesions, skin flaps, boils, suppurations, warts, blisters, eczema, and calluses seem particularly plastic and real; second, and this is the more important innovation, the disease (and with it the observer's gaze) no longer rests on the skin. Instead, for the first time in the history of dermatological illustrations, it eats deeply into the body. We can gauge the nineteenth century's fear of these surface-destroying lesions in light of the change in mentality toward a necessarily closed skin. Dermatological sculptures follow in the wake of a phantasmatical body image that is created only by the symbolic closing of the skin. It would appear that, in the final analysis, it is the persistent memory of the body's state of nonclosure and its fragility that has made dermatology a stigmatized discipline to this day.

The afflicted body in Baretta's moulages is open and porous; the disease cuts a hole into the skin, and the corruption slowly grows into the inside, which is involuntarily exposed. These dissecting wounds are especially gruesome when they corrode the face, exposing the pharynx and nasal cavity and the bones of the jaw or skull. The diseased subject is deprived of the mask of facial skin; all that remains is a questioning open hole of nonidentity. In this respect, destroyed physiognomies like the one depicted in figure 16 do not point to an individual but to the disease itself in its pronounced individualization. (Still, the objects in this encyclopedia of dermal maladies are often personalized after the fact through indications of gender, age, name, or dates pertaining to the history of the disease. This is a common practice in pathology[12] and in striking contrast, for example, to plastic anatomy, which erases the person with the mold by refusing to provide any information.) The size of the collection in the Hôpital Saint-Louis indicates that the curators were interested in a comprehensive panorama of all manifestations of a disease. What Foucault demonstrated in the case of the diagnostic practice of internal lesions around 1800 is true also in this case, namely, that thinking in terms of categories and types slowly yields to thinking in terms of singular variations.

All parts of the human body surface without exception were objects of presentation. Among the venereal diseases we find sections of the afflicted vaginal opening bracketed by spread legs (see figure 15), as well as an exposed, isolated anus. It is these truly macabre portraits of diseases that drive

figure 15

Jules Baretta, *Vegetations vulvaires
nonsyphiliques* (1881)

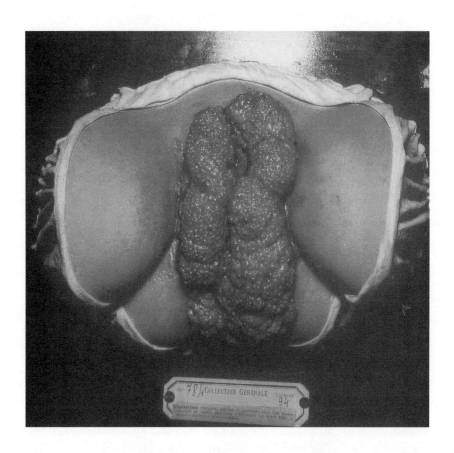

figure 16

Jules Baretta, *Tumeurs des os:*
Difformité faciale (1886)

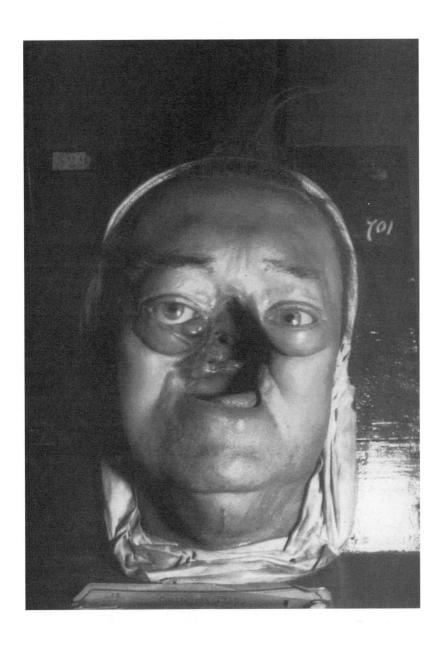

the compulsion toward localization and fragmentation as well as the necessary coldness of the physician's and artist's gaze to this emphatic climax.[13] A new epistemological and artistic approach, compared to earlier methods in plastic anatomy, lies in the fact that the plaster casts were taken from the living body, which, in spite of its individual suffering, functioned merely as a timeless model. Gérard Tilles, the current curator of the collection of the dermatological museum, speaks retroactively of a "privilège d'accéder au sanctuaire de l'iconographie dermatologique" (1995, 207), that is, of the (dubious) honor of gaining admission into this sanctuary of dermatological iconography. Through the process of being cast, the patient's skin disease becomes an identity-bestowing image, which, as indicated, is further highlighted by indications of personal data. Here, the skin bears the unique personal stigmata of the sufferer, which make the afflicted individual singular and unmistakable in the eyes of the dermatologists. This close connection between stigmatized skin and (forcible) individualization will reappear throughout this study in other contexts.

This chapter, which has looked at the symbolic change of the body surface, reveals the extent to which the body still tended to be seen as open in the seventeenth and eighteenth centuries. The skin was a porous surface whose openings served a multitude of medical practices. The surface of the body was not yet regarded as a smooth wall but as a three-dimensional layer interwoven with the world. Not until the late eighteenth century did a hygienic concept appear that no longer identifies invisible fluid relationships inside the body as the cause of a disease but rather attributes it to external infection. Drawing on these and other clues, I have traced the extent to which the collective body image has changed only during the last two centuries to that of a closed, demarcated individual body whose final boundary is the skin. At the same time, there arose a way of thinking according to which diseases bear individualizing characteristics, as is clearly revealed by dermatological illustrations. While skin diseases in the late eighteenth century were depicted as blemishes and spots located on the skin, the nineteenth century saw the creation of the phantasms of dissecting wounds that eat deeply into the skin and (re)open the carefully closed body in a gruesome way.

4 flayings

Exposure, Torture, Metamorphoses

Flaying holds a special place in the history of the piercing of the body boundary. The practice represents a synthesis of the most extreme form of capital punishment (torture) and the medical production of knowledge. The visual arts of the sixteenth and seventeenth centuries, in particular, belabored the theme of flaying to exhaustion. This intense preoccupation reflects the epistemological rupture that was triggered by the emerging discipline of anatomy. The question of violence in the transcending of the cutaneous body boundary and the possibility of depicting a more-than-naked body were addressed iconographically. These works of art reflect the intent to establish the display of the dissected interior as a pictorial theme and to remove the taboo hanging over it. But they also mirror the mental struggle of the artist with the horror of excessive exposure, which one could begin to banish only under the protective cover of a mythical or Christian representation.

The backdrop to this correspondence between anatomy and penal flaying are the facts, often overlooked by medical historians, that the bodies used for anatomical dissection were almost exclusively those of criminals and that in a court of law the mere threat of postmortem dismemberment (or flaying) was regarded as a strong increase in the severity of a punishment. Destroying the bodily integrity of a corpse was not easily done, by any means; rather, breaking open the body was tantamount to a disgrace, an added degradation of the criminal. Anatomists had to struggle hard to free themselves of the stigma of being "flayers of humans" (Bergmann 1997, 45). And there is something both heroic and sinister about the testimony of Renaissance artists recounting dissections they carried out, usually in secret.

Jonathan Sawday has shown that the bodies depicted in the anatomical illustrations of the sixteenth century often take an active part in their own dissection (1995, 110ff.). He argues that this autodissection attests to the fact that the anatomical specimen remained alive and indicates that the body "acquiesced" in its own anatomical reduction. For example, a large number of woodcut and copper engravings from anatomical atlases of the sixteenth and seventeenth centuries depict whole-body figures who lift up their skin like a cloth garment and allow the observer a look at what was previously hidden. They present their underlying, schematized muscles (figure 17), digestive tract (figure 18), or reproductive organs (figure 19) with equanimity or grim delight. These figures clearly reveal the extent to which the skin was understood as a kind of enveloping leather or textile tent in which the true essence was concealed. Especially in figure 19, the female body is depicted as a filled, voluminous hollow space presented to the observer, a space that houses the internal organs.[1] The skin functions as a solid separating layer surrounding the inner body space, further emphasized by the fact that the detail of the opening reappears on the wall as though it were a hole.

The aesthetic effect of this active participation creates the impression that the body desires its own dissection. These images imply that anatomical reduction was something entirely natural, reflected in a willing self-presentation or in a head turned toward the anatomist, as well as in the shift of the scene from the dissection chamber to a rural landscape (Sawday 1990, 123 and 127). Sawday maintains that the convention of anatomical self-demonstration was in essence based on the Calvinist doctrine of *nosce te ipsum*, which made it the duty of every believer to engage in a never-ending process of ruthless self-examination and self-exposure to God (1995, 110–111). Knowledge of the interior and the removal of the skin could find a suitable analogy in the metaphor of self-anatomy. Sawday goes so far as to speak of the late Renaissance in the broadest sense as

figure 17

Standing figure displaying the muscles of the
abdomen, from *Comentaria . . . super anatomia
Mundini* (1521)

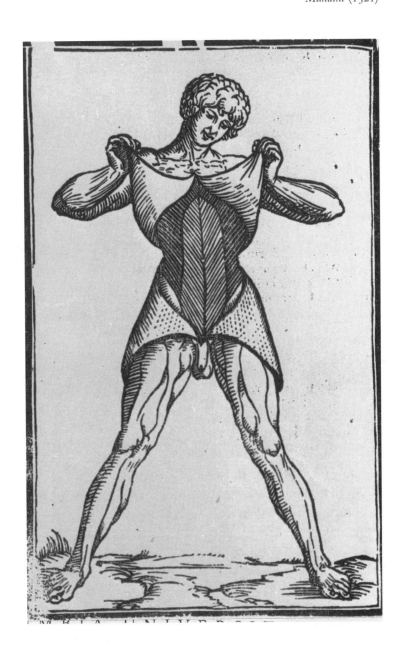

figure 18
Abdominal cavity, from Juan de Valverde
de Hamusco, *Historia de la composicion
del cuerpo humano* (1556)

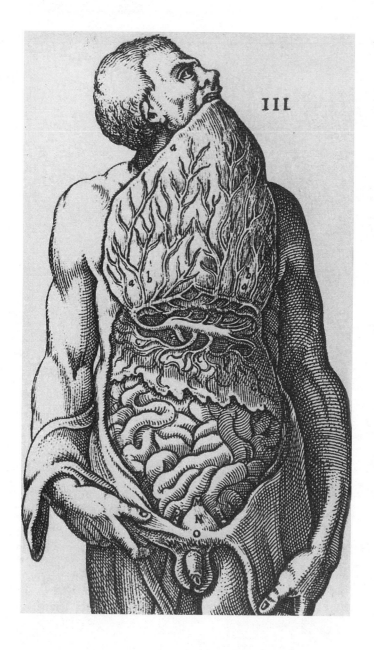

figure 19
Female reproductive organs, from Gaetano
Petrioli, *Tabulae anatomicae* (1741)

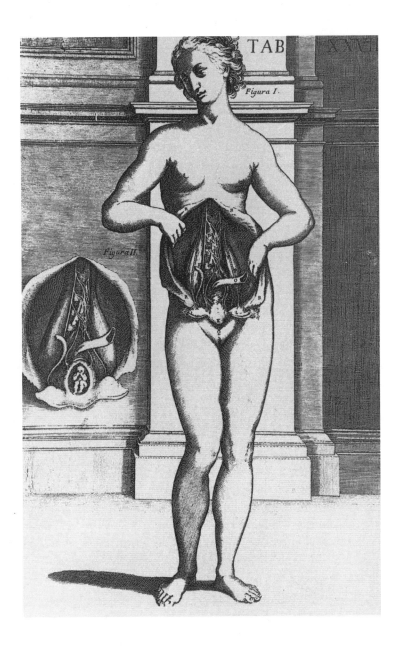

a "culture of dissection" (2–3), which stands in strange discrepancy to the modern consciousness of the autonomous and self-contained individual.

The paradox of a living *écorché* is plainly evident in a woodcut from Juan de Valverde de Hamusco's *Historia de la composicion del cuerpo humano* (1556; figure 20).[2] The *écorché* not only holds up its own skin like a trophy; it also presents to the viewer a knife, indicative of the flaying—as though the figure had carried out an autovivisection. The knife is not a dissecting tool but more like a dagger; in that sense the figure can also be interpreted as a warrior who has fought a battle with his own body and emerged the victor. This anatomical specimen thus represents an early synthesis of two figurative types: that of the flayer and that of the flayed, familiar to us from mythology and martyr legends. In the anatomical studies of Giulio Bonansone, as well, these two figures merge into one (figure 21).[3] The anatomical flaying for the purpose of demonstrating the play of the muscles is here stylized into a process of undressing. With a gesture full of pathos the *écorché* tears off his skin to expose what is of interest to the artist and the anatomist alike.

Flaying, reinterpreted in the anatomical illustrations as an act of voluntary and liberating peeling, has a long and gruesome tradition as a ritual of punishment or an archaic sacrificial custom (for example, in pre-Columbian Mexican cultures). Flaying a person alive was especially common in Eastern cultures, for example among the Scythians, Persians, and Assyrians (Kleine-Natrop 1961, 237 ff.). In European visual arts, the theme was taken over from classical and Christian traditions, whose pictorial conventions partly overlapped. The myth of the satyr Marsyas, who challenges Apollo to a musical contest, loses, and is punished by being flayed alive, and the flaying of the apostle Bartholomew, who is tortured to death for converting Polimius (the brother of the Armenian king Astyages) to the Christian faith and at his resurrection presents his old skin to God at the Last Judgment as proof of his martyrdom (de Voraigne 1993, 109 ff.), are prominent pictorial themes of the *exemplum doloris* in Renaissance, mannerist, and baroque art. Their iconographies increasingly resemble each other. For the present context, the scene of Marsyas and Apollo is more revealing than that of Bartholomew and his torturers, since the mythical constellation deals implicitly also with the relationship of the post-Vesalian anatomist to his object. Since I can select only a few of the very large number of images, the following discussion will focus largely on the myth of Marsyas.

figure 20

Ecorché, from Juan de Valverde de
Hamusco, *Historia de la composicion
del cuerpo humano* (1556)

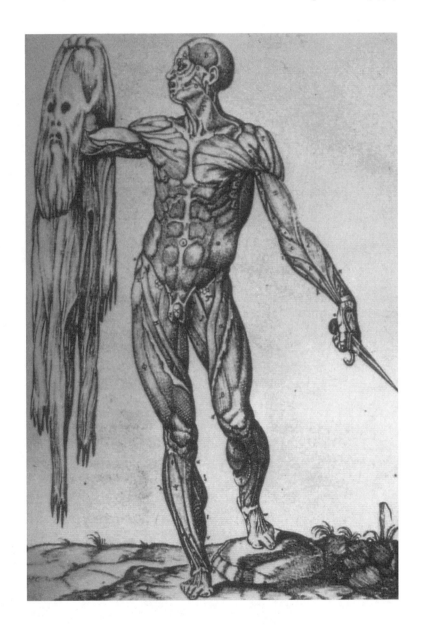

figure 21
Giulio Bonansone, *Anatomical Study* (1565)

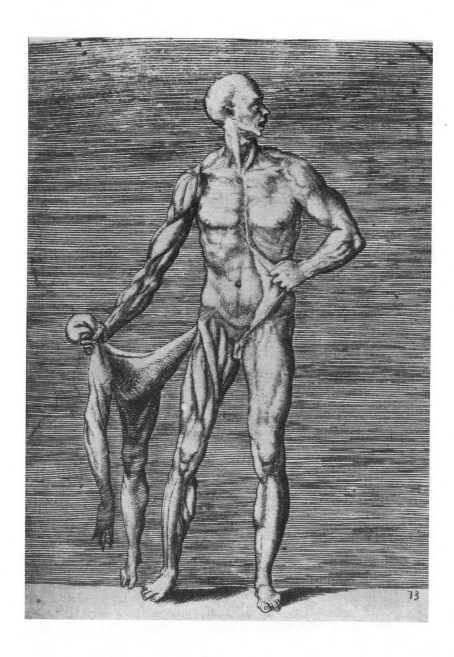

73

Literary accounts of the flaying of Marsyas can be found in Plato, Herodotus, Ovid, and Hyginus. Of these, only the death scene in Ovid's *Metamorphoses* became a model for the visual arts:

> When the story-teller, whoever he was, had related the disaster which befell the Lycians, another man remembered the tale of the satyr whom Apollo punished, after having defeated him in a competition on the reed-pipes, the instrument Minerva invented. "Help!" Marsyas clamoured. "Why are you stripping me from Myself? Never again, I promise! Playing the pipe is not worth this!" But in spite of his cries his skin was torn off the whole surface of his body: it was all one raw wound. Blood flowed everywhere, his nerves were exposed, unprotected, his veins pulsed with no skin to cover them. It was possible to count his throbbing organs, and the chambers of the lungs, clearly visible within his breast.
>
> (1955, 6.382–391)

What impressed artists in this graphic account was especially the description that Marsyas *nisi vulnus erat*, that he was nothing but a wound. But the visual depiction of this more-than-naked body varies because of different conceptions about the representability of physical pain. One prominent sculptural motif in Greek and Roman antiquity has Marsyas suspended from a tree in the moment immediately preceding the flaying, with a knife-sharpening Scythian often added as an ominous counterpart. In the pictorial tradition, by contrast, the actual flaying was taken progressively further, with the satyr eventually turning into an anatomical demonstration object on whom the location and interconnection of the human muscles could be shown. In the visual depictions, Apollo gradually takes an increasingly active part in the act of flaying, until we finally arrive at a kind of unequal duel between a god and a flayed human/animal. This active participation on the part of Apollo places him in an immediate relationship to the anatomists, who, since the time of Vesalius, also directly confronted the cadaver.

The close relationship in the act of flaying between the dissection of a corpse and capital punishment is revealed—apart from the Marsyas scenes to which I will presently return—in Gerard David's famous oil painting *The Flaying of Sisamnes* (1498), a theme that is based on a Persian myth handed down by Herodotus, among others (figure 22). This work is chronologically the later of two paintings, each of which shows a large group of figures in the foreground and a smaller, nonsynchronous group in a corner of the background. Together, the four scenes depict the corruptibility of the judge Sisamnes, King Cambyses' subsequent judgment in the case, the flaying of Sisamnes, and the succession of his son, who takes over the father's office of judge. As an ever-lasting admonition to his future integrity and a reminder of his father's disgraceful misconduct, the son was required to sit on a judge's chair, the seat of which had been fashioned from the father's tanned skin: in this instance, the inscription of the law is incarnated in the skin, which is taken from the individual and placed in the possession of public order.

David's highly realistic work derives from the genre of justice paintings that have been displayed in Dutch and German town halls since the late Middle Ages, which are among the earliest paintings with a secular theme (Rost 1956, 513–514). Here, the flaying alive of the judge takes place on a table, a composition that formally assimilates the flaying to an anatomical dissection.[4] David appears to intimate that the body to be flayed is less than a human being to the torturers; it is mere matter. Having the judge Sisamnes skinned in this demeaning position indicates, by association with the dissecting table, a further degradation that renders him a dehumanized object of display. The reification of the body that is being punished, re-flected in the matter-of-fact and concentrated way in which the flayers go about their business, contrasts with the unspeakable torment that Sisamnes is suffering, expressed only by the concerned look directed at the viewer by a boy (on the right, between two torturers).

In the myth of Marsyas, the martyrdom of the apostle Bartholomew, and the Persian legend of the corrupt judge Sisamnes, quite independent of the different moral-ethical statuses of the victims, the flaying of one man at the hands of others seeks to restore the existing order symbolically through the use of the most extreme means. Marsyas, who dared to compare himself to a god; St. Bartholomew, who committed the sacrilege of converting a king's brother to another faith; and Sisamnes, who sullied one of the foun-dation stones of the human social order, the dignity of the judge's office, by allowing himself to be bribed—all three are lawbreakers who violated the existing order to the core. The infliction of public and lethal harm puts these presumptuous individuals back in their social place, precisely by tak-ing from them the boundary of their bodies. The act of flaying deprives the victims of their identity along with their lives; in extinguishing the skin, it obliterates the person. Philipp Fehl has pointed out that the didactic mo-ment of admonition and deterrence, especially in David's painting but also in the depictions of Marsyas (e.g., the Greek sculptures), was significant for

figure 22
Gerard David, *The Flaying of Sisamnes* (1498)

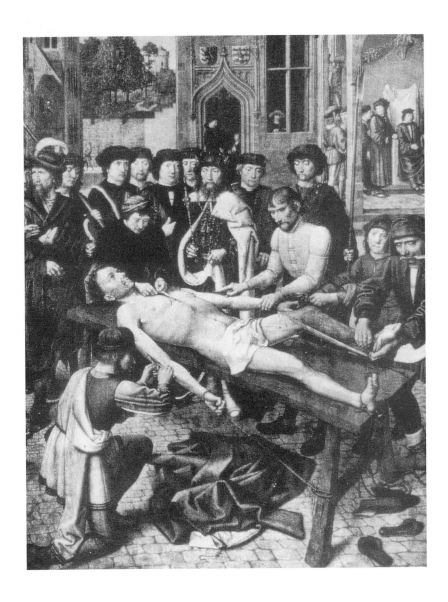

the wide diffusion of the subject and its placement primarily in public spaces (Fehl 1995, 72–73).

In Dirck van Baburen's mannerist painting *The Flaying of Marsyas* (ca. 1623; figure 23), Apollo makes the first cut on the victim's right shin. Marsyas is suspended upside down between a tree and several stumps of wood. One could interpret his position as a symbolic return to the humiliating way in which the brazen satyr lost the contest: Apollo guilefully suggested that they turn their instruments upside down, which is perfectly all right with the kithara but makes no sense with a flute. In this pictorial type, Marsyas is placed, as it were, in the position of the unusable flute, whose uselessness and absurdity is immediately evident.[5]

In Baburen's painting, the eyes wide with pain, the mouth opened in horror, the knitted horned forehead, and especially the redness of the head, chest, and hands reveal the corporeality of the lethal torture and hint at the bloodiness of this form of killing. Compared with the engravings from the sixteenth century (figures 24 and 25), Apollo participates much more actively in the execution, which heightens the cruelty of the depiction. His gaze betrays concentration and curiosity—and probably also pleasure in the deed: he appears to be grinning. Marsyas, naked save for a loincloth, tied down with his legs spread in a feminizing, humiliating pose, is at the mercy of the god's will. The cut, which begins at the lower end of his leg, leads invariably to the sensitive genital area, which is here still in shadow. In this way, the scene is infused with a latent component of sadism. Both medieval and early modern torture as well as the anatomical theater were staged as spectacles of the body and of pain. Artists, too, played to the observer's curiosity when they portrayed the flaying motif as cruel or bloody, as is so compellingly shown in this case. In Baburen's painting, the secret eroticism of this unfathomable torment is grounded especially in the coloration and illumination of the flesh tones. The Caravaggian handling of light allows the smoothness of the skin in its individuality to emerge and makes its fragility painfully apparent. And Apollo's relatively clothed state (compared with earlier depictions) lets the victim's nakedness emerge all the more starkly. The modern consciousness that we are alone in the moment of pain and the fear of death causes the figure of Marsyas not to look toward heaven (as St. Bartholomew does) but to stare into nothingness with eyes wide with terror. In fact, the painting is characterized by the radical absence of the hereafter. The pictorial field is filled with nothing other than the physical presence of the protagonist and the victim's pain.

figure 23
Dirck van Baburen, *The Flaying
of Marsyas* (ca. 1623)

figure 24
Melchior Meier, *Apollo with the Flayed Marsyas and the Judgment of Midas* (1581)

figure 25
Giovanni Stradanus, *Apollo Flays Marsyas*
(ca. 1580–1600)

By contrast, in a series of sixteenth-century engravings that stand in a peculiar relationship of tension to the more sensitive as well as the bloody
adaptations of the theme, the Greek satyr Marsyas is an interchangeable
écorché devoid of identity. And his flayed skin, which is often held up by
Apollo, does not represent a creature half man, half animal; instead, it is an
insignificant, hairless shell, as, for example, in Melchior Meier's engraving
Apollo with the Flayed Marsyas and the Judgment of Midas (1581; figure 24). This
work is a re-creation in mythological garb of the physician's position toward
the dissected body. The myth, with its immanent tragedy—or hubris—of
the vain attempt to measure oneself against a god, is here placed entirely in
the service of the *nuova scienza*. It serves merely as a foil and justification for
depicting an *écorché* and his counterpart, the well-proportioned male nude.

Apollo himself turns away from the *écorché*, which is of no use to him; it
is only the skin itself that is important to him as a trophy, and he holds it up
to King Midas such that the latter is inescapably confronted with Marsyas's
facial mask.[6] The flayed skin resembles a loose cloth that Apollo is wearing
around his shoulders and hips. Compared to the soft and smooth appearance
of Apollo's skin and to the skin he is holding up, Marsyas's flayed body is
hard and rigid: the "clothing" skin of Apollo is depicted as a caressing and
integrating integument that turns the body into living matter in the first
place, a body that exudes warmth and strength—it is no coincidence that this
composition places the god unrivaled in the center. Through his central position, Apollo also symbolically separates the flayed Marsyas from his skin: the
latter is assigned to the group of figures on the right, who, dressed in antique-
looking armor and helmets, stare at the skin without emotion, while the
écorché belongs to the grieving, partially nude satyrs and Phrygian countryfolk
on the left. But they, too, do not look at the skinless corpse; its sight is meant
solely for the viewer. The artist portrays Apollo's body as a muscular body of
ideal shape, as though he wanted to demonstrate that it was only the study
of anatomy that enabled him to shape the perfect body, where all the muscles that are revealed in the sacrificed Marsyas show through the skin.

The satyr is in equal measures an anatomical demonstration object and
mere material for a godlike sculptor, who sometimes portrays himself in the
figure of Apollo. This artistic reference becomes clear, for example, in an engraving designed by Giovanni Stradanus and carried out by Theodor Galle
(between 1580 and 1600; figure 25). The work depicts a Pygmalion in reverse, who creates a sculptural work of art from living matter (though in this
case not a female work of art). The phoebean nimbus of light surrounding

the figure makes this surgical elucidation appear like an allegory of the scientific spirit. That Stradanus is less concerned with depicting a mythical killing than with the act of peeling something out of its (false) form—a shedding of the skin in the positive sense of the word—is also revealed by the fact that the muscle surface of the flayed Marsyas is not a bloody relief, not "all wound," but an aseptic sculptural form, even though the caption refers explicitly to Ovid and his formulation *nisi vulnus erat*. Like a double, the skin falls from Marsyas, whose subcutaneous body is now laid bare in its muscular glory, cast in an ecstatic pose, and bursting with power.

The textile, hairless garment of skin is revealed as a false integument that does not seem quite to fit the muscular body. The skin is, accordingly, a separate, second figure, an alien alter ego: although the Marsyas under the skin is interchangeable, he is long since familiar to the viewer; what is taken from him is his alien shell. Here, the traditional relationship between alien interior and familiar surface has been inverted. The dual aspect of killing versus revelation that is inherent in the act of flaying is limited entirely to the emphatic, transformative regeneration.

Balthasar Permoser, in his ivory relief dating from between 1675 and 1680 (figure 26), depicts the flaying of Marsyas at the hands of Apollo as an unspeakable, cruel, but necessary extraction from the animal shell. The dramatic flaying will deprive the victim of his furry hide. Here, death is depicted as the process of deanimalization; what Apollo removes, as though in a painful birth to humanness, is the noncivilized, the beastly in Marsyas. The untamed, animalistic urge, which longs for the boundless—a victory over a god—is overcome and rendered unrecognizable. The now hairless Marsyas, his face contorted in pain (or anger?), seems more undressed than flayed. And the fact that Apollo's knife does not cut into the body but merely scrapes at it sideways also indicates that this is not so much an act of killing as a violent modification, in which the victim may even participate by a tormented act of pushing himself out. In this work (as in that of Stradanus earlier), Apollo is both the carving artist and the focused anatomist who is cutting off the dermal layer. The medium of the relief is particularly well suited for this depiction of the flayer as sculptor, since it duplicates the process of carving out—the "flaying out" (Herder)[7]—on the surface of the relief.

The two figures are each given half of the pictorial field, with the dividing line running from the lower left to the upper right corner. As a result, Apollo and Marsyas, more so than in other works, stand in a tense, mirror-image relationship to each other, an arrangement further emphasized by the

figure 26
Balthasar Permoser, *Apollo Flays
Marsyas* (ca. 1675–1680)

polar placement of the musical instruments. Drawing on Nietzsche's *The Birth of Tragedy*, one might therefore interpret the flaying scene, perhaps especially in this work, as a struggle between two psychic forces or drives within the subject: the Apollonian and the Dionysian locked in combat. Edgar Wind highlighted that Marsyas belongs to the followers of Dionysus, an interpretive approach that has since been picked up frequently in scholarship (1987, 200). In this regard, the myth of Apollo and Marsyas could also be interpreted as a "primal drama of individuation," as Beat Wyss has suggested, in the sense that the ego attains mastery over the high-spirited, impulsive id (1996, 16). If the skin is taken away—and this may also have been one motive for the interest in this topic during the Renaissance and subsequent epochs—there occurs, psychologically speaking, a splitting of the self. It is no coincidence that the flayed satyr already laments in Ovid, "quid me mihi detrahis"—why are you stripping me from myself?

In the eighteenth century, the flaying of Marsyas (as well as that of Bartholomew) disappears as a pictorial subject as suddenly as it had burst on the scene in the sixteenth century. The humanization of punishment that occurs with the disappearance of penal torture, as Foucault has shown, causes the body of the perpetrator to vanish from public view. Punishment no longer manifests itself in the body, whose walls it previously had to overcome; on the contrary, the body of the delinquent is surrounded by additional (prison) walls and thereby removed from the gaze of the public.[8]

Once the depictions of flaying disappear from art, flaying itself remains present merely as a philosophical and literary metaphor. This cultural shift from real-life practice and high iconographic visibility to metaphorical representation could not be arrested by the scattered reappearance of actual flaying rituals (or their mythologization). For example, some legends about American slavery speak of the flaying alive of slaves. If such events did happen, they represent a return to brutal medieval rituals of punishment, which, much like the later practice of lynching, have a collective character.[9] There are also reports of flaying in German concentration camps during the Second World War. Credible evidence indicates that human skin was used to fashion everyday objects such as lampshades and book covers that graced the living quarters of SS officers (Oettermann 1994, 109ff.). To that end, the choice victims were killed and then flayed, mostly partially, for example, to cut out a tattoo. This reshaping of human skin into trophies and the simultaneous, deliberate degradation of body parts into mere articles of everyday use do not represent practices that were aimed at exposing what was beneath the skin (as in the case of anatomy), nor were they forms of torture (as in the flaying scenes). Instead, they were a symbolic assertion of power over a human being's most elemental possession: his skin. The act of transforming the skin of murdered inmates into parchment and then into everyday objects symbolically denies the dead their human status: their skin is given the same treatment that is usually reserved for the skin of slaughtered and flayed animals. Unlike the painted skin parchment on depictions of justice—for example, the judge's chair covered with the skin of Sisamnes in David's work—we are dealing with real human skin, something we must not forget; the Fascist practice of demonstrating power can therefore be compared more readily to archaic rituals, such as the Native American tradition of scalping dead enemies, which was also about the bodily possession of skin. What I am looking at here, however, is the act of flaying someone alive.

Sylvia Plath, in her poem "Lady Lazarus" (1962), makes reference to the Fascist practice and simultaneously elevates it into the realm of the subjective:

> I have done it again.
> One year in every ten
> I manage it—
> A sort of walking miracle, my skin
> Bright as a Nazi lampshade,
> My right foot
> A paperweight,
> My face a featureless, fine
> Jew linen.
> Peel off the napkin
> O my enemy.
> Do I terrify?

(1981, 244)

This enigmatic, many-layered poem deals with transformation and cyclical suicide; the latter is visualized through active flaying and peeling. Through its (surely presumptuous) identification with Judaism, the lyrical self assumes the role of a victim, which, like Lazarus, enters death in order to be resurrected. The painful process of flaying—what Plath sarcastically calls "the big strip tease" (245)—may be threatening to the observers, but it does not in principle deprive the lyrical self of its self-identity, since it will grow a new skin time after time.

A similar notion of active flaying—as the image of an excruciating but necessary peeling out from old, inauthentic sheaths—can be found in Verena Stefan's novel *Häutungen* (Flayings, 1975). The narrative adopts the image of a liberating metamorphosis as a feminist program, a program aimed at casting off a rigid skin that "has become too tight" (1994, 29). We are told that one has to "separate oneself from the old skin in the first place, it does not detach on its own" (105). "After the flaying comes the identity crisis" (10), writes Stefan in the preface; however, the implicit thesis is that this temporary, painful loss of self leads to a more authentic self.

In terms of cultural history, the topos of flaying as a process of cleansing and growth, as the peeling out from inauthentic forms and identities, as suggested by Plath and Stefan, is the product of a euphemistic reinterpretation and metaphorization of the gruesome flaying ritual. The act of radical self-alienation is stylized into a moment of self-becoming. A process of cyclical regeneration that occurs in the reptile world is transferred metaphorically to human beings. It should be emphasized, however—and will be become clear in the closer analysis of Plath's work in chapter 6—that flaying as a positive act of liberation and a successful process of growth succeeds primarily in male writers. The examples I have cited from the two women writers indicate, through the theme of suicide, provocation, and identity crisis, that we are dealing with a problematic process of transformation.

And so, when we read in a letter from Goethe that "the human being has many skins to shed before he is even somewhat sure of himself and of worldly things" (1997, 433) or, in a letter to Charlotte von Stein, "Oh Lotte, what skins one has to shed, how pleased I am that they get bigger by and by, although I feel that I am still stuck in some of them" (375), this rhetoric corresponds primarily to the masculine gesture of liberation, not to the gesture of psychic agony, of victimization, or of uncertainty. Nietzsche, too, sets up an analogy between a person's mental growth and a shedding of the skin that lets the self undergo a continuous transformation, while the surrounding world often does not notice these changes: "We are misidentified—because we ourselves keep growing, keep changing, we shed our old bark, we shed our skins every spring, we keep becoming younger, fuller of future, taller, stronger, we push our roots ever more powerfully into the depths—into evil—while at the same time we embrace the heavens ever more lovingly, more broadly, imbibing their light ever more thirstily with all our twigs and leaves" (1974, 331–332)

In these literary and philosophical images, flaying changes from a singular act that destroys the subject into a conscious and transforming act of will; it is semantically recoded from a final into a transitory moment. There is no single skin that constitutes humanness, individuality, and vitality; rather, beneath the skin are ever-new layers to discover. The metaphor of the naked truth, which rests on a mechanism of continual uncovering, is here transferred to the gradual nakedness under the skin. Only a very slow and lengthy process, however, makes this second stratum of meaning dominant. In Goethe, the meaning of flaying is still inherent, though here conceived of as a necessary act of violence, as attested by the motto preceding the first part of *Dichtung und Wahrheit* (1811): "Ὁ μὴν δαρεὶς ανθρωπος ον παιδευται" (Man is not educated unless he is flayed).[10] Goethe is referring back to the motto in Jean-Jacques Rousseau's *Confessions* (1782), "intus, et in cute," which promises that the author of these confessions will reveal himself completely, "inwardly and beneath the skin" (2000, 9).[11]

In *Wilhelm Meister's Years of Travel* (1821), Goethe coined the formula "Man without sheath is the true man" (10, part 1:607).* Goethe's protagonist develops this notion in the course of the famous conversation about *anatomia plastica* with an Italian sculptor, who, at work on classical torso of a youth, "was now endeavouring to use his insight in order to strip the epidermis from this ideal figure and to transform what was beautiful and lifelike into a real-life muscle preparation" (Goethe 1982, 16). Here, too, the anatomized male body devoid of its covering is equated with the state of inner nonconcealment that constitutes true human nature.

In his essay on morphology (1806–1807), Goethe presents skinning as an elemental process in the ongoing transformation of shape that all living beings undergo. He goes on to state emphatically that

> life is unable to work at the surface or express its generative powers there. The whole activity of life requires a covering which protects it against the raw elements of its environment, be they water or air or light, a covering which preserves its delicate nature so that is may fulfill the specific purpose

---

* Goethe's original German reads: "Der Mensch ohne Hülle ist eigentlich der Mensch." H. M. Waidson's translation *Wilhelm Meister's Years of Travel* renders this as: "Man in his nakedness is the true man" (1982, 16). Since this translation does not capture Goethe's use of the word "Hülle"—sheath, covering, or shell—I have translated this quotation directly from the German. Waidson's translation is used for the other passages from this work.—Trans.

for which it is inwardly destined. . . . The bark of trees, the skin of insects, the hair and feathers of animals, even the epidermis of man, are coverings forever being shed, cast off, given over to non-life. New coverings are constantly forming beneath the old, while still further down, close to this surface or more deeply hidden, life brings forth its web of creation.

(1988b, p. 66)

In Goethe's view, organic development consists of a continuous shedding of the uppermost layers.[12] His thesis that all living things need to be enveloped indicates, however, that these skins or scales are only shed once the new underlying membranes have formed, which means there is never real exposure. This kind of awareness of the necessity of sheaths and boundaries is increasingly displaced by a scientific desire for knowledge. Anzieu has shown the many functions that arise from primary experiences of touch and distance and are permanently symbolized via the skin. The experiences of self-stability and psychic protectedness and unity are just as central as the libidinous charging of the psyche or the "container function" of the skin ego. The paradigm change triggered by the transformation of anatomy also disregards these basic functions of human self-perception on the philosophical level. The primacy of the visual displaces not only the importance of the sense of touch in the discovery of the world but also the more comprehensive functions of the skin that directly constitute identity.

The Second Book of the Maccabees in the Old Testament recounts the martyrdom of the seven brothers and their mother (7.1–42). As practicing Jews they refuse to eat pork, whereupon they are sentenced to die. The torture begins with the cutting out of the tongue, after which the skin and hair of the head are torn off, "in the manner of the Scythians," as the Bible adds.[13] The refusal to ingest flesh thus leads to the exposure of the offender's own flesh by way of punishment. The agonizing death of all seven brothers and their mother is described in excruciating detail. The last to die is the mother, although in contrast to the execution of her sons, the account leaves open the question of whether she was scalped as well.

That silence is no coincidence, since the flaying or scalping of a woman would evidently violate an existing taboo, one that has not lost much of its force down to this day. In medical history, for example, virtually no female figures are attested as *écorchés*; there are also no partially skinned female torsos or skulls intended to expose and demonstrate the nervous system, the lymphatic system, or the network of veins.[14] To this day, just about the only time anatomical atlases depict the female body is to show the reproductive organs or other organs in the abdomen (see figures 9, 10, and 19); all other illustrations are of male bodies. The male body is understood as the normal, the paradigmatically human body, the female body as a deviant, sexualized, and specific variant of the male norm. Unless the purpose is to show the reproductive organs, a depiction of the female body is not customary, since it is considered erotically charged and its potential sexualization would get in the way of the cold (male) gaze of the physician. And the female whole-body models of wax with opened abdomens produced in growing numbers in the late eighteenth century, along with the female skull models that could be opened up, are no exception. In fact, they further substantiate the thesis that there was a fundamental gender difference within anatomical and artistic images: although the female body is by now also a "public space" (Duden 1991b), closer inspection reveals that this applies only to its deep hollows and its outermost surface. What lies between, the web of blood vessels and muscles, remains taboo, either because of its functionality and its potent power or because of the obscene ugliness that is attributed to bloody wounds. The female skin is understood as a concealing veil. Undressing a woman of her skin would fundamentally destroy the myth of her being other. On the skin, woman is woman, and the same is true for the inside of her (lower) abdomen. The layers in between are fraught with a taboo (to the extent that they are a wound) or bear a male coding (to the extent that they are *écorchés*) and must remain suspended in this state of indeterminacy, for otherwise they would pose a fundamental threat to the existing order of desire. Woman should remain the wounded sex; the skin remains a fetish and a veil, which of necessity conceals what she may not reveal. Plath understood this connection when she has her skin-shedding, lyrical self ask in "Lady Lazarus": "Do I terrify?"

The anatomical atlas *De humani corporis fabrica librorum epitome* (1543), the study edition of Vesalius's *Fabrica*, includes two archetypal figures labeled "Adam" and "Eve" (figure 27), whose proportions, positioning in space, gesture, and shape remind us of Greek sculptures. The male body is presented as a powerful construction of muscles and veins enclosed by a transparent skin, while the female body is characterized as smooth, with hardly any surface contours. The pose of the female figure hints at the classical posture of the Venus pudica; at the same time, the hand covering the vulva refers with a kind of pointing gesture to the reproductive organs beneath the skin and to the woman's ability to create life. The association with the capacity of bearing children is reinforced by the fact that the male figure holds in its mirror image hand a skull, which, as a memento mori, represents the countersymbol to female fertility. Vesalius said of one *écorché* in his *Fabrica* that the surface muscles exposed therein could also be seen in the living body (Roberts and Tomlinson 1992, 150). When it comes to these exceedingly rare depictions of intact figures in an anatomical atlas, Vesalius, in speaking of those surface muscles, has only the male body in mind, which is to him the only one that is characterized by muscles. The transparent, elastic quality of skin is a desirable characteristic in the muscular male body, for what it allows to shine through bears the positive connotation of vitality and virility. The female body, by contrast, needs a covering, concealing, smoothing skin that does not reveal the diffuse interior. The coding of femaleness takes place on the skin, that of maleness under the skin—this, in a nutshell, is how we could characterize the juxtaposition that is already established here but remains valid for many centuries.

Jonathan Swift, in his satire *A Tale of a Tub* (1704), writes about the "wisdom which converses about the surface" (1986, 83)—a wisdom of the surface that stands in contrast to those philosophical endeavors that always seek to plumb the depths. As an example he points to anatomy, where penetration constantly leads to new problems: "I do here think it fit to inform the reader that in such conclusions as these, reason is certainly in the right, and that in most corporeal beings which have fallen under my cognizance, the *outside* hath been infinitely preferable to the *in*: whereof I have been further convinced from some late experiments. Last week I saw a woman *flayed*, and you will hardly believe how much it altered her person for the worse" (84). It is no coincidence that Swift invokes the anatomically flayed women to drive home the point of his thesis, a woman whose "personality," as he so ironically put is, changed so much "for the worse" by the removal of the skin. He emphasizes that this dreadful sight did not advance his knowledge and that the female outside was, by contrast, always to be preferred.

At a time when male muscle figures were already an indispensable part of an artist's training, Denis Diderot, in his *Essai sur la peinture* (1766), wrote about the precarious connection between flaying and femaleness:

Study of the *écorché* doubtless has its advantages; but is it not to be feared that this *écorché* might remain in the imagination forever; that this might encourage the artist to become enamored of his knowledge and show it off; that

figure 27
So-called Adam and Eve, from Andreas
Vesalius, *De humani corporis fabrica
librorum epitome* (1543)

ns:

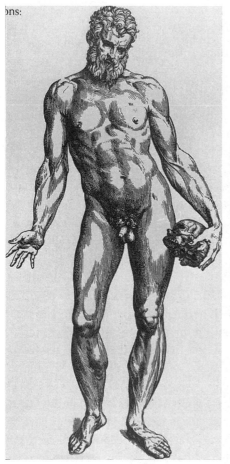
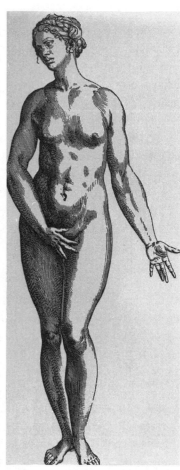

his vision might be corrupted, precluding attentive scrutiny of surfaces; that despite the presence of skin and fat, he might come to perceive nothing but muscles, their beginnings, attachments, and insertions; that he might overemphasize them, that he might become hard and dry, and that I might encounter this accursed *écorché* even in his figures of women? Since only the exterior is exposed to view, I'd prefer to be trained to see it fully, and spared treacherous knowledge I'd only have to forget.

(1995, 193)

While knowledge of the male *écorché* produces an irreversibly disturbing effect both on the contemplation of the reproduced human (male) body, and on artistic production, the passage describes female skinlessness as all but unthinkable and knowledge of it even as "treacherous." Especially striking is the self-reference, indicated by the change from the third person to the first person, from the identification with the artist to the naked self: the horrifying skinless woman, which could now shine through all smooth-bodied female sculptures, paintings, and drawings, poses a fundamental threat to the image of the self and of the other (the fair sex). Such a "desublimation" (Zizek 1997, 78) of the female body is irreversible.

The consistent pattern seems to be that the flayed woman is no longer a woman. Femaleness lies only in the dark and muddy breeding ground in the depths of the body or in the smooth and beautiful sheath-façade that surrounds this body but not in the powerful and vigorous, though profane, intervening layers of muscle and tissue. But woman is not surface *or* container. The two notions, at least from the perspective of subconscious imagery, turn out to be two sides of the same conception: woman as hollow space with an enveloping, smooth external skin. If that skin is removed, her body also ceases to be a "container." Elisabeth Grosz has emphasized that while there is a substantial theoretical literature about female body fluids, there are—with the exception of some medical and biological discussions—virtually none about male body fluids (1994, 198 ff.). She rightly notes that the male body was, symbolically, gradually closed into an "impermeable body," while the female body was construed as "a leaking, uncontrollable, seeping liquid." This process of "phallicizing the male body" thus gave rise to the opposing concept of the female body as "a vessel, a container," something that becomes clearly visible in regard to the skin.

A few additional references culled from the vast field of Western cultural history, some of them very early, will further substantiate the thesis that the skinless woman was and is taboo. According to the Apocrypha, Adam, before Eve was created for him, was given two other women by God. Lilith, the first, refused to lie under Adam in the sexual act because she considered it humiliating. As for the second, Adam could not feel any desire for her because he had witnessed her creation:

> Undismayed by His failure to give Adam a suitable helpmeet, God tried again, and let him watch while he built up a woman's anatomy: using bones, tissues, muscles, blood and glandular secretions. The sight caused Adam such disgust that even when this woman, the First Eve, stood there in her full beauty, he felt an invincible repugnance. God knew that He had failed once more, and took the First Eve away. Where she went, nobody knows for certain.
>
> (GRAVES AND PATAI 1964, 65)

In response, God formed Eve while Adam was asleep. Only now could Adam enter into a union with the third woman given to him. What is revealing about the second woman is that she disappears unknown: the woman who was seen without a skin in her fleshly nakedness did not turn into a legend (like the first wife, Lilith); she became nothing. Even the smoothing skin that enveloped her could no longer expunge the primary memory of what lay beneath. The beautiful appearance of femaleness can no longer exert its effect once the flesh devoid of identity has been exposed to the male gaze.

The motif of desire killed off by the exposure of the female interior also plays a central role in Johannes von Tepl's poem *Death and the Ploughman* (ca. 1401). In this dialogue, personified death seeks to assuage a peasant's grief over the death of his wife by describing to him what a woman truly is beneath her skin, that "painted deception," with all the processes of fermentation and decomposition that occur in her body:

> A thing of disgust, a noisome mass, a vessel of filth, food for worms, an abode of stinks, a loathly slop tub, a packet of carrion, a barrel of scum, a bottomless sack, a dripping sieve, a bladder of wind, a gobbling mouth, an insatiable orifice, an open cess-pool, a stinking piss-pot, a reeking bucket, a foul-smelling swill, a den of thieves, a pit of abominations, a dissembling dummy, a bag full

of holes and a painted deception. . . . Strip the fairest woman of the clothier's colours, and you will see an outrageous doll, a swift-fading flower, a short-lived phantom and a soon-sagging mound of earth.

(1947, 28–29)

Death tells the peasant that if only he had "the eyes of a lynx" and could "see through him [man] within," he would "shudder" (28). To be sure, the passage is addressing the general worthlessness and uncleanliness of the physical body as such, without reference to gender, but the return of the motif from the Apocrypha is no coincidence. The allegorical Lady World figures popular in the Middle Ages—one example being the portal figure by Konrad of Würzburg at the cathedral in Worms (thirteenth century)—also show female beauty richly attired on the front, while the back reveals the interior of the body crawling with worms and maggots. The fact that the interior of the body was, far into the Middle Ages, identified primarily with the female indicates that the tabooing of female flaying encountered since the Renaissance has its roots in this early, collective attribution.

Georg Simmel points to a presumed biological difference between the sexes by tracing it back—characteristically enough in an essay entitled "Zur Psychologie der Frauen" (On the psychology of women, 1890)—to a lack of differentiation in the female body:

When it comes to the area of corporeality, the assertion, first of all, that women lack differentiation holds true. Throughout nature, the female sex is less differentiated than the male sex; the female everywhere bears a greater resemblance to the young of its own species than to the male. . . . The surface of the male body is more differentiated than that of the female. The skeleton stands out more vigorously, it makes itself known through protrusions and recesses, while in woman the more even fat pads make the body appear as a smoother surface that is raised and recessed only in very general ways.

(1989, 2:67).

Claudia Schmölders has rightly emphasized the delusive character of this "soft portrait" when she says that, "like a courtly mask," it "conceals the hideous face of the Gorgon" underneath (1995, 149–150). When Simmel claims that woman simply has more uniform and more "fat pads" that smooth out her surface, we are not told anything about the horror that the male observer associates with the possible exposure of these "pads." Nietzsche, much like Swift, speaks accordingly of a "courage" that consists in stopping at the surface in the quest for truth. And like Swift he illustrates his argument with the image of the female skin:

> Perhaps truth is a woman who has reasons not letting us see her reasons? Perhaps her name is—to speak Greek—*Baubo*?
>
> Oh, those Greeks! They knew how to live. What is required for that is to stop courageously at the surface, the fold, the skin, to adore appearance, to believe in forms, tones, words, in the whole Olympus of appearance. Those Greeks were superficial—*out of profundity*.
>
> (1974, 38)

Living requires that we cling to the surface (of femaleness). The depth of woman would cast this very life in doubt.

Rainer Maria Rilke, in his novel *The Notebooks of Malte Laurids Brigge* (1910), which is disguised as a fictitious diary, describes a scene in which the first-person narrator observes a woman in the streets of Paris who "had completely fallen into herself, forward into her hands." He follows her when she suddenly hears his footsteps: "The woman sat up, frightened, she pulled herself out of herself, too, quickly, too violently, so that her face was left in her two hands. I could see it lying there: its hollow form. It cost me an indescribable effort to stay with those two hands, to look at what had been torn out of them. I shuddered to see a face from the inside, but I was much more afraid of that bare flayed head waiting there, faceless" (1982, 7). Rilke's protagonist, who in the previous scene had flippantly spoken about the fact that human beings have several faces and that most change them constantly, unless they are "frugal, simple people" who always wear the same face (6), is aghast that this woman has literally "lost her face" and that naked flesh lies underneath. He is so horrified by this that he prefers to stare as though transfixed into "the face from the inside," even though this, too, fills him with terror. What he beholds lying in her hands is the face the woman sees of herself—her "inner face," an unbounded and frightening intimacy. There is no description of what he perceives in the hands, nor does the author indicate what kind of skinned physiognomy of the woman would await his gaze. Instead, the text goes on to address the general problem of fear and thus leaves the flayed face merely hinted at.

The real history and practice of the violent penetration and destruction of the female body (Duerr 1993; Theweleit 1993:1; Cameron and Frazer 1987) attests to a constantly recurring assault on woman's lower abdomen and her primary and secondary sexual organs; what we do not find are attacks on the layers directly beneath the skin or on the skin itself. The sheer peeling off and removal of the surface layers seems to be an act of violence that men perpetrate against other men—at least according to classical and biblical sources and medieval penal practice. The generalizing conclusion we can draw is that in terms of cultural history (in torture, medicine, and sexual crimes), the skin of the woman is pierced while that of the man is stripped off.

The film *The Silence of the Lambs* (1990)[15] for the first time took as its theme the flaying of women: a psychopath who has been denied a sex change operation because of prior criminal offenses abducts young women. After a period of imprisonment, during which the female victims (whom he addresses only as "it," like an animal) have to treat their skin with a special lotion until it is sufficiently smooth, he kills the women and removes the flat skin from their backs. From these pieces, which he subsequently tans, he intends to sew himself a second, female skin. The central symbolic animal of the film, the caterpillar, is used to indicate that this is the attempt at a magical ritual of transforming sexual identity—that is, a transformation from the (ugly) male body to the (beautiful) female body.[16] Meanwhile, hardly anything is revealed about what lies beneath the skin of the young women: what is flayed is a part of the back, that is to say, one of the most sex-neutral sections of the body. Moreover, the body is brought into the picture only fleetingly, as though this kind of skinless corpse can not be shown. The motive for the actual act of murder is neither punishment nor the gaining of knowledge; the killing merely serves the "profane" purpose of possessing the skin, which Buffalo Bill misunderstands as "the essence of femaleness" (Halberstam 1995, 168). The fact that the film in the process touches—as though by coincidence—on the phantasm of the skinless woman accounts for its subtle horror; as a result, the film can expect the collective revulsion of both female and male viewers. The object of the pathological desire is the female skin, which, from time immemorial, in some form or another, has been the goal of male desire as a "fetishized signifier" (Halberstam 1991, 42). The film therefore does not reveal any real change; rather, it is a confirmation of the old attribution whereby woman is reduced to a smooth surface or to the characteristic that she encloses hollow spaces. The skinless backs of the corpses, by contrast, are "abject"—they are the place of the female body "where meaning collapses" (Kristeva 1982, 2). And so this film, too, shows once again that the archaic fear attached to the loss of the skin (as a container of the body fluids as well as a symbolic boundary) was displaced only onto female skinlessness. The flayed woman thus represents a threat to "the inner and the outer borders in which and through which the speaking subject is constituted" (69).

This excursion through the cultural history of flaying and the practice of its depiction has demonstrated the close connection of flaying and the production of knowledge, a connection that ties together art and anatomy and characterizes conceptions of (self)-knowledge in general. The fact that the medical dissection of human bodies is a boundary-crossing act is covered up by having the anatomical specimen itself perform the removal or lifting of the skin—or, as in the case of some Marsyas scenes, by having the person being flayed actively push himself out of his skin. In this way, the skin is represented as an inconvenient membrane, an obstacle to inspection and knowledge. Flaying stands for a number of contrary processes and layers of meaning: on the one hand, for example, it denotes the most extreme inscription of power in the form of torture and killing; on the other hand, it is understood as an allegory for an act of liberation or (violent) modification. It thus signifies both the loss and the gaining of the self.

Juxtaposed to this singular loss of skin is the image of a continual shedding of skin, in which the constant casting off or self-flaying of skins and sheaths is interpreted as a process of maturation and transformation. Even if some female writers also deal with the theme of this kind of exfoliation as a self-transformation process, the notion of the skinless body as a positive image in Western culture is still radically masculine. The male subject can, as the ultimate liberation fantasy, free itself of its skin, while the female subject remains bound within it. The female skin is understood as a mask; although woman is "upright" in "countenance," the male, in order to stabilize the sex difference, must not forget that she is at the same time "a bag of rot inside the skin" (Logau 1872, 2:103). The taboo of female skinlessness is grounded in the fact that male authors and artists seek to exclude the other in themselves. That which is not a potent muscle structure under the skin but rather a bloody mass of flesh is unwanted as part of the male body and must be projected onto what is defined as formless femaleness.

5 mirror of the soul

The Epidermis as Canvas

It was not polite, indeed, that he should have permitted himself this jest on my name; for a man's name is not like a mantle, which merely hangs about him, and which, perchance, may be safely twitched and pulled, but is a perfectly fitting garment, which has grown over and over him like his very skin, at which one cannot scratch and scrape without wounding the man himself.

—GOETHE, *Autobiography*

In this passage, Goethe establishes a direct connection between a person's name and skin by characterizing both as indispensable components of identity.[1] The name is something external, something bestowed by others, while the skin is given to a person at birth. By connecting the two, Goethe is also saying indirectly that the skin is fundamental in establishing identity, for it identifies the individual like a name. It is this connection between self and skin that I shall presently examine.

In Michelangelo's fresco *The Last Judgment* (1534–1541), the resurrection of the apostle Bartholomew is depicted in a central location, with Bartholomew showing his skin to the judge of the world as proof of his martyrdom. Scholars discovered only a few decades ago that Michelangelo portrayed himself on the martyr's flayed skin (figure 28) (Poseq 1994).[2] In fact, the flayed face is believed to be the only known self-portrait of the artist. It was by no means uncommon during the Renaissance for a painter to insert himself into a religious scene; however, it is unique that Michelangelo would lend his features to the saint's crumpled, flayed skin (and not, for instance, to the voluminous, powerful figure of the risen apostle). Leo Steinberg's interpretation of the scene is that Michelangelo himself is asking for mercy in the form of the skin, an allegorical reference to the possibility, exclusively reserved to God, that the artist's skin could be given new flesh after death. Steinberg refers to a quotation from Job, which states that each person carries within him the hope of individual resurrection, that he will rise from the earth and be clothed again in his old skin, whereupon he will behold God in his flesh.[3] What the Bartholomew scene in the fresco depicts is the brief moment that decides the individual's fate: "whether one rotted vesture is to be fleshed or not, salvaged or dropped" (435).[4] This interpretation strikes me as significant in that it implicitly posits the skin as a representation of the soul—and thus of what is individual about a person and remains constant. The skin (and not the soul) is what remains of the person after death, can be revived, and makes a person identifiable. In Michelangelo's depiction of Bartholomew's plea to have his mortal skin filled up again, the vitalizing and essence-imparting aspect is reserved to God, but the identity- and character-imparting element, which manifests itself on the outer sheath of the body, is reserved for the self and its history. In one of Michelangelo's sonnets, which he dedicated to his lover Tommaso Cavalieri, the poetic self expresses the wish that after the poet's death, the beloved be enveloped in the skin of the departed.[5] This gesture of complete devotion identifies the self with the external covering of the body, which thus represents the only thing of value that can be passed on. The gift of one's own skin refers to the archaic notion of dressing oneself in a second skin as a magic doubling of protection (Anzieu 1989, 50).

The idea of refilling the skin, as depicted in the Bartholomew scene, makes reference also to the mythical belief that a person's soul remains alive for as long as an intact bodily envelope ensures individuality (50). A very different take on this topos appears in Kleist's *Anekdote aus dem letzten Kriege* (Anecdote from the last war, 1810), which tells the story of the execution of a soldier who requests a final wish. When the colonel asks what it is he wants, "he pulled down his pants and said: could they please shoot in his . . . so that there wouldn't be a h . . . in his h . . ." (1961, 2:268). The soldier's last wish,

figure 28
Michelangelo, *Last Judgment* (detail)
(1534–1541)

that his "hide" stay intact, exemplifies this symbolic significance of an un-scathed skin without a "hole" even after a person's death. Kleist's macabre variant of a shot into the bottom makes drastically clear just how pitiful this last wish is.

These two variations on the notion that the external sheath represents the individual person correspond to one of the two conceptual models out-lined earlier of how subjectivity is conceived with regard to the skin. I looked at a number of idiomatic expressions that equate the subject with its skin and the skin's individual (or also stereotypical) characteristics. What follows are some explorations of the issue of identity and interpretation re-volving around the dermal surface and its visual semantics.

The notion of the skin as true self entails the desire of shielding this sur-face—which identifies and reveals—from the foreign gaze. Mechanisms of concealment and masking set in. The primeval clothing of the naked body, as prefigured in Genesis, for example, is preceded by the desire for knowl-edge: it is the eating of the fruit from the tree of knowledge that opens Adam's and Eve's eyes, "and they discovered that they were naked" (Gen. 3:7). Before that they were unclothed without being aware of it. The newly discovered nakedness, which goes hand in hand with becoming mortal and being expelled from paradise, is posited as the human condition: in contrast to animals, human beings must cover their bare skin. This critical difference between the species is further emphasized by the fact that God will fashion "tunics of skins" (Gen. 3:21) for Adam and Eve at the gate of paradise to clothe them with: what is given to animals at birth, Adam and Eve must appropriate as a second skin in order to become human in this primal cul-tural act of the emerging sense of body shame.

After discovering their nakedness following the eating of the forbidden fruit, the human couple stitched loincloths of leaves. This is about the recognition of sex differences: the human sense of shame is initiated by the fact that man and woman are not the same and that they conceal from each other what is perceived as different. Even though Adam immediately iden-tified his (third) wife Eve, after God had created her, as a creature like him-self, "flesh from my flesh" (Gen. 2:23), and not like all the animals, this sameness, as it now turns out, was based on a primal misjudgment. Only when God approaches do both hide themselves completely, from head to toe, in the trees. Now the mere fact of being seen triggers shame. This is the kind of characteristic shifting of shame from the sex to the face and the entire body (which must remain hidden from the eyes of God) that we can also observe in the socialization process: the body shame that is taught to small children gradually gives rise to a more broadly conceived, psychological notion of feeling ashamed (which, however, continues to be conceptualized by way of body analogies).

"Man alone comes from the woman, / bare as he is with mother-naked body / without scales, bristles, or horn, brings nothing to the light of / day, by which he could henceforth defend his skin" (Martin Opitz, quoted in Grimm 1984, 10:col. 703). Existential bareness as the condition of human existence, which Martin Opitz describes in these verses, is grounded in the nakedness of the human skin.[6] This nakedness is even "external in a more radical sense than the outside of the world," as Emmanuel Lévinas has noted: "Human nakedness questions me—it puts the self that I am in question—it questions me in its unprotected and defenseless weakness as nakedness" (1987, 9). The human being must protect himself or herself against the penetrating gaze of others. That requires covering oneself—even if, as in many cultures, this is done merely through symbolic ornaments or a specific inner attitude that regulates the act of looking. What we are dealing with is the archaic fear of the magical, possession-taking gaze of the other, a fear of a look that could rob one of something if one is not careful, and at the same time with the fear of being fascinated and blinded by what is seen, the desire for possession and incorporation.[7] Various studies have shown the extent to which the shedding of clothes has led to an increase in the regulation of looking and to prohibitions of perception (König 1990; Duerr 1988). This kind of restriction of the visual field applies to nudist beaches as well as to the so-called primitive peoples: the essential thing is to ignore systematically the surfaces that are coded as sexual or erotic in a respective culture or to de-sensualize them symbolically through cursory and uninterested-seeming glances. Moreover, and this is occasionally overlooked, glances that perceive the body of the other as a naked body in the original sense, that is to say, as a fragile, aging, fleshly body are taboo. For the uncovered skin is not only an erotic surface but also the defenseless state of being in its most elemental form.

Only love is in a position to permit this vulnerability and lack of covering. During a session of the Viennese Psychoanalytical Association, Otto Rank made the revealing statement that the human being had "perhaps taken off his hairy hide in order to embrace more passionately" (Nunberg and Federn 1976, 328, quoted in Knigge 1989, 102). Roland Barthes takes this a step further, going so far as to describe love as a condition of skinlessness. This is his definition of the entry "flayed" (*écorché*): "The particular sensibility of the amorous subject, which renders him vulnerable, defenseless to the slightest injuries" (1978, 95). The biblical use of the verb "to know," which means "to see" as well as "to love" and "to impregnate," still incorporates this interweaving of gaze, desire, and possession. It signifies that the seeing of the naked person must be empathic so as to be able to grasp the individual nature of the other in its discontinuous being.

The word "shame" and the word "skin" share the same Indo-Germanic root, which means "to cover."[8] Shame and skin are therefore closely related etymologically and conceptually. Accordingly, the desire to conceal oneself is inseparable from the philosophical as well as psychological concept of shame. Leon Wurmser has argued that shame about "exposing one's sexual organs, activities, and feelings" is a paradigm of the feeling of shame; in most Western languages, in fact, "shame is practically synonymous with sexual exposure and with the sexual organs themselves" (1981, 32). From a psychoanalytical perspective, shame, at its most basic levels, is the conviction that one is not worthy of love because of an inherent sense of being "dirty," "untouchable," or "rotten" (92).[9] Shame always appears with the fear of rejection, ridicule, or abandonment. The forms of perception that are constrained by shame are primarily visual, but also tactile or auditory. Shame represents an "interface effect" (Seidler 1988, quoted in Wurmser 1993, 251) that manifests itself in a transitional space. What a person needs to come to terms with is the polarity or tension between one aspect of the superego, the idealized image that I have of myself, and the ego function of self-observation, the image of myself that I have in reality (Wurmser 1993, 76).

According to psychoanalytic theory, shame serves as a defensive attitude against the two partial drives of exhibitionism and voyeurism (or scopophilia). Wurmser argues that we should expand our concepts of these drives: the former "to a more general and very early manifest need for self-expression and for attaining aggressive and libidinous aims through such expressive means, the latter to encompass the equally archaic wishes to gain love and power, communication and mastery through looking" (1981, 97). To that end, he introduces the new terms "theatophilia" and "delophilia," defining the former as "the desire to watch and observe, to admire and to be fascinated" and the latter as "the desire to express oneself and to fascinate others by one's self-exposure, to show and to impress" (158). These two partial drives, which are operative from earliest childhood, have both an active and a passive form. For theatophilia, these are active inquisitiveness and visual curiosity (by seeing, to incorporate others into oneself, to merge with them, to penetrate into their interior) and passive exhibition, the sense of being helplessly overcome and fascinated by others. The active form of delophilia is a magical self-display and the desire to please, while the passive form is the experience of exposure and unveiling and the fear of being overwhelmed, devoured, or rejected (162). The active expression of the partial drives is desired, the passive expression, however, is feared—and therefore shameful. The concepts developed by Wurmser seem useful in that they do not adopt the pathological connotation of the old terms and at the same time avoid what Georg Simmel has rightly criticized as the "predominant sexual coloring" of the concept of shame (1986, 143), since they refer to every kind of perceptual and expressive contact with one's environment.

In phenomenological terms, shame is an obstructed "away!" (Schmitz 1982b, 41). The free expression of this flight impulse is blocked by the fact that the atmosphere of shame attacks concentrically from all sides, as suggestively symbolized by a circle of fingers pointing at the shamed person (41). The individual who is encircled and pierced by shame has no other means of escape than the futile attempt to withdraw into himself. Hans-Thies Lehmann has therefore interpreted shame as "anti-affect" and "expressive *obstruction*" (1991, 824). He believes that the mask can be seen as a veritable synonym for shame: blushing, which accentuates the corporeal boundary, represents a kind of "symbolic death," which, as a physiological reflex, resembles the death-feigning reflex (thanatosis) in animals (828). Another way out of the menacing shame situation is to redirect the affect into anger and aggression (and thus to overcome it by taking on the burden of guilt). In contrast to guilt, which refers to a "code of ideal actions," shame, according to Wurmser, makes reference to an "image of the ideal self" (1981, 74–75); it is therefore more existential, because in terms of individual history it is more archaic and less differentiated. Accordingly, psychologists have noted that a congenital body defect arouses far more shame than one caused by an accident; it is the original body that symbolizes the self and is therefore shaming (Lehmann 1991, 832).

The connection between shame and skin plays a central role in this chapter and the next. I will look first at shame as the visible manifestation of inner sensations (e.g., in the act of blushing). The link between shame and one's inescapable being will come into focus in the next chapter. The sources I examine there repeatedly address the issue of shame in connection with stigmatized skin. But what was the historical process by which the unadorned face and the naked body became a surface on which a person's being could manifest itself?

I have already mentioned the collective conceptual change that, in the second half of the eighteenth century, gave rise to the archetype of a smooth and self-contained skin-canvas—a canvas that became interpretable as a result of the distance that was created by this change. There is also a second aspect that seems important in this context: cosmetic practices, which underwent a fundamental transformation in the eighteenth century. After a phase of ostentatiously made-up skin in the baroque period, characterized by emphatic artificiality, a cosmetic paradigm shift took place. Previously, makeup had an equalizing effect, in that not only skin defects but also affects and emotional states could be hidden beneath a mask of color and were largely shielded from perception. As a result, makeup was in principle vulnerable to the accusation that it was a kind of cover-up and fraud. In the late eighteenth century, by contrast, cosmetic practice was transformed by the emerging ideal of naturalism, which was influenced, not least, by the new medical knowledge of the skin (Dane 1994).

Central to this new concept of cosmetics was the distinction, going back all the way to Galen, between *comotica ars* and *cosmetica medicamenta*, or, as Zedler's *Universal Lexicon* (1743) puts it, between "the art of cosmetics" (*Schminckkunst*) and "cosmetic medicines" (*Schminckarzneyen*) (1961, 35:cols. 447 and 454). In a nutshell, the former represented the attempt—common in the seventeenth and early eighteenth centuries—to cover up and hide irregularities and blemishes of the skin, especially the pox scars that were so widespread at the time. The goal was a uniform white foundation, much like a neutral canvas, which was then artificially animated and reindividualized with rouge and beauty spots. *Cosmetica medicamenta*, on the other hand, was characterized by the attempt at reducing, in a healing and nourishing way, the impurities, spots, scars, and wrinkles of the skin with the help of a variety of "tinctures," "pomades," and "balms" (Dane 1994, 52),[10] though without trying to cover them up. Toward the end of the eighteenth century, there thus arose a new ideal of smooth, transparent skin whose veins and reddening naturally shone through.

It is surely no coincidence that this ideal of a nonconcealing skin emerges at the same time as physiognomy is popularized as the art of reading the "natural" being. The two phenomena are closely connected, for it was only after the practice of the concealing *comotica ars* was fundamentally questioned in the late eighteenth century and hardly used any longer that the epidermis was able to develop into a surface that could bear semantic meaning and on which individuality could reveal itself. It was therefore only this historical process of uncovering that constituted the skin in its authentic nature and changeability. Only now did skin become the "parade ground of physiognomy," to use the graphic language of modern dermatology (Fritsch 1985, 565). But in addition to the rather static expression of physiognomy, the animated self-revelation of pathognomy also had to be considered in the knowledge of man—something that Georg Christoph Lichtenberg had already pointed out in his polemical tract *Über Physiognomik; wider die Physiognomen* (On physiognomy; against the physiognomists, 1777), which was directed at Johann Caspar Lavater's physiognomy (1983, 78 ff.). Compared to physiognomy, defined as the "technique or art of discovering temperament and character from outward appearance (as from facial features)" and concerned more with a fixed portrait, pathognomy, "the study or recognition of emotions and passions through their outward signs or expressions," allowed for a much more differentiated interpretation of the face.

Literature in general, but especially the psychologized realistic novel of the nineteenth century, employed the classical color code of painting in its pathognomic and physiognomic descriptions (for example, women usually have a lighter skin tone). When it comes to descriptions of the skin, there are times when one can all but speak of literary painting: "Does each passion have its own color? Does this remain unaltered through the various moments of a given passion? The color of anger has its nuances. If it inflames the face, the eyes become fiery; if intense, causing the heart to contract rather than expand, the eyes wander, a pallor spreads over the forehead and cheeks, the lips become whitish and begin to tremble. Does a woman have the same coloring when anticipating pleasure as when in its embrace or taking leave of it?" (Diderot 1995, 201). According to Denis Diderot, the color tones in the face of portrayed figures, together with expressions, can be interpreted pathognomically by means of a scale of emotions. Tractates on painting repeatedly emphasize that flesh color posed the greatest challenge to the artist. For Diderot, one reason for the difficulty in achieving "a feeling of the flesh" (646) lay in the complexity of these color mixtures. Another reason was the constant transformations on a person's face, which was continually changing through shadows, coloration, and highlights—like a landscape altered by clouds passing overhead:

> But what drives a great colorist to distraction is flesh's mutability, how it can become more vivacious or moribund in the blink of an eye. This is because

while the artist's gaze is focused on the canvas and he's doing his best to trap
me with his brush, I move on, and when he looks up again he no longer finds
me as I was. . . . Because I picture Grimm or my Sophie, and my heart beats
fast, tenderness and serenity becoming visible on my features; joy is released
through my every pore, my heart dilates, my small sanguinary reservoirs are
set vibrating and the barely perceptible color of the fluid thus activated aug-
ments the bloom and life of my flesh. Even fruits and flowers change under
the perceptive gaze of La Tour or Bachelier; what torment for them, then, is
the human visage, this canvas that becomes excited, animated, flushed, or
pale, that expands or contracts in tandem with the infinite multitude of al-
ternatives sustained by this light, fleet expiration we call the soul?

(DIDEROT 1995, 201)

The emotions that seem to push through the skin turn the face into a trans-
parently lucid, mediating foil. As such, it compares to the painter's canvas,
which absorbs the colors, fixing them and making it possible for the observer to experience them.

The nineteenth-century literary technique of creating a semiotics of
character types by means of the skin's structures and shadings is especially
pronounced in Honoré de Balzac, who is also cited in the secondary literature as a first-rate physiognomist (Scheel 1961). Balzac's literary pathognomy of the skin creates a differentiated system. Selected facial descriptions
from his novel *The Woman of Thirty* (1842) illustrate how the skin—as a
"canvas that becomes excited"—is put to literary use.

It is striking how often the faces in this novel are described from the perspective of another character (and not from that of the narrator), which
means that a figure is physiognomically introduced through the eyes of another. This interpretation usually takes place without the observed figure
returning the gaze. What becomes clear here is the modern change of behavior that Elias and others have identified as the increasing necessity of the
unnoticed observation of an interaction partner: against the backdrop of the
internalization of emotions, it becomes important to decipher the emotions
and thoughts of others that are no longer openly revealed. This gives rise
to a number of unveiling techniques. In nineteenth-century literature, as
the example of Balzac shows, this constant observation without the observed person returning the gaze has already been strongly internalized. On
a narrative level, the situative gaze with which one figure looks at another
fulfills the function of creating both authenticity and an atmosphere of pres-

ence. Already the introductory scene of the novel follows this narrative pattern, so that the reader meets the title character, Julie, and her father from the perspective of the other person. Both characters discover a multitude of emotions in the face of the other.

Skin tone in the novel varies depending on the age, gender, and social standing of a protagonist. The individual complexion is subjected to the standard of classical norms: at the beginning of the story, the face of the young woman, Julie, has a "pink and white freshness" (1909, 4), while her fiancé, Victor d'Aiglemont, has a "strong, dark face" (14), her elderly father, on the other hand, "a yellow skull" (3), and the village priest a "rubicund face, but aged and wrinkled" (96). Balzac elaborates further on the face of Colonel d'Aiglemont: "His full, highly-colored cheeks were remarkable for brown and yellow tones, which denoted unusual physical vigor" (14). Character traits are tied to specific skin tones. For example, we are told the following about Julie, later the marchioness d'Aiglemont: "Like almost all women who have very long hair, she was perfectly white. Her skin, which was wonderfully fine,—a sign that rarely deceives,—indicated true sensibility, confirmed by the character of her features, which had the marvelous 'finish' that the Chinese painters give to their imaginary figures" (116). Leaving aside the somewhat bold notion that the length of a woman's hair influences her skin tone, it is striking how matter-of-factly Balzac taps into the meaning of physical characteristics as though into a universally valid system that can be accepted as a given. The quality of the surface of Julie's face is described as an unerring "sign" that allows the physiognomist—who stylizes himself as a doctor—to draw inferences about her character.

The interpretation of the skin of the marchioness's children then proceeds to all but invert the gender-coding established in the introductory scene: while son Charles has fresh, white skin, which makes him resemble a little girl, according to the authorial narrator, daughter Hélène, despite "the brilliancy of her complexion," conveys the impression of a "sickly boy"; moreover "her very whiteness had an indefinable sallow, greenish tinge—the symptom of an energetic character" (143–144). In a later chapter, the now-grown Hélène is introduced once more physiognomically: with a smooth, white forehead, "on her upper lip she had a few tokens of courage which made a faint dark line beneath a Grecian nose" (160.). In Balzac, light skin, in both adults and children, is indicative of a sensitive, feminine soul, entirely in keeping with classical physiognomy, while a more darkly shaded complexion is the mark of a dynamic, masculine type. Arthur

Ormond, a young nobleman Julie meets after her marriage to d'Aiglemont and with whom she falls in love, has "one of those typically Britannic faces whose texture is so fine, whose skin is so soft and white, that one is sometimes tempted to think that they belong to the body of a young woman" (25). Balzac seems to imply that only a feminized man, instantly revealed as such by his pale, fine skin, will be able to understand Julie's subtle emotions. Although a genuine, mutual understanding is presented as potentially possible, it is not a sure thing, since Balzac leaves open the question of whether the Englishman does in fact see the "moist, glistening track" that Julie's tears (of unhappy love for him) briefly leave behind on her cheeks before the wind quickly dries it (26). Her husband, in any case, in a later scene that picks up the same motif, explicitly does not notice the traces of tears on Julie's face (54), which reveals him as an unfeeling, uninterested person and makes him the guilty party in the failure of their marriage.

While skin tone, wrinkles, and other individual features of a complexion are considered physiognomic characteristics, Balzac resorts in equal measure to pathognomic interpretations, indicated by sudden, emotion-induced changes. These include less facial expressions than traditional signs of sensitivity and refinement (blushing, blanching) but also modifications that bespeak deeper changes of mood. For example, in the phase when Julie is most deeply in love with Victor d'Aiglemont, her "cheeks had taken on an extraordinary flush." But only a few pages later, when Balzac describes the marriage between her and d'Aiglemont as a disappointing illusion, the young woman's face, "still delicate in outline, had lost the rose coloring which formerly gave it such brilliancy"; her black hair heightened the "whiteness of her face, whose vivacity seemed to have become deadened." Beneath her eyes, the "lids were dark violet rings on the worn cheeks" (15, 22).

In a state of happiness, the complexion of the grown daughter, Hélène, possessed an air of "Oriental poesy" (201); the face of her sister, Moina, was "flushed and bore the impress of stormy thoughts" (230). The radiance and lovely colors of the skin of a woman's face are interpreted as clear signs of emotional well-being, while a dull, pale skin tone indicates unhappiness. But despite the cultural unambiguousness of such attributions, Balzac does render problematic the fundamental ability to read the other by using, as a literary device, misreadings among the protagonists. For example, one of the d'Aiglemont aunts misinterprets Julie's paleness as sadness over the im-

pending separation from her husband (and not as the consequence of unhappy love for another man). Over the course of the novel, Julie's face,
time and again, is a screen on which is revealed what the aunt believes is
going on inside her niece. Here are two examples: "The old lady observed,
not without surprise, the changes that took place in Madame d'Aiglemont's
face. The vivid coloring that seemed to set her cheeks on fire gradually
faded, and her complexion took on dead-white, pallid tones. As she lost her
early brilliancy, she became less depressed" (31); "The marchioness was
reading and did not hear: her friend, watching, saw the most intense feeling, the most dangerous excitement, appear on her face, as she turned red
and white alternately" (78). Balzac shows the extent to which the perception of the other is fundamentally an act of interpretation—for the reader is
not enlightened about whether the emotions manifesting themselves on the
surface in fact correspond to what the observed individual is experiencing.
The "fading" of the skin tones in the first passage, or the emotions that "appear" on the face of the marchioness, as in the second passage, are present
as signs on the transparent canvas of Julie's face, but whether these signs can
be translated remains an open question.

That this is so is also revealed by the reference to undisguised childhood,
in which all emotions show themselves as they are, turning the child into an
"incorruptible witness": "Childhood has a transparent brow, a diaphanous
complexion; and, in childhood, a lie is like a bright light which reddens even
the glance" (147). Children are thus characterized by the same diaphanous-
ness that Balzac uses to describe the skin of young women.[11] It is especially
in the portrayal of Hélène that Balzac strives to evoke the quality of translu-
cence: he notes the "transparence of her delicate skin" (161) and her "strong
white hands, through which the light shone, giving them a transparent, almost fluid flush" (162). In another passage we are told that there was "happiness and love . . . in her blue veins" (207). By means of the childlike, transparent skin of the young women, Balzac thus portrays a state of being in
which the mechanisms of self-concealment, which are created through the
internalization of feelings in the socialization process, have not yet taken
hold. Julie as a young woman and later her growing daughters are shown in
a primal state of involuntary feeling, a state they only lose through the negative experiences and suffering in their later years. All this is explicitly revealed through the quality of skin tone: that the "language of dissimulation"
(Geitner 1992) also manifests itself—as paradoxical as this may sound—on

and in the skin is intimated by the transformation, suggested as the story unfolds, of a vivid and transparent complexion that speaks involuntarily into one that is dull, lusterless, and at times in itself mute.

It is only when Julie is an old woman of fifty that her face has become truly "cold." The narrator describes it as one of those "terrible poems" (*une de ces poésies terribles*), for "in old age, a woman's whole being has spoken; the passions have carved themselves upon her face; she has been sweetheart, wife, mother; the most violent emotions of joy and sorrow have at length discolored and distorted her features, by inscribing themselves thereon in numberless wrinkles, each of which has its language" (223). The pathognomic signs have become physiognomic characteristics that have engraved themselves on the face. The aged woman, like the aged man, is furrowed by wrinkles in which history has inscribed itself. But a gender difference remains in that the face of an old woman is "awe-inspiring," while the male face makes a "keen impression" on the observed by the "profound sorrow graven upon that downcast forehead" (19) or by the "physical courage written in the wrinkles of his cheeks" (159).

In his physiognomic reflections toward the end of the novel, Balzac deals only with the female face, contrasting the appearance of a young girl with that of an old woman. In keeping with a long tradition of imagery, the skin is analogized to the surface of water and to the earth:

> A young woman's face has the tranquility, the smoothness, the freshness of the surface of a lake. In truth, a woman's physiognomy does not really begin before she is thirty. Before that age the painter finds in their faces only pinks and whites, smiles and expressions which repeat the same thought, a thought of youth and love, and unvarying and superficial thought. But in old age, a woman's whole being has spoken; the passions have carved themselves upon her face. . . . If we may be permitted to pursue this curious metaphor, the dry lake then shows the marks of all the torrents that originally formed it.
>
> (223)

The actual drying of the skin in old age becomes allegorically elevated in the image of the dried-up lake. Young skin, by contrast, is like the smooth, calm, and cool surface of water. In Balzac, it is only the skin of the old woman that attains three-dimensionality through the wrinkles that engrave themselves deeply, thus destroying what was originally a surface smooth as glass. This "biography" (Serres 1985, 332) in the literal sense of the word, which has inscribed itself on the face of Madame d'Aiglemont in old age, speaks

> of the suffering that had been sharp enough to ravage that face, to wither the temples, to hollow the cheeks, to redden the eyelids, and to strip them of their lashes, which give charm to the glance. . . . The nature of her wrinkles, the way in which her face was creased, the pallor of her pain-ridden glance, all bore eloquent witness to those tears which, being consumed by the heart, never fall to the earth. . . . Genuine suffering is in appearance so calm in the deep bed it has made for itself, in which it seems to sleep, while it continues to corrode the whole being like the terrible acid that eats glass!
>
> (BALZAC 1909, 224–225)

Bound up in this passage about the destructive effect of suffering is a poetic reflection about the limits of the art of writing, which in the final analysis is not able to render the individuality of faces adequately: "Painters have colors for such portraits, but ideas and words are powerless to draw them faithfully . . . ; a recital of the events, to which such terrible transformations of the features are due, is the only means that the poet has to make them intelligible" (225). This qualifying remark about the descriptive power of literature, which can intimate feelings but cannot produce adequate visual images of them, in the end puts in question the analogy between artistic and poetic portraiture. In Balzac's semiotics of surfaces, the (inevitably) inadequate visual description is supplemented by a penetrating gaze, which conveys through language what the colorations, shadings, and wrinkles truly mean to say about psychological character.

The example of this one novel must suffice for the present context. The skin semiotics of literary painting reaches its high point in the nineteenth century (and possibly with this very author).

Nietzsche pointed to the insurmountable dilemma confronting every artist who seeks to indicate a psychological state by means of the external appearance:

> That the painter and the sculptor, of all people, give expression to the "idea" of the human being is mere fantasizing and sense-deception: one is being tyrannized over by the eye when one says such a thing, since this sees even of the human body only the surface, the skin; the inner body, however, is just as much part of the idea. Plastic art wants to make characters visible on

the outside; the art of speech employs the word to the same end, it delineates the character in sounds. Art begins from the natural *ignorance* of mankind as to his interior (both bodily and as regards character): it does not exist for physicists or philosophers.

(1986, 85)

Nietzsche rightly opposes the traditional descriptive practice in literature and painting (which I have examined in the example of Balzac's work) that uses the painted or described surface of the body in such a way that it functions as a surface reproducing the essence. After all, as Nietzsche states elsewhere, it is one characteristic of every surface that it, "like every skin, betrays something but *conceals* even more" (1966, 234). It is only in the late nineteenth century that the ability of character to be translated by means of the skin is rendered problematic. As a result, an unambiguous semiotics would cease to be available in the twentieth century. The "natural ignorance" of the inside that Nietzsche talks about again and again thwarts the physiognomic-pathognomic methods of reading the skin.

6 mystification

The Strangeness of the Skin

In his miniature "Clothes" (1913), Franz Kafka equates the second skin of clothes with the body's surface, what he calls the "natural fancy dress."[1] With his use of the clothes analogy, a "master trope" in his work (Anderson 1994, 3), Kafka points to the ephemeral nature of youthful beauty. Growing old is portrayed as a sad and ridiculous process of remaining captive in the skin, which marks the individual for a lifetime and cannot be taken off. We are dealing with an absurd allegory that captures the tragedy of wearing one's skin: the one thing we would never do with clothes—namely, wear the same outfit for an entire lifetime—is the very thing we must invariably do with the unique skin we possess. Because, according to Kafka, the process of growing old and becoming dirty and wrinkled is a matter of negligence and fault, the skin is not only a garment but also a straitjacket and fate. The motif of the skin becoming dusty over time that Kafka picks up in this miniature—an image that is not based on a living, moving individual but rather on a static sculpture or a clothes-draped mannequin—recurs repeatedly in Kafka's writings.[2] That a skin turned dirty, "outdated," and old by life is "hardly wearable any longer" is something Kafka also notes in his diary in the description of a gentleman at the opera, in which he comments on the "worn, bloodless skin of his face" (1976, 885).[3]

For a literary history of skin, Kafka's diaries (1909–1923) are a unique document of physiognomic description, a mode of description that uses the structures and qualities of the surface of the body and the face. I will therefore take a closer look at central aspects of Kafka's obsession with observation and description. Nearly all portrayals of individuals in the diaries are written in the present tense, thus creating the impression of a discursive observation of someone who is physically present. The ideal on which this approach is based is the word-becoming gaze that captures the living expression instantly and without delay. In contrast to Kafka's literary works, which largely dispense with facial descriptions or employ them merely in a conventional way, similar to the realistic writers of the nineteenth century, the rendition of detail is central to the diaries, as a result of which they hold a preeminent place in the history of the literary portrait (von Matt 1989, 13 ff.).[4]

The production of literary portraits in Kafka represents primarily a "ritual of defense against the encountered person and the possible consequences of that encounter" (37), which leads von Matt to speak of an "enigmatic tendency" (24) of facial descriptions that strike us as odd and bizarre. The practice of portrait writing thus functions in the opposite way from the love magic of popular belief (which invokes presence), in that Kafka uses the portrait he creates to keep the described person at arm's length. The microscopic description of individual aspects of the face, to which the gaze "clings in clamlike fashion" (44), causes the person to vanish as a human counterpart, turning him into a foreign body, into a merely objectified entity. The following parenthetical sentence in Kafka's famous entry about his first encounter with his future fiancée, Felice Bauer, "I alienate myself from her a little by inspecting her so closely" (lit., by getting so close to her body) (1976, 722), encapsulates this mechanism, which is also found in a similar form in Sylvia Plath.

In his diaries, Kafka repeatedly noted the aspect of the skin's tautness that we encounter in the miniature "Clothes." The skin is imagined as a membrane stretched over the individual and individualizing skeletal frame, a membrane that, like a dress, fits more or less well: "The dancer Eduardova is not as pretty in the open air as on the stage. Her faded colour, her cheekbones which draw her skin so taut that there is scarcely a trace of motion in her face . . . , the large nose, which rises as though out of a cavity"

(594–595); "Inaesthetic transition from the taut skin of my boss's bald spot to the delicate wrinkles of his forehead" (634); "In the carriage: pointed nose of the old woman with still almost youthful, taut skin. Does youth therefore end at the tip of the nose and death begin there?" (638); "Bernard Kellermann read aloud . . . painstakingly close-shaven, a sharp nose, the flesh over his cheekbones often ebbs and flows like a wave" (604); "Miss Gerloff, teacher, owl-like, vivacious young face with animated and alert features. Her body is more indolent"(904). All these entries are about the relationship between hard and soft matter in the shaping of a face. These are the perceptions of a sculptural gaze, one that probes the proportions and structure of the forms without the observer being able to change these sculptures with his own hands. One entry about a Hungarian Jewish woman, with whom Kafka is sharing a train compartment, describes her explicitly as having a "large, well-worked face."* In another passage, Kafka notes about a woman he observes on a train to Paris that "her nose seemed to come too abruptly to an end" (882).

Yet the act of seeing also incorporates the animation of the malleable face, which changes from a frozen, masklike state (in the first passage about the dancer) to a liquefied state (as in the passage about Kellermann). In Kafka's descriptions, the capacity for both mimic expression and an undefined self-acting movement of the facial features depends more on the individual nature of how the skin is stretched across bones and cartilage than it does on a person's real age or active changes of expression. It is also interesting that in the passage about Miss Gerloff the body is described as "indolent" (*nachlässiger*): the German adjective that Kafka uses implies once more a dressing of oneself, that is, an act subject to individual will and taste. But Kafka does not apply this to the clothed body but to the body shapes as such and through the use of the comparative also to the face of Miss Gerloff. In a different entry he writes about a young woman: "Unnecessarily thin cheeks" (898). Comments such as these indicate that the person being described also bears responsible for his "natural fancy dress." Kafka the diarist cannot accept that body, face, and skin unavoidably express something that simply is the way it is.

---

* The English translation of Kafka's diaries by Joseph Kresh renders the original German, "großes, gut ausgearbeitetes Gesicht" (1994b, 738) as simply "well-proportioned face" (1976, 808). This does not capture the connotation of the German "*ausgearbeitetes*," which suggests the way a sculptor works clay or stone.—Trans.

The narrowly focused gaze at individual fragments of the face approaches the way in which human beings in fact, and often involuntarily, stare at some blemish in the face of a stranger if that person is not looking at them and if they believe that they are not being watched themselves. Kafka's dictum of rigorous self-observation (Kremer 1989, 118) leads him to a ruthless recording of his own perceptions. His fascination with the details in people's faces makes him capture the special spots and shadings of faces like an impressionistic painter trained in dermatology: "Mrs. Tschissik was beautiful yesterday. . . . The hair separated into two waves, brightly illuminated by the gaslight. Somewhat bad complexion around the right corner of her mouth. . . . The powdering that I have so far seen I hate, but if this white colour, this somewhat cloudy milk-colored veil hovering low over the skin is the result of powder, then every woman should powder" (658); "Rowohlt: young, red-cheeked, breads of sweat between his nose and cheeks, moved only above the hips. Count Bassewitz, author of *Judas*, larger, nervous, expressionless face. The movement in his waist, a strong physique carried well. Hasenclever, a lot of shadow and highlights in a small face, bluish colours too. . . . Pinthus, correspondent for the *Berliner Tageblatt*, a round, rather flat face" (891–892). Kafka not only keeps the described individuals at a distance, as von Matt maintains. With his gaze he simultaneously gets close to them in an almost unseemly manner, so that he sees the bad complexion hidden under the powder of the actress as well as the small beads of sweat next to the publisher's nose. The four men he describes appear almost to be hastily sketched, with merely the most prominent spots on each face captured so as to create the strongest possible contrasts among them.

Another striking aspect in all these entries is the fact that, despite the animation of the faces, one cannot speak of a pathognomic expression, since the meaning of the respective features remains enigmatic. Of course, one must take into account the genre in question here: in a literary text, an author will be more concerned to intimate the characteristics of individuals through their expression and appearance than is the case in a diary. Still, there is an undeniable relationship of fundamental alienation, even hostility, with regard to the other, who is described as fleshy-bony material but not as a human individual. This stylistic quality is not merely grounded in a particular aesthetic interest, that is, in the exploration of how the human physiognomy is actually constructed. It is also connected with the relationship between the self and the world. Kafka's descriptions of bodies and faces outline a premodern, grotesque notion of the body, one that does not experience the body of the other as essentially final and closed but "in the act of becoming" (Bakhtin 1984, 317) and interwoven with the self. Kafka's alien body images are therefore often broken open, images that allow a glimpse into the inside or jut out into the world through central, inordinately projecting parts: "Her face, something I saw only partially at first, had such deep wrinkles that I had to think about the uncomprehending astonishment with which animals must look at such human faces. Her small, angular nose, especially in its somewhat upturned end, protruded from her face in a strikingly corporeal manner" (1990, 213);* "Pretty girls. One with a flat face, unbroken surface of skin, rounded cheeks, hair beginning high up, eyes lost in this smoothness and protruding a little" (1976, 676); "Miss Kanitz. Coquetry that ill suits the kind of person she is. She spreads, points, pouts her lips as if her fingers were invisibly shaping them" (832); "Tall, vigorous actor with delicately painted nostrils; the black of the nostrils continued to stand out even when the outline of his upturned face was lost in the light. . . . Man in a box opened his mouth when he laughed until a gold molar became visible, then he kept it open like that for a while" (875).

It is the grotesque quality of faces that simultaneously fascinates and repels Kafka in these passages. The very moment when physiognomic ways of reading the face fail because the grotesque explodes their system, the face becomes a body part like any other. It is then corporeal: an animated, structured mass that attracts the observer, repels him, or leaves him indifferent but is deprived of its expressive dimension. The sole reason why the face in Kafka receives special attention is that it is usually the only part (in addition to the hands) whose uncovered surface is visible. The protruding and receding quality of the face is so dominant that Kafka needs to make a special point of mentioning that a face is "smooth" and has "unbroken" skin surfaces, as in the second example.

Although it is faces that are being described, these are motifs of the grotesque, which are frequently—though not exclusively, and that is the point—represented by the lower abdomen. Bulging eyes and gaping mouths also play an essential role. What is unusual is that Kafka (in the first example) creates an astonished animal gaze from whose perspective the face with its deep wrinkles appears grotesque in the first place. He inverts the

---

* This passage is not found in the English translation of Kafka's diaries. I have therefore translated it directly from the German edition.—Trans.

carnivalesque motif by depicting the genuinely human as grotesque, where-as it is really the animal elements in the human figure that possess this bizarre characteristic (Bakhtin 1984, 316). The grotesque is invoked not only in the preoccupation with deep openings and the protruding parts of the described faces but also, and especially, in the focus on only one element of the whole, which appears as though magically enlarged.

With respect to the opening and closure of the body, Kafka in his diaries also mentions his own body, for example, when he notes, "For the length of a moment I felt myself clad in steel" (612). Or when he writes: "When I lay in bed this afternoon and someone quickly turned a key in the lock, for a moment I had locks all over my body, as though at a costume ball, and at short intervals a lock was opened or shut here and there" (1990, 723).* While Kafka certainly experiences the imaginary openings distributed over his body—and arbitrarily opened and closed by strangers—as a secret pleasure, his description of young women is marked not only by a closure of the skin but also by the careful enwrapment of their bodies, a way of escaping the threatening (or longed-for) stream of intermixing: "Yesterday in the factory. The girls, in their unbearably dirty and untidy clothes" (703); "The girls, tightly wrapped in their work aprons, especially behind. One at Löwy's and Winterberg's this morning whose apron flaps, which closed only on her behind, did not tie together as they usually do, but instead closed over each other so that she was wrapped up like a child in swaddling clothes. Sensual impression like that which, even unconsciously, I always had of children in swaddling clothes who are so squeezed in their wrappings and beds and so laced with ribbons, quite as though to satisfy one's lust" (661); "The girls in the adjoining room yesterday. . . . She seemed to me in my mind to be overdressed not only because of the clothes she wore, but also because of the entire room; only her shapely, naked, round, strong, dark shoulders which I had seen in the bath prevailed against her clothes" (624). Women require an additional skin of sturdy, body-shaping clothes to keep from dissolving. It is only this diaperlike enwrapment in a second skin that makes them erotic. The loose wrapping of the Czech workers in his father's asbestos factory in the first passage strikes Kafka immediately as "unbearably dirty." In like manner, he documents with horror the descriptions by Anton Max Pachinger, who was reporting on the

---

* The phrase "fancy-dress ball" in the English translation has been changed to the more common expression "costume ball."—Trans.

nude pictures of the shapeless "darlings" of his friend Alfred Kubin. In one picture, which showed a massive woman in bed, "the breast, they way they look spread out and swollen and virtually coagulated, and the belly rising to the navel are like equal mountains" (1990, 275–276).** The fleshy, female body becomes a grotesque, vaguely defined, fluid and hilly landscape that frightens but also fascinates the writer.

Klaus Theweleit has revealed the degree to which the collective male fantasy of the armored women is based on the fear of the desire to blend, hence its primary purpose is that of deanimating the object (1993, 1:211). He draws on more recent insights of psychoanalysis, according to which fears of the dissolution of the ego boundary—of phantasmatical penetrations and blurring object relationships—are derived not from the oedipal triangle but from an earlier phase of a symbiotic one-on-one relationship with the first person to whom the child relates. Michael Balint has described disturbances on this early relational level, where the child does not yet perceive itself as an object separate from the mother, as the area of "fundamental disorders." At this stage, the psychological authority of the ego does not yet exist (or is considerably disturbed). When Anzieu, paraphrasing Freud, talks about the ego as derived from feelings that are created on the body surface and says that an intact ego represents a psychological sheath, it becomes clear that the notion of such a given enrobement, one that simultaneously protects, delimits, and makes contact possible, is quite distant in Kafka's body images. In Kafka, the skin is described as one that is stretched over the bones (i.e., a secondary skin), or it is encumbered with birthmarks, wounds, or other openings (it is both permeable and repulsive). Or it is fluid (and thus neither protective nor graspable) or hardened like leather.[5]

Several of the Jewish myths that Kafka notes in his diaries are connected with the skin as a protective barrier and with the prohibition against the touching of one's own body. This indicates the high symbolic importance that attached to the body boundary as the problematic place of contact between the inside and the outside. We are told that the "evil spirits gain entry into a person who drinks out of an imperfect glass" (646) or that, in Russia, tablets with cabalistic symbols are hung above the doors "to protect the mother from the evil spirits during the time between the birth and the circumcision" (686). According to another superstition, in the morning, on

**This passage is missing from the English translation of Kafka's diaries. The page reference is to the German edition.—Trans.

awakening, one must "dip the fingers three times in water, as the evil spirits have settled during the night on the second and third joints of the fingers." Kafka, however, interprets this explanation as a purist excuse aimed at preventing "the fingers directly touching the face," since the hands might have accidentally touched the body during sleep, "the armpits, the behind, the genitals" (646). This ambivalent relationship to the touching of one's own body (and the bodies of others), which Kafka identifies here as a phenomenon of Jewish culture, is simultaneously a theme that runs through his literary work like a convoluted thread.

"In the Penal Colony" (1919) is Kafka's famous story about an ingenious torture machine that, in a lengthy procedure, penetrates the offender's body surface with countless needles, inscribing his sentence and eventually killing him. Most literary scholars have interpreted this story as describing a process by which the law is inscribed in the body. Although Kafka undertakes an "exemplary retranslation of verbal rituals of punishment into actual physical ones" (Abraham 1990, 260), the painful transfer of text onto and into the body was rarely conceived of in its physical extremity. Kafka's "literal reading of metaphorical sayings as principles of artistic representation" (Müller-Seidel 1987, 124) notwithstanding, most scholars have interpreted the process of inscription on the body allegorically (as the embodiment of abstract facts such as mercy, justice, or law) or in terms of textual theory with regard to the written nature of the execution of the sentence, which transformed the body into a book.[6] It is significant that these interpretations often end with the officer's report on how the apparatus functions and the process of the tattooed inscription and pay scant attention to the end of the narrative. While the first part of the story deals only with the description of the precisely programmed killing process, it is the second part that deals with the real, anarchical self-destruction of the machine, in which its erstwhile masters destroy themselves as victims. What happens here, however, is a critical change in the semiotic level of writing and ornamentation on the epidermis of the body (in the report) to the no longer merely semiotic level of the actual perforation and destruction of the body surface.

The story, especially its second part, thus revolves around the body image of the perforated skin. Anzieu speaks of the skin ego as "colander" to describe extreme forms of this phantasm: an ego representation that continuously empties itself, offers no protection of any kind, and is subject to the danger of depersonalization. In such patients the "container function" of the skin ego has been fundamentally destroyed, which is reflected in the anxiety "of a flowing away of vital substances through holes" (Anzieu 1989, 38). This, then, is not a fear of dismemberment and fragmentation—as Jacques Lacan described in his well-known "mirror stage" essay (1977)—but an explicit fear of emptying, for which some patients, according to Anzieu, use a memorable metaphor, describing "themselves as an egg with a broken shell being emptied of its white (actually of its yolk)" (39). The story deals explicitly with this perforation of the skin, which Kafka expresses in graphic and vivid form.

What is striking in this context is the frequency with which naked bodies are juxtaposed in the narrative to very firmly wrapped, clothed bodies. For example, the officer, who later becomes a pitiful victim of his own apparatus, is wearing, despite the heat of the shadeless valley, a "tight-fitting full dress uniform coat, amply befrogged and weighed down by epaulettes" (1983, 142). The condemned prisoner, on the other hand, has his shirt and pants cut from behind so that they fall off and leave him standing naked: the undressing of the defenseless prisoner as a traditional ritual of public humiliation is heightened by the suddenness of the stripping and the irreversible destruction of the protective sheath of clothing. The cutting of the clothes anticipates symbolically the goal of the torture: the destruction of the integrity of the surface and with it the emptying of the inside. This violent stripping of the condemned stands in stark contrast to the slow and careful way in which the officer later in the story undresses before lying down in the apparatus himself. As he takes each garment off, he handles it with "loving care" but then proceeds to fling it "with a kind of unwilling jerk into the pit" (162–163): his protective layer is not taken from him; he gives it up voluntarily. But then, in the cruel culmination, his body is not inscribed and punctured but pierced, causing his body fluids to drain away:

> The Harrow was not writing, it was only jabbing, and the Bed was not turning the body over but only bringing it up quivering against the needles. The explorer wanted to do something, if possible, to bring the whole machine to a standstill, for this was not exquisite torture such as the officer desired, this was plain murder. He stretched out his hands. But at that moment the Harrow rose with the body spitted on it and moved to the side, as it usually did only when the twelfth hour had come. Blood was flowing

in a hundred streams, not mingled with water, the water jets too had failed
to function. And now the last action failed to fulfill itself, the body did not
drop off the long needles, streaming with blood it went on hanging over
the pit without falling into it.

(165)

The officer does not die from unbearable pain (as is intended by the conception of the apparatus); he bleeds to death. The killing is not a form of
torture dependent on an ingenious system and a functioning apparatus but
the mere whim of an anarchic machinery that, in the end, even regulates
its deadly touches. On several occasions, the narrator indicates that it appeared as though the apparatus could feel the weight and form of the body
lying in it and moved to meet it. In this story, the relationship between anthropomorphized machine and body is described as an ambivalent one of
contact and destruction.

This central phantasm of the torture of the skin is reminiscent of the one
that appears in deeply masochistic patients: faced with the threat of depersonalization, according to Anzieu, it is often only the experience of a sheath
of pain that can convey the integrity of the self. What is important for this
feeling is the sense of being one and being held—which is precisely what
the apparatus in Kafka's story does in an exaggerated and deadly form.
Anzieu maintains that an infant learns to differentiate two fundamentally
different forms of skin contact: those that communicate excitation (or, in
the negative case, pain) and those that communicate information. The former are related to masochism; the latter to narcissism (Anzieu 1989, 43).
When it comes to Kafka's penal colony, there is a transition from the level
of meanings—and the deciphering of the script "with his wounds" (1983,
150)—in the first part of the story to the level of stimulation in the second
part. In the second part, the apparatus thus no longer conveys meaning; instead, what takes place is a perverse, excessive, and lethal stimulation. What
this means, in generalizing terms, is that Kafka does not conceive of touching as message (e.g., the demonstration of affection or hatred) but essentially as pain.

The description of the initial contact between the condemned man's
skin and the machine also makes clear that the story fundamentally revolves
around perverted forms of touching (in the broadest sense of the word).
Kafka portrays this contact as ambivalently erotic and painful: "When the
needle points touched him a shudder ran over his skin" (150). Through the

narrative conjoining of paper and skin, Kafka makes tactility as such into a problematic issue: while the skin of the condemned man is touched too strongly—namely, exclusively with needles—the officer, in explaining the apparatus, "outlined the script with his little finger, holding it high above the paper as if the surface dared not be sullied by touch" (161). On the paper are traced, like a pattern, the needle pricks the machine must carry out. During the torture itself, the respective page lies inside the "Designer," above the glass harrow, through which—conveyed through a media channel, as though through a screen—the same design becomes visible on the skin. The fact that the paper, which represents the skin, like some holy parchment must never be touched, while the skin itself is touched in a penetrating, destructive form, reminds us of the generally highly ambivalent attitude toward nakedness and touching that is evident in various passages of Kafka's diaries.

For example, in 1915 he wrote this entry: "I am as incompetent and dreary as always and should really have no time to reflect on anything but the question of how it happens that anyone has the slightest desire even to crook her little finger at me" (1976, 802). He uses the touch from the hand of another person, both longed for and feared, to illustrate his existential self-doubt over having any worth and physical attractiveness at all. In his diaries, Kafka frequently talks about his despair over his "physical condition": "Nothing can be accomplished with such a body" (668); "I write this very decidedly out of despair over my body and over a future with this body" (594); "a loneliness . . . that is organic with me—as though I consisted only of bones" (881). Loneliness is experienced as the absence of contact in the original sense of the word, as the existence of a person who feels only his bones, because the skin is sensually felt and experienced only through touch. Just as the skin of the people he sketches in his diaries is described primarily as fleshy material and as such as repulsive, in these passages, as well, his own skin is not a place of contact but merely of closure.

Much as in Kafka's diaries, the skin descriptions in the poetry and prose of Sylvia Plath are interesting for their strategies of enigmatization and their gestures of defense and aggressiveness. Moreover, in Plath's autobiographical writings, the image of the wound and the scar plays an important role, along with the perception of her own skin as either an impenetrable wall or a highly fragile protective layer. Exemplary in Plath is also the connection among (female) skin impurity, physical injury, and self-rejection. Present are not only detailed physiognomies focused on the individual skin quality of other characters. In many prose texts, the first-person narrator explicitly perceives herself through her own skin as seen in the mirror or imagined. In Plath's poetry, the shedding of the skin is a central metaphor for a change of roles or the fragility of the ego. Moreover, her work can be used to show the extent to which the complexion and the structure of skin had already largely lost their meaning-laden clarity in the literary descriptions of the twentieth century.

I will begin with a few example of the enigmatic skin images in Plath's prose, which will reveal the degree to which skin is no longer used as a means to make character visible. In Plath's novel *The Bell Jar* (1963),[7] the skin of a young woman has "a bronzy polish under the pale dusting powder"; her face is "dusky as a bleached-blonde Negress" (1971, 6, 9). The first-person narrator, Esther Greenwood, says about herself: "The city had faded my tan, though. I looked yellow as a Chinaman" (6). Both complexions are contextualized with the skin color of other ethnic groups, but this reference does not point to the characteristics of these groups. A young man's tanned face "seemed almost black" (67), while a prostitute has "rat-colored skin" (64). Although the latter comment is clearly derogatory, it says nothing concrete about the person described. Esther's mother has a face that is as "sallow as a slice of lemon" (107), while that of her roommate at the clinic looks "like maps of the craters on the moon," for it "had at one time been badly pitted with acne" (174). To be sure, Plath is drawing analogies to other creatures and objects (lemon, moon, rat). But these analogies do not actually individualize the described persons or illustrate their natures (in the sense that the external points to the internal); instead, they merely emphasize their obscurity. The only person in *The Bell Jar* who is characterized by neutral skin is a young professor whom Esther chooses as her first lover; he has the "pale, hairless skin of a boy genius" (186). What is surprising here is the logic of the attribution of hairlessness and paleness to the nature of the young genius, which seems like an arbitrary insertion and is not pursued.

In Plath, much as in Kafka, the coding of skin types and skin colors, which modern literature has largely abandoned, is replaced by a heightened interest in the physical materiality of the skin. This microscopic gaze at the surface inspects individual peculiarities, inquires into their origins, or searches for analogies. Here are two examples from the prose works "Johnny Panic and the Bible of Dreams" (1968) and "Above the Oxbow" (1977): "Her face, hefty as a bullock's, is covered with a remarkable number of tiny maculae, as if she's been lying under water for some time and little algae had latched on to her skin, smutching it over with tobacco-browns and greens. These moles are noticeable mainly because the skin around them is so pallid" (1979, 158); "The raised scar running diagonally from his right eyebrow across his nose and deep into his left cheek showed white against his tan. Pale, almost dirty, the scar tissue had a different texture from the rest of his skin; it was smoother, newer, like plastic caulking a crack" (167). The narrator describes the facial skin like someone who is gazing at an unfamiliar culture, like a plastic surgeon or a dermatologist. The observations of the discolorations and the structures are inquisitive and thorough; they possess a precise language but do not engage in psychological or aesthetic interpretations of any kind—in the sense, for example, that a scar signals courage or that a profusion of birth marks is unattractive. The describing eye looks with a closeness not permitted by the culture: faithful in detail, medical, objective. It looks at the face of the other as though it were looking at dead flesh and not a human visage. That alone explains how there can be comparisons to "plastic" or "algae," other forms of physical matter. The other person is something foreign that is perceived neither with empathy nor antipathy but merely with a distanced stance.

What is striking is that the skin in Plath's prose is perceived with all the senses except touch. While we repeatedly hear about the visual impression of characters (a device common in literature), it is unusual that attention is also given to taste sensations, acoustic impressions, and olfactory sensations.[8] By contrast, the elimination of the body surface encountered through touch and feel is connected with an unspoken prohibition on touching, which psychoanalytical theory attributes to the original denial of separation (the loss of the common skin with the mother or the unconscious desire to return to a symbiotic condition). The fact that the skin does not come into play as a place of touch, as a libidinally charged boundary and contact surface, may have something to do with the pervasive motif "of wanting to incorporate and be incorporated" (Biven 1982, 215) or, as Plath put it in her diary, "to crawl back abjectly into the womb" (1983, 59).

In an autobiographical childhood memory, Plath describes the traumatic situation after the birth of her younger brother, when she suddenly experienced the drastic separation from her mother's body, who had been nursing her until then: "As from a star I saw, coldly and soberly, the *separateness* of everything. I felt the wall of my skin: I am I. That stone is a stone.

My beautiful fusion with the things of the world was over" (1979, 23). Here, the skin is experienced as a barrier that separates the self from the world; the other, too, is stone. The I who is describing this is in an extremely distanced position relative to this (her own) skin, on which it casts a "cold" and "sober" eye. The exclusion of the tactile dimension in Plath, and the feeling of separation from one's own body and the bodies of others, creates a heightened awareness of the discrepancy between inner self and outer sheath. Physical contact in Plath, when it does occur, takes the very aggressive form of biting, cuts, surgeries, accidents—a form of contact that is in every respect separating. We are thus dealing with boundary issues, and it is therefore no coincidence when Esther Greenwood, the protagonist in *The Bell Jar*, recounts the beginning of her psychic suffering as the painful inability to prevent the involuntary penetration of the outside world (in this case, light): "I feigned sleep until my mother left for school, but even my eyelids didn't shut out the light. They hung the raw, red screen of their tiny vessels in front of me like a wound. I crawled between the mattress and the padded bedstead and let the mattress fall across me like a tombstone" (1971, 101). The skin ego is so fragile that the protagonist needs an additional support to preserve the unity of the person. The fact that this support then becomes a tombstone is interpreted by the narrator as an unsolvable, paradoxical conflict. The eyelids do not represent protective membranes but are raw, injured skin flaps incapable of keeping out the light. The narrator thus imagines herself as so unprotected and vulnerable that later, as a logical consequence, fear at the prospect of electroshock therapy makes her face "stiff, like pergament" (117). The other person, by contrast, is as though armored by a thick, masking skin; for the female protagonist in "Stone Boy with Dolphin," for example, the face of her companion becomes a wax or rubber mask behind which he hides himself: "his wax mask escorting her," "intent, behind a glistening pink rubber mask" (1979, 177, 184).

It is especially the passages in which Plath tries to come to literary terms with her psychosis following a suicide attempt that show a painful split between a fragile self and the external sheath.[9] In *The Bell Jar*, the narrator, who awakens in a hospital following a suicide attempt, looks first at her body and then at her face in a mirror, though without being able to identify with this person, who seemed strange and misshapen to her: "I looked down at the yellow legs sticking out of the unfamiliar white silk pajamas they had dressed me in. The skin shook flabbily when I moved, as if there wasn't a muscle in it, and it was covered with a short, thick stubble of black hair" (1971, 141); "One side of the person's face was purple, and bulged out in a shapeless way, shading to green along the edges, and then to a sallow yellow. The person's mouth was pale brown, with a rose-colored sore at either corner. The most startling thing about the face was its supernatural conglomeration of bright colors" (142–143). The first-person narrator experiences the external appearance as a disgusting, discolored sheath that confronts her like an alter ego—as is made clear by the impersonal articles, the distanced descriptive style, and reference to "the person." She feels no compassion of any kind but rather disgust and aversion toward this body, which is described as a soulless, dirty marionette.

This encounter with the blemished face in the mirror is already prefigured in the earlier story "Tongues of Stone" (1955), whose title captures the impossibility of the suffering subject's expressing itself or receiving comfort. Moreover, this earlier version of the theme also sketches the image of a contaminated body vessel that collects mountains of refuse, to the point where the toxic garbage even becomes visible through the eyes:

> She imagined the waste piling up in her, swelling her full of poisons that showed in the blank darkness of her eyes when she stared into the mirror, hating the dead face that greeted her, the mindless face with the ugly purple scar on the left cheek that marked her like a scarlet letter.
>
> A small scab began to form at each corner of her mouth. She was sure that this was a sign of her coming dessication and that the scabs would never heal but would spread over her body, that the backwaters of her mind would break out on her body in a slow, consuming leprosy.
>
> (1979, 270)

The phantasm that the wounds would not heal but instead slowly spread like leprosy over the entire body surface to form an infected, dark crust is an expression of the existential shame of a person who tried to resolve a narcissistic crisis through suicide and failed—even at this (Henseler 1974). The scar mentioned here is directly related to Plath's own facial scar, which she perceives as a lasting stigma after her suicide attempt and tries to come to terms with in her writing, though it was barely visible to those around her.[10]

The stigmatized body is experienced as a prison. It condemns its bearer to wander forever, like Cain with his mark, never to find peace (death). For example, in the relevant scene in *The Bell Jar*, we are explicitly told about the body: "It would trap me in its stupid cage" (1971, 130). The protagonist imagines her body as a cage that simultaneously traps and exposes her—a nightmarish situation similar to the one in which Kafka's "Hunger Artist" find himself. In "Tongues of Silence," Plath describes this situation in ever-new metaphors. We hear of "soulless flesh," a "dead brain," of being "caught in the nightmare of the body," of being "sallow-skinned" with "purple bruises," raw open scars and scabs, and of being jolted "back into the hell of her dead body" (1979, 267ff.). This kind of split between the psyche and the soma, as described in the image of lifelong imprisonment in a continuously rotting body, is, in the stage of psychosis, the final option of preserving an integral self against the danger of total destruction (Anzieu 1989, 132). The feeling of being a unitary person in whom psyche and body are integrated poses a potential threat insofar as an attack on one of the two parts would mean a destruction of the entire person; one part of the Self is sacrificed to save the other. In Plath's literary body images it is the somatic part that is split off in order to preserve the integrity of the psychic part. Corporeal self-awareness is negated so that *the* body may be perceived as a marionette controlled by some other force, an object with no libidinal cathexis: "a dull puppet of skin and bone that had to be washed and fed day after day after day" (Plath 1979, 262).

The individual's skin is burdened with shame in a special way when it is experienced as afflicted with blemishes and flaws. Psychoanalysts and psychologists have noted in many of their analysands an intense, sometimes even excessive concern with their own skin, whereby the body surface is in most cases experienced as much more inflamed, scarred, and impure than is objectively the case.[11] On the level of visibility, the stigmatized skin shows the hidden, bad character; on the level of the sense of touch, it prevents any empathic contact that could eliminate this feeling of uncleanness and worthlessness. The skin imagined as repulsive forms a kind of blockade rendering impossible the touch that is both longed for and feared. A genuinely disfigured skin is, literally, such an encompassing stigma that the subject is not able to distance itself from this blemish. In psychic illnesses, this experience, which some sufferers of neurodermatitis and psoriasis make firsthand on their own bodies (Schulte-Strathaus 1994; Holzegel 1995; Lévy 1997), can become a heightened imaginary symptom in which the suffering is reflected in the body image. Such sufferers also inflict deliberate injuries to their skin by irritating it through hard scratching or maltreat it with objects, in an attempt thereby to preserve a pain envelope that conveys anew the lost feeling of unity, cohesion, and protectedness.[12]

In her diaries, Plath records the following self-portrait, which clearly re-veals the intertwined relationship between the perception of the individ-ual's skin and the feeling of self-worth:

> Nose podgy as a leaking sausage: big pores full of pus and dirt, red blotch-es, the peculiar brown mole on my under-chin which I would like to have excised. Memory of that girl's face in the med school movie, with a little black beauty wart: this wart is malignant: she will be dead in a week. . . . Body needs a wash, skin the worst: it is the climate: chapping cold, dessi-cating hot: I need to be tan, all-over brown, and then my skin clears and I am all right. I need to have written a novel, a book of poems, a *Ladies' Home Journal* or *New Yorker* story, and I will be poreless and radiant. My wart will be nonmalignant.
>
> (1983, 286)

In Plath's self-perception, her bad skin and the potentially malignant mole on her chin reflect the depressing situation of being unsuccessful in her writing. If, however, something of hers were published, the conclusion is that her skin would become "poreless and radiant." Writing as a remedy in Plath, a "cure" (Axelrod 1990), is to prove itself here explicitly as a psy-chohygienic cleansing of the skin. Plath uses the current condition of her skin with its large, dirty pores as a figurative stand-in for her unwellness: only the "poreless" state, in which her skin would no longer be a porous sieve but a smooth canvas, would give her well-being and self-assurance.

In Plath's poetry, the body often functions as "an embarrassing reminder of the self's failures, an icon of the poet's vulnerability" (Lant 1993, 625). In contrast to the work of contemporary male poets (for example, Robert Lowell and Alan Ginsberg), where the naked body shedding all its cover-ings stands for self-liberation, authenticity, and strength, the female body, "in terms of the dominant figurative system of Western discourse . . . is vul-nerable in that it is sexually accessible, susceptible to penetration, exploita-tion, rape, pregnancy" (626). The naked female body—for centuries sym-bolically overloaded, idealized, and demonized in the arts—is also unable in modern poetry to represent a person's positive, true self in the unques-tioned way the male body is able to. The philosophical tradition of the naked truth—whose metaphorology Hans Blumenberg has examined (1960)—is thus exclusively a male tradition, in which the female body func-tions merely as a model. While male poets, beginning with Walt Whitman, celebrate nakedness as a gesture of honesty and freedom, female poets since

Emily Dickinson rather tend to present their poetic self as one that is armored, concealed, and hidden in masks (Diggory 1979, 136).

To that extent, it is not surprising that nakedness in Plath goes hand in hand with a wounded or blemished state and not with liberation. In her poetry are images of masks, bandages, and mummification, which have in common that they simultaneously support and conceal the skin. Although there are transformations in her work, these do not result in a more naked and thus more authentic self. In the already quoted poem "Lady Lazarus," the shedding of the skin is a metamorphosis that is both growth and death. Plath describes a passive body presented as an object, displayed to the eager crowds in a carnival freak show and yet still preserving an inner consciousness of itself:

> *The peanut-crunching crowd*
> *Shoves in to see*
> *Them unwrap me hand and foot—*
> *The big strip tease.*
> *Gentlemen, ladies*
> *These are my hands*
> *My knees.*
> *I may be skin and bone,*
> *Nevertheless I am the same, identical woman.*
> *The first time it happened I was ten.*
> *It was an accident.*
> *The second time I meant*
> *To last it out and not come back at all.*
> *I rocked shut*
> *As a seashell.*
> *They had to call and call*
> *And pick the worms off me like sticky pearls.*
> . . . .
> *For the eyeing of my scars,*
> *There is a charge*
> *For the hearing of my heart—*
> *It really goes.*
>
> (1981, 245–246)

The poetic self, continually alternating between active self-control and corpselike passivity, periodically sheds its skin and kills itself, though without becoming clean in the process. Plath refers explicitly to her suicide attempt in the basement when she says that the second time she did not intend to "come back at all." The scars remain despite the shedding of the skin; she is still "the same, identical woman." The poetic self stylizes itself into a suffering, passive object whose wounds the voyeurs can inspect for a charge and whose heart they can hear beating. It does not seem immediately evident that this worm-eaten persona is still alive. She is a kind of marionette: the metamorphosis is not an active process; it, too, happens to the poetic self.

Like "Lady Lazarus," the poem "Getting There" (1962) deals with the shedding of skin and purity but at the same time also with the constant presence of death:

And I, stepping from this skin
of old bandages, boredoms, old faces
step to you from the black car of Lethe,
pure as a baby.

(249)

Already in "Face Lift," Plath had used this image of the self peeling itself out of the skins of its history until it returns once again to its longed-for origins, where it was still "pink and smooth as a baby" (156). The secret cosmetic surgery recounted there, although we are quite realistically told of a face wrapped in gauze bandages, of painful sutures and surgeons, is presented at the same time as a kind of imagined "draining of age" from the body:

For five days I lie in secret,
Tapped like a cask, the years draining into my pillow.
Even my best friend thinks I'm in the country.
Skin doesn't have roots, it peels away easy as paper.

(156)

It is not made clear whether this rejuvenating lifting is the draining of inner fluids leaking out from the tapped "body-cask" or whether it is not instead a peeling away of the outer, rootless layers of the skin. Both processes are part of a complex transformation. At the end of the poem, the now rejuvenated self gazes at a test tube in which the shed, drained part of the self, visualized as old flaps of skin ("dewlapped lady" and "sock-face" [156]), is now captured.

A split of the self into two personae—an artificially created but loved persona and a hated but more authentic one—is found even more starkly in the poem "In Plaster" (1961). In this poetic account, written in a narrative prose style, the lyric self speaks about the double it lives with in a forced, inexplicable symbiosis: "This new absolutely white person" (158)—which suddenly appears beside the I and at the same time surrounds it, because it is also its second skin—stands for the desired pure and marblelike surface of the woman and simultaneously for her social masking. This porcelain sheath becomes the ideal body mask of the fragile self, since it possesses all the qualities the I longed for all its life. And yet this sheath creates in her a profound feeling of unease. Plath describes a symbiotic dependency relationship, in which both parts support each other. At first the I lies next to the white body mask, "shaped just the way I was," a mask that is cold, inanimate, and "unbreakable" (158). Gradually, since they complement each other, the two merge: the I gives the white sheath content, warmth, and volume; the mask gives the I support and an external identity. The third verse captures this relationship in the image of the vase and blooming flower: while the vase ("she") receives the flower ("I"), stores vital fluid, and gives the flower support, allowing it to stand upright, the flower makes the vase whole in the first place by filling it with life and vitality—"I gave her a soul" (159). Here, already, is an intimation of a rivalry between the two, because the I must insist that "it was I who attracted everybody's attention" (159). In the fourth verse, the I slowly grows weaker and begins to admire the porcelain "she," "her tidiness, and her calmness and her patience" (159).

The I is now revealed in its fragility, its unstable bones in need of support from the plaster form. In this way, the two are welded together more and more. Although we are initially told that the relationship between the two was intensifying, this closeness is subsequently lost, and the I feels increasingly threatened and impeded by its body mask; at the same time, it senses the loss of its brace. Then it becomes clear that the plaster/marble/porcelain skin has covered the real skin so closely that there is no longer any space between the two. For some time "I" and "she" formed a common body, but now the porcelain skin lets air through (it loosens its embrace), which causes the skin, now oversensitive and no longer able to cope with direct contact with the outside world, to detach and flake off:

She stopped fitting me so closely and seemed offish.
I felt her criticizing me in spite of herself,
as if my habits offended her in some way.
She let in the drafts and became more and more absent-minded.
And my skin itched and flaked away in soft pieces
simply because she looked after me so badly.

(159)

Anzieu has described to what extent the normal skin ego is made up of a double surface: an external sheath that receives external stimuli and a sheath of internal excitation (1989, 123). Some distance necessarily exists between the two layers, which allows for a certain free play, thus making it possible to differentiate between internal and external perceptions and also between the image that others have of the person and the image the ego has of itself. The loss of this distance becomes clear in the motif of the mummy, which has stolen the face of the poetic I and now wears it like a painted face:

And secretly she began to hope that I'd die.
Then she could cover my mouth and eyes, cover me entirely,
and wear my painted face the way a mummy-case
wears the face of a pharaoh, though it's made of mud and water.

(1981, 159)

According to Anzieu, a narcissistic person "needs to be self-sufficient in his own psychical envelope, to give up that skin shared with another, which is a sign and a cause of his dependence upon that other." In order to reinforce the weakened (or still weak) skin ego, the person can reduce and, if possible, abolish the space between the two surfaces. The result is that while the double sheath conveys a sense of security, it lacks flexibility and tears or becomes brittle at the smallest narcissistic injury (1989, 123–124). This psychic structure of strengthening the skin through a melding of the inner and outer surfaces into a thick, rigid layer, to which Plath gives shape in her poem "In Plaster," evokes many associations, which Plath also explicitly picks up: the notion of lying in a coffin alive, the image of the mummified body, and the real double embrace in the uterus of the mother's womb: "Living with her was like living with my own coffin; / Yet I still depended on her" (1981, 160).

The poem deals with the impossibility of the I to separate itself from a mask with which it has grown together at the skin: "She had supported me for so long I was quite limp—/I had even forgotten how to walk or sit" (159). The urgent desire to free herself from the mask experienced as a coffin and a prison gradually gives rise to the realization of the essential dependency on this supporting layer. Unlike "Getting There" and "Face Lift," "In Plaster" does not end with the cleansed, naked, vulnerable innocence of the baby but with the desperate hope of one day being strong enough to free herself of her "own coffin." It is a testament to her captivity in roles that make her seem a "saint" on the outside, while inside she continues to feel "ugly and hairy" (160). In the end, the doubled, reinforced skin, which becomes a mask and an armor, offers no escape from the problems of ego fragility and self-boundary, to which Plath gave exemplary literary expression.

7 armored skin and birthmarks

The Imagology of a Gender Difference

This chapter will look at two skin motifs that are scattered throughout Western literature and cultural history: the mythical motifs of the male armored skin and of the female *macula materna* (lit., mother's mark), the birthmark. Both encapsulate gendered body images, a recurring theme in this study.

In Greek mythology, Achilles was famous, apart for his strength and courage, for a nearly invulnerable skin. The myth tells us that Achilles' mother, the goddess Thetis, burned off the "mortal shell" of her first six sons and then anointed it with ambrosia to make them immortal like herself. Achilles, the seventh son, was torn from her hands by her husband, Peleus, when his entire body except for his heels had been rendered immortal in the fire (Graves 1960, 1:272; Grant and Hazel 1993, 9). His skin is therefore invulnerable except for his heels. But this secret is not known to his enemies, only to the gods. Eventually, after countless battles in which he was undefeated, Achilles is killed by Apollo with an arrow to his heel as punishment for his arrogance and excessive cruelty against the Trojans.[1] What is revealing about this myth is that mortality and potential vulnerability are equated:

only a skin completely resistant to physical attack would make a subject divine. Once again the naked, sensitive skin is the *conditio humana* that situates humankind hierarchically between the immortal gods and the animals with their thick fur or scaly skin.

The myth of the hero's invulnerable skin also forms the basis of the legend of "horned" Siegfried, who in the *The Nibelungenlied* (around 1200) also possesses skin so hard "that no weapon will bite it" (1969, 28). Siegfried acquired this armored skin by bathing in the blood of a dragon he had slain, an act that transferred to him the "lindworm's scaly armor," as Hebbel puts it in his 1860 Nibelungen cycle (1964, 2:122). The invulnerable skin is a mark of distinction Siegfried receives for his heroic courage and ability to overcome his revulsion at bathing in the dragon blood "while it was still steaming hot" (134). Similar to the Achilles myth, what occurs here is a kind of tanning and anointing of the skin that endows it with additional strength and thickness. But even Siegfried's "skin of horn" (120), this armor fused with flesh, has a spot where it remains vulnerable: between the shoulder blades, where a linden leaf landed while he was anointing himself with the dragon's blood. As in the case of Achilles, this place of vulnerability, this "open door" (as Siegfried himself describes the spot in Hebbel [120]) in the otherwise sealed body container leads to his death. Both of these literary-mythological figures are therefore not quite immortal-divine. The continued existence of an opening in their skin causes them to remain human.

During his first night with his bride, Kriemhild, Siegfried reveals to her the site of his vulnerability—the "door" in the skin thus becomes an intimate entryway of the human element in this otherwise godlike body. Through its placement within the context of a lover's confessions, the divulging of the vulnerable spot is symbolically equated to the loss of Kriemhild's virginity on the wedding night: it equals the sacrifice of her erotic surrender and is thus also in part a feminization of the hero.[2] Hagen of Troneck coaxes a concerned (but unfortunately also naive) Kriemhild into revealing the secret of the vulnerable spot, that ominous place "already recounted in songs." She confides where Siegfried is "weak" when Hagen professes that in future battles he will protect this "spot" on his friend with his own body (187). He even talks Kriemhild into sewing a barely visible cross onto her husband's clothing to mark the exact location.

Once he knows Siegfried's weakness, it is so exposed that Hagen, in a monologue, can compare him to an insect, whose skin is so transparent (and thus virtually nonexistent) that it "looks as red and green / as its food"

(190). Soon after, in a moment when he is not observed, Hagen kills the horned-skin Siegfried with an arrow between his shoulder blades. Kriemhild, kneeling beside her dead husband lying in the dust, laments that there are still so many places on his body untouched and unkissed by her, for they had vainly believed that the future lay ahead of them:

> I only half-embraced the living man, this I now learn from his dead body. Oh that it were the other way around! I'd kiss him still, not even on the eyes! Everything new! We thought we had time. . . . There is no feast day anymore! The silk, the golden sumptuous robes and the linen, bring it all here! Do not forget the flowers, he loved them! Tear it all off, even the buds of those yet to come, for whom should they still bloom! Put this into his coffin, my bridal dress on the very top. And place him gently on it, then I will do thus, *she spreads her arms*. And cover him with mine own self!
>
> (209)

She wants to cover and protect the many libidinous places on his skin that she still has not touched by enveloping Siegfried completely with her bridal dress and with her own body. The dress as the doubling of her skin, together with Kriemhild's real body surface, could completely embrace the wounded armored body and thus symbolically restore its integrity.

It is revealing that Siegfried himself describes his death as a "draining away" and uses the image of melting wax to picture his body as a kind of container that has sprung a leak: "I am dripping away, / like a candle that has started to run" (203). This hints at a body image I have already examined (in reference to Kafka's phantasm of the perforated skin in his story "In the Penal Colony"): in contradistinction to Theweleit's thesis (1993, vol. 2), here the armored, steely man does not possess a body phallically hardened through and through but merely a hard skin that contains the liquid inside only as long as it is closed.

In the *The Nibelungenlied*, Kriemhild demands that the men suspected of murdering her husband stand next to Siegfried's corpse: according to an old belief, wounds will start to bleed again "if one sees the man stained with the murder next to the victim." Hagen steps forward and the wounds "flowed abundantly" (167)—an eloquent sign of his guilt. As a communicative sign, the revealing wounds with their oozing body fluid revoke the separation between the inside and the outside, so starkly drawn by the armored skin.

The armored skin is a male body image, and it is no accident that it characterizes two paradigmatic heroes of Western cultural history. Although I have presented only two examples of this type, it is nothing less than the overarching concept of the narcissistic male fantasy of an invulnerable, impenetrable, phallic body. As the complementary constellation to this iron skin (with a single, vulnerable spot), literature offers the motif of the female body marked with a birthmark. This vulnerable skin with a superimposed, thickened mark forms the counterpart to the male body image of the reinforced sheath with a fragile spot. Here, the woman possesses a smooth, soft, permeable surface on which a dark callosity—an entryway for evil?—can be found.

Whether in Heinrich von Kleist's *Michael Kohlhaas* and *Käthchen of Heilbronn*, Friedrich de la Motte Fouqué's "Undine," Nathaniel Hawthorne's "The Birthmark," Robert Musil's *The Man Without Qualities*, or Toni Morrison's *Sula*—in all of these really quite different texts—it is always a woman who bears such a dark skin mark. The macula has the most varied functions: for example, it allows the recognition of lost family members, marks individuality, or signifies moral depravity. On a metalevel, the authors can also use it as a projection surface reflecting the multifarious interpretations of other protagonists. For instance, the title character in Morrison's novel *Sula* (1973) has a birthmark above her eye that looks like a rose with a stem (1982a, 52). As she grows older, the birthmark darkens, this "scary black thing over her eye" (97–98). Other characters interpret it not only as a rose on several occasions but also in succession as a moccasin snake (103), a rattlesnake (104), the stigmatizing ashes of her dead mother (114), and a tadpole (156). Sula's birthmark acts as a mirror for the gaze of others; in her face, they see what corresponds to their preconceived images.

This kind of birthmark is not necessarily a stigma that turns the person, as Goffman (1963) has argued, into someone who is discredited or (if the stigma is not known) discreditable, even though it does constitute social information.[3] But it can be declared a stigma, as was historically the case for a long time. The superstition that birthmarks, skin discolorations, and growths were attributable to bad influences during pregnancy persisted far into the eighteenth century. The German word for birthmark, "*Muttermal*" (like the Latin *naevus maternus, macula materna*), shows to what extent a woman bore sole responsibility for the appearance and the blemishes of her offspring. Especially powerful was the belief in transmission by sight: if a woman perceived something shocking, repulsive, or ugly during pregnancy (in another version, even at the moment of conception), this impression was invariably imprinted on the surface of the fetus in a process of transmission by analogy (Stafford 1993, 306 ff.). If she beheld an African man or woman, her child could have dark splotches; if she looked at an animal, the child could end up with hairy patches of skin, warts, or calluses. In Lavater's interpretation, for example, the mushroomlike skin flaps and hairy excrescences on a girl's body (figure 29) appeared because the mother, during pregnancy, supposedly quarreled with a neighbor over some venison (316). Instead of holding fate or an ominous punishment by God responsible for such bodily deformities, observers turned mothers into the guilty parties. Unlike the smaller liver spots, birthmarks are generally congenital and less common, which therefore makes them especially susceptible to these kinds of interpretations.[4]

Hawthorne indirectly alludes to this tradition of mystification and association with female impurity in his story "The Birthmark" (1843), although the mother herself never appears as a protagonist. "The Birthmark," set in the second half of the eighteenth century, tells the story of the fanatical scientist and alchemist Aylmer and his wife, Georgina, whose perfect beauty is marred only by a birthmark on her left cheek. The very first time we hear Aylmer speak, he is already suggesting to his wife that she have the birthmark removed, a thought that keeps haunting him as the tale unfolds. The birthmark resembles a tiny hand, which, depending on the hue of Georgina's skin, is more or less obvious:

> In the usual state of her complexion,—a healthy, though delicate bloom, the mark wore a tint of deeper crimson, which imperfectly defined its shape amid the surrounding rosiness. When she blushed, it gradually become more indistinct, and finally vanished amid the triumphant rush of blood that bathed the whole cheek with its brilliant glow. But if any shifting emotion caused her to turn pale, there was the mark again, a crimson stain upon the snow, in what Aylmer sometimes deemed an almost fearful distinctness. Its shape bore not a little similarity to the human hand, though of the smallest pigmy size. Georgina's lovers were wont to say that some fairy, at her birth-hour, had laid her tiny hand upon the infant's cheek, and left its impress there, in token of the magic endowments that were to give her such sway over all hearts.
>
> (1982, 765)

As in a fairy tale, Georgina's admirers interpret the birthmark as the sign of a good fairy, who touched the child with her gentle hand and gave her the

figure 29

Girl with birthmarks from Johann Caspar
Lavater, *Essays on Physiognomy* (1792)

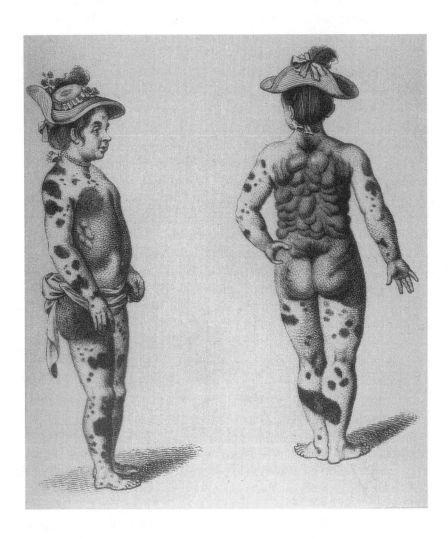

power henceforth to enchant all hearts. The mark stands out more distinctly only when Georgina is not feeling well and her face loses its color. The tiny crimson hand thus becomes an indicator of the sensations and moods displayed on her skin; blushing in vivid and positively excited moments makes the contours of the birthmark fade or even disappear, while a pale complexion reveals it in all its sharpness. This is significant insofar as Aylmer in his imagination explicitly links his wife's birthmark with death. Having paid little attention to it before their marriage, the birthmark now becomes the mark of Cain of human guilt and mortality, since Aylmer himself identifies with his wife's body (771).

Jules Zanger has argued that Aylmer's change in attitude is connected with Georgina's menstruation, which terrifies him (1983, 364 ff.). According to Zanger, in the nineteenth century it was by no means a given that men would know about menstruation prior to being married (which would apply to Aylmer as well as Hawthorne, who had been married a mere six months at the time he wrote "The Birthmark"). The fact that the mark is perceived as a "crimson stain" supposedly alludes to the woman's monthly "maculation." Zanger notes that the superstition that plants wilt if touched by a menstruating woman persisted into the early twentieth century. Hawthorne picks up this motif in a later scene in Aylmer's laboratory, when Georgina touches a plant and it is instantly charred down to its roots.

Apart from this possible association to menstruation, the mark also evokes the Christological context of a postulated sinfulness of woman, which crystallized into sin via the eating of the forbidden fruit and the seduction of Adam. It is therefore no coincidence that it is a hand that appears on the young woman's cheek. It symbolizes Eve's intemperate grasping of the fruit, the resultant mortality through the expulsion from paradise, and the hardship of physical labor and giving birth (and the female cycle!), all of which henceforth characterize earthly life: "It was the fatal flaw of humanity, which Nature, in one shape or another, stamps ineffaceably on all her productions, either to imply that they are temporary and finite, or that their perfection must be wrought by toil and pain. The Crimson Hand expressed the ineludible gripe, in which mortality clutches the highest and purest of earthly mould, degrading them into kindred with the lowest, and even with the very brutes, like whom their visible frames return to dust" (Hawthorne 1982, 766).

The mark as a sign of transience and a "symbol of imperfection" (766) on the female skin is directly related to the vulnerable spot in the hero's armored skin, which, as I have indicated, is also to be understood as a *signum humani* on an otherwise godlike body. Hawthorne explicitly tells us that it is a mark of mortality—just like the vulnerable spot of Achilles and Siegfried. But while the fragile site on the male skin forms in visual terms an indentation or depression, the birthmark is a protrusion on the smooth, marblelike surface of the female skin—a "bas-relief of ruby on the whitest marble" (767), as Hawthorne put it. Aylmer thinks he can remove it because it seems to sit *on* his wife's skin. But a dream conveys to him (what he later is forced to discover during an actual attempt at removal) that the birthmark is possibly more deeply ingrown that he initially believed: "But the deeper went the knife, the deeper sank the Hand until at length its tiny grasp appeared to have caught hold of Georgina's heart" (767).

Because of the stigma, the young woman is—metaphorically speaking—not untouched, another way of interpreting the mark.[5] The hand is "stamped upon her cheek" (774): something has taken possession of her, branded her, and marked her as belonging to it; it is this that the patriarchal husband wants to extinguish after Georgina has become his wife. In Georgina's face are combined two antipodal sexual images of the female: in Judeo-Christian culture, the female body has traditionally stood for either that which is pure and untouched (and hence one's own) or for the exact opposite, the dirty other (von Braun 1997, 19). These two quite contrary concepts find themselves united in a single face, as a result of which the compulsion to separate them forcefully becomes almost a cultural necessity. The split into a depraved part and a lovable part, which is inherent in the face, is articulated in the following lines: "Her husband tenderly kissed her cheek—her right cheek—not that which bore the impress of the Crimson Hand" (Hawthorne 1982, 768).

Georgina, who herself comes to see the birthmark as a disfiguring blemish as the story unfolds, eventually agrees to have it removed by her husband. Aylmer, overjoyed in his mad perfectionism, compares the "ecstasy" that awaits him upon reaching this goal with the ecstasy the second creator of Pygmalion must have felt "when his sculpted woman assumed life" (768). The human experiment takes place away from daylight in a "boudoir" (770) furnished with rich hangings and carpets, a room adjoining the laboratory. It is a uterine cave in which Georgina is to be reborn. This second birth also represents a kind of initiation into a closer bond with Aylmer, in which the woman mutates into a sacrifice to sacred science. This is implied by the scene at the entrance to the laboratory: as in the Christian marriage ritual, Aylmer must carry his wife across the threshold—not into their shared home, however, but into his nebulous laboratory.

In the laboratory, Aylmer, "the pale philosopher" (769), shows her a number of compounds he has developed as a way of proving to her the chemical miracles of which he is capable. Among them is a tincture that can remove freckles as well as the blushing of a face: both of these two very different phenomena are here understood as externally overlaying the skin. But unlike these external cutaneous changes, her birthmark—as Aylmer has by now realized—required "a remedy that shall go deeper" (773). He concocts a mysterious potion; after taking it, Georgina falls into a deep sleep that lasts for days. At the side of the sleeping woman, the experimenter watches as the mark grows fainter and fainter, until it disappears entirely. The now immaculate beauty awakens long enough to forgive her husband's hubris and then dies: perfect beauty is like death.

While the myth of the armored skin shows that a completely hardened skin equals divinity and immortality, here the state of bearing a blemish is defined as a basic aspect of being alive and as an anthropological determinant. Following a sudden impulse, Aylmer kisses the tiny hand on his wife's cheek while Georgina is lying in her sleep of transformation and death: he realizes too late that the hated birthmark actually embodies her individual essence, without which she will no longer be able to live. The dream in which a connection had been made between the mark and her heart had already prophesied as much.

In Musil's *The Man Without Qualities* (1930–1952), the character Clarisse has a birthmark "in the hollow of her groin, half hidden on the inside of the thigh and close to where the pubic hairs somewhat raggedly made room for it" (1995, 1:475). She talks about the birthmark in connection with her father's incestuous advance: it was the "black medallion" (1:318) that stopped her father's hand moving down her body, bringing him to his senses and making him turn away. In Musil, the birthmark is not seen but felt by Clarisse's father—even if she herself calls it "the Devil's Eye," with "a gaze that pierced through any clothing and 'caught' men's eyes and drew them to her, spellbound" (1:475)—for the night when he came to her bed was pitch-black. Recalling the event, Clarisse touches herself, "felt with her fingertips through her robe, searching for that velvety-black birthmark that had so strange a power" (1:475). Here, Clarisse's mark is not a visible but a tactile sign. Moreover, it functions not as the stigma of a postulated depravity but, quite the contrary, as a magical protective symbol of (sexual) purity: "It is the mother's macula on the skin of the daughter that protect her from being sullied by her father" (Meisel 1990, 181).

Other authors, by contrast, employ the birthmark as an unmistakable identification mark on their female protagonists in situations where family members become estranged or later find each other again. Here, it is not a stigma or protective symbol but an individual, immutable, identity-conferring sign. For example, in Kleist's *Käthchen of Heilbronn* (1810), an angel appears to Count Ritter von Stahl in a feverish dream and announces that his beloved and future wife is actually the daughter of the emperor. And "after the angel had told him that she was a daughter of the emperor, it showed him the reddish birthmark inscribed on the child's neck" (1961, 1:471). A short time later, von Stahl unties the kerchief from the neck of Käthchen, the daughter of a weapon's blacksmith, and she shows him her birthmark. The emperor of Swabia acknowledges her as his illegitimate daughter, and she marries the count. In this constellation, the mark indubitably attests noble descent, which seemed highly improbable at first, and socially elevates its bearer.

In Fouqué's "Undine" (1811), the motif is used in exactly the opposite way.[6] Bertalda, an orphan adopted by a duke, has been living a pleasant life at the court since her early childhood, until she discovers, on her name day, that her birth parents are still alive. Undine, her girlfriend and rival for the favor of the knight Huldbrand, claims that Bertalda is the lost daughter of the old fisherman and his wife who live secluded in the forest and had raised Undine. Bertalda is outraged at this assertion in front of the assembled court and subjects. When the old fisherman and his wife stagger from the crowd and embrace her as their long-lost daughter, she rebuffs them harshly. The duke and his wife ask for proof of this extraordinary claim: "With that the old fisherwoman approached, bowed deeply before the duchess and said, 'You have spoken to my heart, noble, God-fearing lady. I must tell you, if this evil young girl is my daughter then she has a birthmark shaped just like a violet between her shoulder blades and another just like it on the instep of her left foot' " (2000, 97). Bertalda is asked to leave the room with the duchess, and when they return she is "deathly pale." It is announced that Bertalda is indeed the child of the fisherfolk and has to live with them henceforward. What is striking here is that the birthmark is not merely an

undefined dark spot; rather, as in Hawthorne and Morrison, it has a concrete shape—in this case, that of a flower. In this way, it is elevated even
more to the status of a sign, something that can be read and interpreted by
human beings.

Kleist and Fouqué use the birthmark as a sign of authenticity, as something that can provide information about true kinship and is incapable of
lying. While Kleist's Käthchen bears on her back a birthmark resembling the
one her late mother had, which she thus, in the sense of a genetic transmission, "inherited from her late mother" (1:434), Bertalda's *naevus maternus* is
known to her birth mother, though she herself does not seem to possess it.
What becomes clear here is a significant, class-specific familiarity with or ignorance of the bodies of one's own children: while the weapons' smith
Theobald in Kleist and the fisherwoman in Fouqué know their daughters'
skins very well, the duchess is as surprised as everyone else to hear about her
adoptive daughter's birthmark. The higher social classes have no access to
their children's bodies, which are cared for exclusively by servants.

Both authors chose the back as the location of the birthmark because it is
more foreign, a semiotic surface over which the bearers are unable to exercise any control and that they themselves cannot perceive. The birthmark on
the back becomes the paradigmatic unknown at the outer edge of one's own
body. Accordingly, Käthchen's father, in the play's courtroom scene, uses
the birthmark as an analogy to state that his daughter had never before laid
eyes on Count von Stahl: "Not with her eyes did she see him since the time
she was born; her back, and the birthmark on it, which she inherited from
her late mother, she knew better than him" (1:434). The birthmark as conceived by Kleist and Fouqué has a secret existence of which those who bear
it have no knowledge. Their lives are determined—literally, behind their
backs—by a genetic sign that can have both positive and negative social consequences. The fact that it is only the body that bears the truth about a subject's identity is made clear in both texts by the emphasis that is placed on
the process of uncovering the signifying mark usually hidden from the gaze.

The following two chapters—which examine the problem of racial
identification on the basis of skin color—focus on this question of the genetic marking of the skin. Here, too, the concern will be not only with
processes of semioticization but also—as this chapter has already made
clear—with the duality of the skin as either a closed, protective layer or a
permeable, transparent membrane.

8 different skin

Skin Colors in Literature and the History of Science

It is not possible, within the framework of the present book, to examine all the complexity of the racist practice of othering—the demarcation and devaluation of the other—and its attendant value judgments. Instead, I will merely ask what specific role the skin and its colors play in this context. At the center of my inquiry will be the juxtaposition of "white" and "black," which, historically, is paradigmatic for all thinking about skin color:[1] both biological-physiological as well as cultural-anthropological interpretation always revolves initially around the opposition between light and dark.

As early as the seventeenth century, visually differentiated skin color becomes the primary characteristic by which ethnic difference is defined. The French naturalist François Bernier "first eschewed the prevailing geographical classificatory system of human beings by locating skin as the single characteristic on which human organization would depend" (Wiegman 1995, 27–28). Georges-Louis Leclerc du Buffon, in his treatise *Dissertation physique à l'occasion du Nègre blanc* (1744), posits "white" as the basic anthropological color and downgrades "black" to a degeneration (Blankenburg 1996, 143). Claude-Nicolas LeCat's

Traité de la couleur de la peau humaine (1765) also reveals the degree to which binary thinking sought to differentiate ethnic otherness by means of the opposites "white" and "black": apart from the "general question of color," LeCat investigates specifically dark skin, the so-called *couleur étiopienne*. Part three of his study examines "La métamorphose du Nègre en Blanc & du Blanc en Nègre" (xii)—for example, in the occurrence of albinism among "blacks" or of vitiligo among "whites."

These works do not discuss skin tones other than these extreme poles, whose potential mixture the eighteenth century finds fascinating and demonizes in equal measure. One illustration from Buffon's *L'histoire de l'homme* (1749), depicting a chubby "black albino child" with an even black-white skin pattern, clearly shows the horror of "mixed skin" (figure 30). The skin that stands between the "races" here constitutes maculation in the literal sense (Lat. *macula*: stain, blot, blemish)—an association picked up by many authors.

Jean-Bernard Delestre's *De la physiognomie* (1866) has this to say about the skin: "Among the inhabitants of the North, it remains white in those places that are hidden by thick clothing. The skin color of natural peoples in tropical countries is uniform. . . . The coloration of the skin varies in large gradations within the human race. From the white Caucasian complexion to the black of Africa, skin spans the gradations of yellow, red, and copper brown. It is a useful document as a basis for classifying the members of the countless families whose name is mankind" (346). What is interesting in this passage is not only that the skin of the inhabitants of the northern hemisphere "remains" light, a notion that, by extension, classifies the color tones of other peoples as something additional and secondary, but also Delestre's thesis that the skin color among "natural peoples" should be regarded as uniform. Such homogeneity is not claimed for the lighter skin types. A classification of the "yellow," "red," and "copper brown" skin tones between *blanc* and *noir* is by no means self-evident, since in color theory, for example, white and black belong to an entirely different category from yellow, red, and brown: the former are achromatic colors, while the latter are part of the color spectrum and are therefore considered chromatic. In racial discourse, however, "black" becomes a chromatic color pure and simple (which is today still echoed in the German word "*Farbige*" or the English term "Colored"), while the "white" skin color is thought of as the basic complexion and a neutral noncolor.

Entries for "skin" in older scientific encyclopedias generally also address the question of the genesis of skin colors. The search for the "origin of the

figure 30
Black albino child, from Georges-Louis
LeClerc de Buffon, *L'Histoire de l'homme* (1749)

negro blackness" (Herder 1966, 147) is at the center of this discussion. As in printing technology or in painting, the "white" skin is understood as a kind of color-neutral canvas or blank sheet, a tabula rasa, and the dark skin as its colored or written-on counterpart. "Colored" as opposed to light skin is thus interpreted as a marked epidermis; it becomes a skin that departs from the neutral norm. The fact that this was a prevailing scheme of Western discourse is revealed, for example, by the fact that countless attempts were made early on to destroy or decolorize "black" pigment cells—as opposed to coloring light cells dark, which would also be a possibility.

Johann Heinrich Zedler's *Universal-Lexikon* (1735) offers this explanation for the cause of dark skin color: below the "upper skin" lies the "Malphagi membrane," which is "a very thin pad . . . with countless tiny holes" in which the pigments can be localized. Zedler then reports that "among us Europeans it is white in color, but among the Moors it is black, even though the skin itself is entirely white; among incomplete Moors it is dark brown, which is why the human color, especially the black color in the Moors, comes from this pad" (1961, 12:col. 925). The color-imparting layer is thus found in the form of a ramose tissue directly under a neutral upper skin layer; this tissue is the same color in all "races." The entry goes on to describe an experiment in which a piece of "Moorish skin" was immersed in ethyl alcohol in an attempt to decolor it: a doctor, "took a piece of skin from a Moor, along with the epidermis, which had been loosened on one side and was hanging off, and immersed it in *spiritu vini*. This made the skin completely white, like that of a European; the outermost layer of the epidermis was black [*sic*], but the inside, where the membrane had been taken away, was black. Wherefrom it is revealed that the membrane is the primary cause of the black color" (col. 925).

The idea of intracutaneous tissue is also discussed in Herder's *Ideas on the Philosophy of the History of Mankind* (1785). Herder relates that neither "the blood, the brain, nor the seminal fluid of the negro is black, but the reticular membrane beneath the cuticle . . . is more or less colored"; however, that membrane is "common to all," independent of ethnic affiliation (Herder 1966, 149). He emphasizes that "the reticular membrane beneath the cuticle" is more or less colored depending on the body part and external conditions. This theory of the intracutaneous, colored membrane is picked up in the *Allgemeine Encyklopädie der Wissenschaften und Künste* (General encyclopedia of the sciences and arts, 1828). The increasing importance given to the question of "colored" skin is apparent from the fact that this encyclopedia already contains, in addition to the general essay on skin, a separate entry on "the skin of the negroes." As in Zedler, mention is made of experiments aimed at flushing out the color pigments: "It is generally assumed that the location of the black color of negro skin is neither in the skin (*cutis*) nor in the *epidermis*, but in the *rete Malphighi* between the *epidermis* and the skin, for if the latter is washed and kept in lukewarm water for some time, it does not change its color and remains black, while the skin and the *epidermis* look nearly as white as they do in other humans."

As the entry notes, there were different opinions about the "cause of the black color of negro skin." It gives preference to the model according to which skin color

> is produced in the same way as the pigment in the eye. . . . One should not picture either the pigment in the eye or the Malphigian phlegm of negroes as dead matter deposited by the vessels; they are netlike tissues of very finely branched vessels that carry black liquid, just as every other kind of vessel carries its specially colored liquid. The redness of blushing appears so suddenly that we cannot regard the coloration of the liquid contained in the capillary vessels as a direct effect, that is, as independent of the general circulation.
>
> (ERSCH AND GRUBER 1828, 204)

Accordingly, what produces the coloration of dark skin is that "the stimulus of the air pulls the carbon-filled negro blood to the surface," where it becomes deposited "below the upper skin in irregular little globules connected by cell tissue" (205). The process of coloration is likened to that of blushing, in that for both cases an "additional" color substance is posited, a substance not found in the blood but in a weblike intermediate layer.

The fact that the "Malphigian phlegm of the negroes" is here interpreted as a thickened, deposited liquid that is found in the finest vessels in the midst of the skin, makes clear why questions concerning the coloration and so-called contamination of the skin became relevant in the first place: the dark complexion is understood as something that gradually accumulates between the epidermis and the dermis and changes the skin secondarily. The coloration imparted by the intracutaneous membrane is thus described as a chemical process—akin to oxidation or clotting—that is not completed until after birth: "In the Negro fetus in the womb it is not yet black, only in the newborn is it reddish; thereafter it becomes yellow, then dirty brown, and finally black" (204).

Buffon's *Histoire naturelle* (1749–1803) had already spoken of the dark skin and the "bodily deformity" of the peoples in the earth's hotter and colder climatic zones as constituting a "degeneration" of the prototype of the human genus living in the temperate zones. Based on the "observation" that the children of these peoples still showed a whitish skin coloration at birth, which supposedly disappeared only after a few days of contact with the air, Buffon inferred that there was a high degree of dependency on the environment and on the particular climate affecting the skin (Buffon 1861, 1:404, quoted in Kohl 1986, 144). According to Montesquieu, who was the first to elaborate the climate theory into a coherent system in his work *De l'esprit des lois* (1748), cold air constricts the skin, while the warm climate "relaxes" and "lengthens" it. The elasticity of the tissue produces greater sensitivity of the exposed nerve cells and with it a heightening of taste, imagination, and sensibility (Montesquieu 1958, 474, quoted in Gay 1973, 517–518). In Montesquieu's scheme, an organism is less sensitive to external sensory stimuli the more constricted its external tissue. This leads him to conclude that the peoples of the north are stronger, bolder, more frank, and less passionate than those of the south, since they are less exposed to the constant overstimulation of the senses attendant on a "slackened" skin.

Kant differentiates four "races" in his treatises *Von den verschiedenen Rassen des Menschen* (Of the different races of man, 1777) and *Bestimmung des Begriffs einer Menschenrasse* (Defining the concept of a human race, 1785). He establishes that "negroes and whites should be regarded as basic races"; lying between them are the reddish-brown "Kalmuckian race" and the olive-yellow "Hindustani race" (1977, 16). The origin of these races, whose primary distinguishing feature is supposedly the skin, which Kant regards as "eminently suited for classification" (68), lies in the influence of the sun, air, and climate. He explains the genesis of "Negro skin" as follows:

> The growth of the spongy parts of the body of necessity increased in a hot and humid climate; whence a thick pug nose and thick lips. The skin had to be oiled, not only to moderate the strong transpiration, but also to prevent the harmful absorption of the putrid humidities of the air. The excess of iron elements, which are otherwise found in the blood of all humans and are here concentrated in the weblike substance through the evaporation of the phosphorous acids (of which all Negroes reek), causes the blackness that shines through the upper skin; the strong iron content in the blood also seem necessary to guard against the slackening of all parts.
>
> (22–23)

While a humid and warm climate was decisive for the constitution of the "Negro," the "Kalmuks," for example, live in a dry and cold environment. Kant is here drawing on classic humoral theory, and on this foil he—like many other thinkers of his time—locates four races that correspond to the four temperaments. It is probably no coincidence that "Negroes" represent precisely those humoral qualities that have been assigned to women since time immemorial (humid and warm), while the qualities of the "Whites" (cold and dry) traditionally embody the male type. Because skin type is invariably determined by climate, the psychological temperament corresponding to humoral theory emerges almost naturally—which means in the case of the "Negro" "strong, fleshy, supple, but, given the abundant provisions of his homeland, lazy, soft, and philandering" (23).

The "difference in the organization of the Negro skin from ours" is, Kant argues, "quite noticeable already to the touch" (79). Herder, too, pointed to a palpable difference in black skin, which was "not as tense and dry as that of the whites." As to what caused this difference, Herder pointed to the "heat of the sun having drawn from their inner parts an oil, which, ascending as near as it could to the surface, has softened their cuticle, and coloured the membrane beneath it" (1966, 150). While Herder (like Kant in his earlier treatise) is here talking about a dark-colored "oil" inside the skin, which renders it supple and makes it appear tinted, Kant in his later treatise already points to a different substance that was now believed to cause the coloration:

> For now we know: human blood becomes black only because it is overloaded with phlogiston (as can be seen from the underside of clotted blood). Now the strong smell of the Negroes, which cannot be avoided by any kind of hygiene, in itself gives reason to suppose that their skin is removing a large amount of *phlogiston* from the blood and that nature must have organized this skin in such a way that the blood can be *dephlogistonized* by it to a much greater degree than occurs in us, in whom that is for the most part the business of the lung.
>
> (1977, 79).

"Phlogiston," "discovered" in the late eighteenth century, was defined as a substance emitted by all flammable materials during combustion. According to Kant, the organism has to rid itself of this substance, which in the "Negro" is accomplished primarily through the skin. This conduction through the skin is necessary because far more "phlogiston" is generated as a result of the more extreme climate than is able to escape through the lungs. The substance of the "Negro's black" is described as a harmful matter, a foul-smelling and polluting residue the organism must expel. The skin of these human beings is thus a priori thought of as unclean. It is the skin, "seen as the organ of the excretion" and "bearing in itself the trace of this difference in natural character, that justifies the classification of the human types into visibly different classes" (68).

From the Enlightenment until the nineteenth century, the question about the genesis of the different skin colors was considered very crucial and became the topic of numerous treatises.[2] From the very beginning, various attempts were made to establish a physiological basis for the difference and thereby undergird it with scientific evidence. In the process, the African peoples were all but reduced to their skin—which allowed such an eminent naturalist as Lorenz Oken, in his *Lehrbuch der Naturphilosophie* (Handbook of natural philosophy, 1811), to speak of the African "skin person" in contrast to the European "eye person" (345–346). Oken goes on to say: "The ape man is the moor. The interior of his body does not show through his skin, which, like plants, is characteristically colored—he is black and cannot display his inner emotions by means of color. The human man is the white. His inside shows through the skin because the latter is transparent, uncolored. A person who is able to blush is a human being; the person who is not, is a moor" (355). This passage condenses many aspects I have already noted: it combines the transparent—because "uncolored"—skin of the "whites" with the ability of the emotions to shine through, which in turn is equated with the condition of being human. It is therefore the "colored" skin of the "moors" that puts their humanness in question. They cannot visibly blush and are therefore dismissed as devoid of feeling. Those who engaged in slavery invoked this very argument to justify the harsh labor and brutal punishments they inflicted.

To this day, it is not entirely clear why humanity developed different skin colors and whether specific shades should be considered mutations of a primal color. Scientists have not been able to provide unequivocal confirmation for the dominant theory of the eighteenth century that the skin color of a specific "race" is evolutionarily connected with the intensity of solar radiation and climatic conditions. For example, there are a number of exceptions to this scheme, to wit, light-skinned peoples on or near the equator and the reverse (Rogers 1990, 23–24). In certain respects, skin color thus presents a problem not only as a cultural phenomenon but also as a matter of science, a problem with no simple, one-dimensional solution. Every explanatory model remains partial, as is also revealed by the present-day dermatological perspective: the use of the electron microscope has put to rest talk of a colored, phlegmy reticulum that gradually acquires an increasingly "dirty" color, of intracutaneous "oils" or "phlogiston" pushing to the surface. Instead, scientists have now identified individual cells (melanocytes or ceratocytes) that are filled with pigments of various color. Brown-black melanin (Greek for "black") is only one of five pigments, another being, for example, the yellowish-orange carotene (4–5). A recent German standard work in anatomy offers this description:

> The color of the skin and its hues are determined by the number, size, and distribution of the melanosomes *within the carotenocytes*. Negroes possess more, oval, and larger melanosomes than Caucasians, although they have the *identical* number of melanocytes. Because of their size, the melanosomes in Negroes occur singly in the carotenocytes (result: the dispersion and absorption of light by a few large melanosome complexes is less than it is from many smaller melanosomes lying by themselves; Negroes therefore appear darker).
>
> (FRITSCH 1985, 572)

Quite apart from the fact that it may seem astonishing how thoughtlessly the outdated word "Negro" (*Neger*) is used here, it is striking that the special interest of medicine is still focused on the "darkness" of the skin and not on the paucity of pigments in light-skinned people.

The difficulty in coming to grips with the "cultural construction of whiteness" (Mercer 1994, 215) lies in the postulated invisibility of white skin. Just as the European gaze was long regarded as neutral in cultural history, "white" skin is still seen as nonsignificant and is therefore not considered to be a construct. In the next chapter I will try to counter this invisibility of "whites" and of "white" skin by adopting an inverted stance to examine "whiteness" (and "blackness") from the perspective of African-American writers. First, however, I will draw on selected texts and passages from German writers to contextualize the semantic field that was opened up by this look at medical, anthropological, and encyclopedic texts. However, these literary texts should not be seen as a supplementary discourse that merely illustrates what has already been said. Instead, they are a textual corpus different in kind but equal in weight to the anthropological-physiological debate.

In Kleist's story "Betrothal in St. Domingo" (1811), the binary structure of European versus African skin color is broken at the very outset. To be sure, the first sentence, in placing the slave revolt on Haiti narrated in the story within a historical context, refers to a time "when the blacks were murdering the whites" (1997, 324). But this clear duality, reminiscent of the battle on a chessboard, is presently destroyed when we hear about an "old mulatto . . . Babekan by name." Babekan has a daughter, a "mestiza by the name of Toni." During the slave revolt, Toni, thanks to her yellowish complexion, at times pretends to be a European in order to lure the Europeans into a deadly trap. Their ethnic origin places Babekan and Toni between the "races." Although Toni is described as a "mestiza" (i.e., of mixed Indian and "white" blood), her status is actually situated between "white" and "black." As the story begins, though she is only one-quarter African and three-quarters European descent, she identifies unquestioningly with her mother and her stepfather, "a terrifying man, Congo Hoango by name," to whom the plantation owner assigned Babekan "in lieu of a wife" (324–325)

The black portions in Toni's ethnic makeup, though small in terms of percentage, determine her social status. She is identified as "black" since she is seen as belonging genealogically to her mother: the dark-skinned element in the next generation is predicated as the female element—a stance that picks up the pattern of rape within the institution of slavery. It would appear that it was unthinkable to the "white" colonizer that a child could be the product of a relationship between an African man and a European woman. A brief story that appears within the larger narrative reveals that Kleist had this context of the sexual control of women "from the tribe of the negroes" in the back of his mind, and it may very well have been his intention to raise it as a problematic issue. That story tells of a young slave girl who resisted the sexual wishes of a "white" planter and was sold as punishment (331). During the uprising, the young woman takes revenge on the planter by pretending that she wants to save him, only to infect him with the plague (which is thus reinterpreted into a venereal disease) during a staged intimate encounter: here, the popular description of the plague as the "black death" becomes a personified threat.

Toni's ambiguous status between the hostile camps of the "whites" and the "blacks" becomes the fulcrum of the story when the fleeing Swiss officer Gustav von der Ried appears at the house of the absent Hoango. He is encouraged to stay by Babekan and her daughter and is attracted by Toni's moderate exotic beauty, which "aroused in him a mixture of desire and fear" (335). His stay at the house is characterized by his careful observation of the young woman in an effort to fathom her true ethnic identity (and thus find the desired confirmation that he is in fact in a safe place). His tale about the plague-infected girl is a foil for his own fear of being likewise lured into a trap, and this should be seen as the motive for his searching glances. The link is reinforced by the semantic tension between Toni's yellowish skin and the potential infection with yellow fever. When Toni, with the feigned submissiveness of a maid or mistress, prepares a footbath for the stranger, he examines her closely:

The officer, without a word relieving himself of his cravat and waistcoat, sat down on the chair; and beginning to remove his footwear whilst the girl, crouching on her knees in front of him, was busy with the little preparations for washing his feet, he dwelled on the attractiveness of her appearance. Her dark hair, copious and wavy, had tumbled down over her young breasts when she knelt; there was a play of extraordinary grace about her lips and about the long lashes showing over her downcast eyes; but for her colour, which he found repellent, he would have sworn that he had never seen anything more beautiful.

(333)

Especially striking in this passage is a discrepancy between color and form, between the "repellent" hue of her skin and the graceful features of her face. This discrepancy is so unsettling because it is contained within a single perceptual paradigm, namely the physiognomic one. Toni's mother, Babekan, by contrast, the stranger had recognized—also by the "form of her face"—as a "mulatto and, what is more, of African origin" (328). And so the story installs on the level of the daughter's body a fundamental ambivalence, one that intensifies and heightens the dialectic of appearance and reality.

The characters observe each other with respect to their pathognomic-emotive signs and those parts that might possibly be feigned. The involuntary body gestures of Toni's blushing and later of Gustav's tears during an intimate conversation between the two of them trigger in both feelings of trust and love. When the stranger "whispered into her ear the teasing question whether perhaps only a white man would ever win her favour, abruptly, after a moment's dreamy reflection and her dark face blushing in an altogether charming way, she pressed herself against him" (333).[3] Toni's face, though described as "burnt" in keeping with a popular prejudice, is just light enough to make her blushing apparent. This sign of womanly grace, which corresponds to the "semiotics of shame" (Weigel 1991, 212) at the time, temporarily suspends Gustav's doubts about Toni's ethnic identity and the possible inauthenticity of her behavior—from that moment on he identifies her as "white."

The faces of the characters, with their individual hues, function in Kleist's story like identity cards that promise to provide information about each person's ethnic identity. That is why Toni, when she meets the stranger for the first time, "was careful . . . to hold the light so that the full beam of it fell on her face," and Babekan professed astonishment that Gustav with his "white face" had been able "to travel that vast distance through a land of blackamoors in revolt" (Kleist 1997, 326–327). The fact that we never read of "skin color" but always "facial color," even though there are moments when body skin also becomes visible, indicates that Kleist generally thinks of a person's complexion as something that is carried in the face. And so, in another passage, the Europeans in Haiti are explicitly described as "all whose color was white" (161).

It is also revealing that Kleist uses not only the term "Negro," which was common around 1800, but also "blacks," a term that remained unusual until well into the twentieth century. The anachronism of the term "blacks" (and the heightened attention to the problem of color that goes hand in hand with it) makes clear the extent to which the dichotomy of black-white employs cultural patterns that draw on the associations of light and darkness.[4] The striking light metaphors and the staged lighting in "Betrothal in St. Domingo" bring together topoi from Enlightenment philosophy, especially the postulated connection between light and knowledge and the contemporary discourse of race (Charbon 1996; Weigel 1991).

The dramaturgy of the story is defined by countless light changes: from daylight to night, from darkness to artificial light, from the closing of windows to the lighting of lamps. And the faces of the protagonists, too, can be illuminated by a bright shimmer. At one point, the stranger says to Babekan: "To you I can entrust myself. There is in the colour of your face a glimmer of my own colour, and it shines forth at me" (Kleist 1997, 327).

Babekan, on the other hand, who in the conversation juxtaposes her own face to "pitchblack night," behaves toward the stranger as though she was just as much in danger from the "pack of thieves and murderers from hell" as he was. We hear her complain: "How can I—whose father was from Cuba, from Santiago—help it that a shimmer of lightness dawns on my face when daybreak comes?" And though she goes on to say of Toni, "And how can my daughter, conceived and born in Europe, help it that the full daylight of those parts is reflected in hers?" she contradicts herself a few lines later when she declares that the "shadow of kinship" with the dark-skinned rebels that is "visible in our faces" does not protect her and her daughter from persecution (328). The African shadow that competes with the European shimmer in the faces of the two women triggers in the stranger's gaze a changing uncertainty that parallels the only seemingly ordered affairs on St. Domingo. The physiognomic readability of skin colors is fundamentally put in question, reflected on the narrative level in contradictions and on the level of the characters in mutual misinterpretations.

The imagery of other-skinned male and female protagonists in the work of Jahnn is disturbing in a very different way. Consider the following exemplary passage from the novel *Perrudja*: "Africa, holy, mother of humanity, unknown, black. Desert, lakes, naked humans. . . . Negroes and Arabs have large procreative tools. I want to go to Africa. South. To sleep in mud huts, on mats. Silky skin against mine. Black breasts. I drink. . . . I love dark-colored humans. Am a little brown myself. Also of even growth. They speak languages unintelligible to me" (50–51). The many African characters who appear in Jahnn's work are, on one level, quite clearly screens onto which the author projected his longings (and prejudices). But at the same time they unmask such ascriptions in their dominant collective form by exposing the manner in which they work.[5]

Although highly problematic images of women appear consistently in Jahnn's work, especially in his trilogy *Fluß ohne Ufer* (River without banks, 1949–1961), and although there are hardly limits to the physical violence against female bodies (Hamann and Venske 1994), female figures, provided they are of African or some other non-European extraction, are also transfigured into objects of desire. The fascination exerted by these women has to do in particular with the velvety texture and dull sheen of their dark skin—qualities, however, that they share with the male figures of the same ethnic background and that therefore do not constitute clear gender attributes. What follows are a few examples of how the other skin is depicted and described in Jahnn.

Gustav Anias Horn, the narrator of "Niederschrift" (the monumental main section of *Fluß ohne Ufer*), recounts how he got his hands on "the photograph of a Negro girl," whose "dark, shimmering skin" fascinated and aroused him to such a degree that he pesters his companion, Alfred Tutein, to go to Africa with him (1986a, 399). Since the fin de siècle, it was time and again the African and exotic child-woman who fired the erotic fantasies of men and who, moreover, represented the prototype of dark-skinned people, who were interpreted as "childlike" to begin with (Gilman 1986, 44). Another thing that characterizes such young, maturing African girls in Jahnn is the fact that they have no body shame whatsoever.

Before the actual trip to Africa takes place in "Niederschrift," Tutein, shortly after Horn expresses his desire to go there, brings a "brown-skinned girl" of around fourteen to the hotel room they both occupy: "Even before there was an exchange of any words, she began to fidget with her dress. It suddenly fell off of her, and the young negress offered me the full glory of her unchapped, dull-shining skin" (1986a, 400). The meek and at first nameless girl, with cheeks "grainy as rough marble, yet dark as tar-soaked rigging" (400), is raped by Horn on the spot in front of Tutein. She suffers it passively and in silence. Her emotions are not given a voice by Jahnn.

It was only after he has violated Egedi that Horn notices a horrible stench on her: "The skin of the black companion smelled of garlic and asafetida" (401). Tutein's response to this observation, which Horn relates to him "with concealed horror" after the girl has left, is short: "Negroes have a strong smell" (402). Different and oftentimes unpleasant and strange smells have been invoked for centuries "to label the other as other" (Gilman 1986, 40). Jahnn both picks up this theme and exhibits it. In the subsequent conversation about the body odor of "Negroes," Horn declares that he has heard that "a full, nutlike scent is supposedly among the smells," while Tutein associates the girl's odor more with "decomposition" (402). Tutein then goes on to assert that the human (female?) skin already smells of decay and putrefaction while the body is still alive, even if one does not notice this in young bodies right away. This comment, which picks up the Lady World motif—a popular contemporary association in regard to the "black" body (Gilman 1985, 235)—triggers shame and disgust in Horn: "I brought my hands in front of my face to cover it. Instantly I yanked them back. They reeked of the horrible stench of the dark human skin. I examined the palms of my hands. They had been given an oily coating" (Jahnn 1986a, 402). The oily layer on Horn's hands, with which he had touched the "dark human skin," echoes the eighteenth-century thesis that Africans excrete through the skin "cooked oil" that is pushed out by heat. Only later do we discover that Tutein, out of jealousy and in order to kill off Horn's desire for women once and for all, had prevailed on the girl "to stain her skin with the juice of white onion" and to rub her body with asafetida, a "brown sap, the devil's swab, as they say" (404). The fact that Tutein's strategic deeroticization of the female body is aimed so directly against the dark skin marks the latter as the sole locus of Horn's exoticizing desire. This interpretation of desire as a desire for the other skin is further reinforced when Tutein, right after Egedi's departure, lies down next to Horn, and his body, as Horn notes positively, gives off a "scent of human skin and English soap." The next day Tutein brings the girl back to Horn's room: "Her skin was fresh, it smelled in deep tones of nut and English soap, of herself, a faint scent of burned horn and decay" (405). Horn not only smells "horn"—that is, himself—he describes, apart from the nut scent foretold by Tutein, precisely those smells that Tutein's freshly bathed body exuded, as well as the scent of "decay" Tutein had prophesied. It is easy to decode that the olfactory impressions are made up of elements of Horn's expectations and prejudices. In retrospect, what lingers, alongside the "stench of her skin," is its color hue, which was "brown-black," so dark that Horn in his life "had rarely seen skin so black" (440).

At one point in the story, the woman who runs the inn where Horn and Tutein live during Horn's relationship with Egedi steps up to their table and declares that a "decent person" does not enter into sexual union "with animals." Whereupon Tutein turns to Horn and explains: "She means the black skin," which was, after all, "a point of attack" (407). That this aggression is directed quite materially at the foreign skin becomes clear in the subsequent scene, in which two men brutally beat up Egedi on the street. It is obvious, even though it is not directly stated, that the attack was initiated by the racist innkeeper. While one man holds her up by her hands, the other takes a club to the nearly uncovered thighs of the screaming girl: "Her skin must have split" is Horn's sober comment, who watches the scene from the window but does not intervene (408).

In "Niederschrift," Horn recounts several other erotic encounters with young African women, whose sexuality appears to be always available to the wealthy friends. Another scene deserves to be singled out with respect to the skin motif. Here, Horn and Tutein are hooked up with two prostitutes along the coast of southern Africa. Horn is left behind with one of the two women in a bedroom: "While I was lying there . . . the Japanese silk dress fell from the shoulders of the Negress. She stood there, fresh, with dry glowing skin, trembling. . . . The lamp was extinguished. I reached out into the dark. Suddenly the room was deep and wide. In the middle of the room the moon painted a violet-yellow shape; it invented a color that was blacker than black, the inversion of the glowing flame. It was so beautiful that my fear grow stronger" (488–489).

This scene has a striking resemblance to the first encounter with Egedi, with its reference to the dress suddenly dropping to the floor and the young African woman standing there dressed in nothing but her "glowing skin." The real significant experience for Horn lies in the young woman's unusual skin coloring caused by the light of the moon. The next morning, when he relates his experience to his friend Tutein, he speaks of how "the moon" had showed him something he had "never dreamed of": "a color." The colored skin of the young women thus becomes a substitute for the person, who does not even seem to exist as such when Horn ends by saying: "I was alone last night with the skin colored purple by the moon" (489–490). His memory transforms the erotic experience into an aesthetic one. Even after the travelers are aboard ship, Horn continues to search the sea with his gaze for "the incredible color. And in the color the dissolving figure. What was dissolving was transitory. The color outlasted the form" (490).

Having arrived in the Canary Islands, Horn notices that "the dark skin color had given way to lighter tones" (497). Still, he is fascinated by the unusually dark skin of a few young divers who jump into the water of the harbor to entertain the tourists, perform little stunts for a few coins, and "naked and wet, with shining pearly skin," offer themselves to the desirous gazes: "Two or three among them had blue hair. And skin as full as an animal hide. Black. And yet not Negro black" (503). An unequal friendship forms between Horn and one of the divers, whom Horn, without "evil thoughts," looks upon as "a beautiful animal, day in and day out" (506). He describes his appearance as follows: "The nipples were as though of iron, set off with sharp edges, you could think you might hurt yourself if you touched them. His ears were small, almost perfectly circular, the skin red-black, only one arm had a patch of light skin, a white inlaid ring" (504). The diver with the unusual nipples and the red-black skin with its paradoxically light stigma, puts himself in great danger when, in order to present his show to a group of tourists, he swims around a moving boat. Just as he is diving, the gurgling propeller sends a churned-up stream of water "over the plumbed skin of the harbor bay. The eyes of the strangers hit the surface of the water. They were searching for the spot where the black slave would resurface" (508). When the diver does not appear, the ship indifferently lays in a course toward the open sea.

Horn, who rows out into the bay to search for his friend, finds a mutilated corpse floating in the water: "Instead of the full brown skin of the belly I recognized pale pink and gray torn shreds" (509).[6] In the image that precedes the mutilation, Jahnn deliberately contrasts the smooth "skin of the harbor bay" with the sea churned up by the propeller. In this way, he implicitly anticipates the image of the destruction of the original smoothness and integrity of the brown body. The human skin in its inscrutability is equated to the dark depths of the sea.[7] In the confrontation with the corpse, we can feel Horn's sober realization that the inside of this body is as "pink and gray" as every light-skinned body; the illusion of otherness is irreversibly destroyed by death. When Horn later claims that the dead man is his brother, he knows how incredible this must sound, for his own skin was, after all, "white as cherry blossoms, and that of the dead man brown-black as Macassar wood" (515). But the difference between the two is only skin deep. Shortly before, Horn had noted that it was time for him to "tear the tissue of pity, of secret lust for the dark figures" (463). Now, before his very eyes, the diver's death symbolically tore the skin that had marked the place of otherness.

The awareness that the skin has the character of a garment, and the realization that ethnic identity is merely a worn identity, becomes clear in Jahnn in phrases such as "the bearers of dark skin" (410) or in the observation recorded in *Perrudja* that human beings see each other as "mutually marked": "In their skin: white and brown and black and yellow" (1985, 236). Jahnn's protagonists, so it would seem, experience not only the dark skin as a stigma (or a false promise) but also the pale European skin: human beings can "disappoint each other with the black and the pale of our skin," as he puts it in the drama *Straßenecke* (1993, 42).

This first excursion through the problem of skin color began by discussing anthropological and physiological theories, specifically their notions of the difference between African and European skin. While the "coloredness" of African skin was conceived of as a visual category of otherness, experiments were already under way in the eighteenth century to manifest the "substances" of this difference in the skin itself. The thesis of a secondary darkening and of the leakage of tinted "oils" degraded the non-European skin into a "discolored" and "dirty" epidermis.

Kleist's "Betrothal in St. Domingo" is exemplary for the way in which it takes as its subject matter efforts to read ambiguous skin colors and the resultant uncertainties this causes for the observing subjects. Moreover, the tale establishes a direct connection between skin colors and light metaphors, which shifts the connection into the realm of the aesthetic. "Facial color" is defined as one that is worn in the face and marks the characters. Jahnn's work shows the problematic linkage of an eroticization of dark skin, which goes hand in hand with a reflection on this phenomenon. Here, the aggression of the "whites" is directed concretely against "black" skin, which is time and again identified as the cause of otherness. In the next chapter, these exemplary images of "colored" skin (and the corresponding postulated neutrality of "white" skin) will be confronted with literary texts from African-American culture, in which the "white" is defined as the other. As I shall show, the African-American authors are struggling to come to terms with an anthropology and science of skin colors that has persisted for centuries.

9 blackness

Skin Color in African-American Discourse

In the prologue to Ralph Ellison's *Invisible Man* (1947), the unnamed first-person narrator speaks about the invisibility that marks him. But this invisibility is not a "matter of biochemical accident or my epidermis," that is, it has nothing to do with the factual darkness of his skin. Instead, it has to do only with those who look at him and with the "construction of their *inner* eyes" (1990, 3). The narrator attributes the impossibility of appearing as a subjective individual to the refusal of his environment to actually see him: "Like the bodiless heads you see sometimes in circus sideshows, it is as though I have been surrounded by mirrors of hard, distorting glass. When they approach me they see only my surroundings, themselves, or figments of their imagination— indeed, everything and anything except me" (3). The projected ascription that the narrator experiences is cast as "distorted" reflections in several ways: one sees only the outer, dark, "hard" shell of the person, imaginary ideas about him or the reflected observer himself. The "white" gaze bounces off the body and is reflected back in a distorted manner. The dark skin is nontransparent, a mere empty shell offering no insight of any kind into the person's state of being.

Ellison returns to the analogy between a mirror and black skin in the first chapter, where the protagonist and a group of other young African-Americans are called by the discriminatory name "little shines" (18). "Shine" is generally used as a derogatory term for "Negro." It is an abbreviation of "shoe shine," which refers to the fact that blacks, especially in the South and still to this day, earn a living by cleaning and polishing the shoes of "white" customers with their "black" hands. The shiny black or brown shoes and the skin of the shoe shiner are metonymically equated—both are shiny, leathery, and serve the so-called lower activities.

Both the material colors black and white as such and the processes of blackening or whitening function as leitmotifs in *Invisible Man*. For example, in a New York storefront window, the narrator catches sight of signs advertising skin-whitening products: "You too can be truly beautiful. . . . Win greater happiness with whiter complexion. Be outstanding in your social set" (262). Ellison deliberately raises an issue that is taboo and shameful among African Americans to this day: the use of bleaching agents, "ointments guaranteed to produce the miracle of whitening black skin" (261).[1]

The odyssey through New York in search of work leads the "invisible man" first to a paint factory that produces white paint—"the purest white that can be found" (202). In this factory, which should also be understood allegorically, the narrator, through no fault of his, has an accident the very first day on the job: the temperature gauges fail and the giant cauldrons of white paint boil over. Unconscious and injured from the accident, the narrator later awakens in a hospital ward: "Suddenly my skin itched, all over. I had on new overalls, strange white ones" (231). The boiling white paint had burned his skin so badly that he finds himself enclosed from head to toe in a tightly sealed, sterile container and wrapped in an artificial (not coincidentally, white) cloth skin.

During weeks of excruciating pain, his old, burned skin gradually peels off: "My side began itching violently and I tore open my pajamas to scratch, and suddenly the pain seemed to leap from my ears to my side and I saw gray marks appearing where the old skin was flaking away beneath my digging nails" (318). In describing this peeling "gray" skin (as the color halfway between white and black), Ellison deliberately uses the verb "to flake," thus implying the connotation of peeling old paint: the protagonist undergoes an identity-altering metamorphosis that changes his social skin color. This image of a transforming shedding of the skin is reinforced by the thought that comes to the narrator's mind at the sight of his worn, old clothes, which he now wishes to cast off for good: "I'd have to shed them" (315). The whitening of the young man from the South in the northern metropolis is described as a violent process, a concrete attack on his "black" skin, the manifest site of his otherness.

The events fundamentally alter his relationship to his skin, which, as *pars pro toto*, stands for his whole identity. During the course of the novel, the narrator on several occasions becomes aware of his entire body surface, which he feels intensively in phases of psychological tension and inner transformation. For example, one passage reads: "My entire body started to itch, as though I had just been removed from a plaster cast and was unused to the new freedom of movement" (499). The protagonist, by now a popular speaker of a political group, feels the skin all over his body itch after he has been publicly mistaken for someone else. He associates this feeling with the situation in the hospital, where he was forced to lie in a sterile container for days on end.

Similarly, a later scene, in which he finds himself anonymously in the middle of a disturbance in the street, revolves around the questioning of his externally defined identity. He experiences the liberation from his public role as the sensation of his skin in a vivid state of alertness, as a heightened consciousness of the contact surface between himself and his surrounding: "I went into the crowd, walking slowly, smoothly into the dark crowd, the whole surface of my skin alert, my back chilled" (550).

When the narrator was engaged as a speaker by the political group shortly after his accident, he had to listen to a woman complaining that his skin was not really dark enough for the role of a symbolic figure: "So she doesn't think I'm black enough. What does she want, a black-face comedian? . . . Maybe she wants to see me sweat coal tar, ink, shoe polish, graphite. What was I, a man or a natural resource?" (303). Blackness is supposed to serve as a badge of authenticity: the darker the speaker's skin, the more credible his membership in the group of the socially discriminated. The protagonist is outraged at this instrumentalization of the "black skin." His role might just as well be played by a "white" man in black face, as was common in the black-face minstrel shows popular since the nineteenth century (figure 31), in which slaves were systematically imitated and caricatured by white-skinned performers with blackened faces (Pieterse 1992, 132 ff.). The impulsive refusal to let his body be abused as a "natural resource" that continuously exudes black color contains a sobering realization about the performative character of ethnicity, which functions only

figure 31

Black-face minstrel show (Georgie Hunter, "In the Town Where I Was Born")

in accordance with stereotyped visual attributes. The notion of oozing substances picks up on early anthropological theories, with their abstruse ideas of "blackness" as an oily-slimy liquid in the skin that leaks out or is driven to the surface by sweating.

Just as the dark skin of the political speaker is to be used strategically to generate emotional responses among listeners, the "white" skin of a young women is used as fetishized bait for the narrator and his African-American companions when the young men, for the voyeuristic pleasure of the "white" establishment, have to fight each other for a college scholarship. Before the beginning of the fight, they are confronted with a woman, "a magnificent blonde—stark naked" (1990, 19). The naked woman, who stands with her back to the audience, performs a deeply erotic dance in front of the young men. The weakness of the African-American men is staged in an exceedingly brutal manner by presenting them with an unattainable sexual object in such a way that they are forced to desire it and by staging this symbolic degradation as a voyeuristic spectacle.

The sudden frontal view of naked skin triggers in the young men intense and contradictory reactions of helplessness, uncontrolled sexual arousal, fear, and shame. The narrator speaks of strong feelings of fear and guilt: "I felt a wave of irrational guilt and fear. My teeth chattered, my skin turned to goose flesh, my knees knocked. Yet I was strongly attracted and looked in spite of myself. Had the price of looking been blindness, I would have looked" (19). What Ellison describes here is the form of overpowering fascination that Wurmser has called passive "delophilia" (1981, 158). The urge to look is not only deeply shameful for the person who feels it, it can also be psychically devastating—attested by the formulation "in spite of myself." The fact that he would be willing to sacrifice his eyesight for a look at this naked woman hints at the sense of an overpowering force that corresponds to the archaic blinding. Being blinded is connected with an excess of light—which Ellison in this case intends to be more than ironic, as he brings into sharp focus the Western equating of light, beauty, knowledge, and "white" skin.

However, Ellison's attempt to destroy the fields of meanings associated with darkness and lightness and to expose the mechanisms connected with them ends up turning "white" into that which is strange and other. In the scene following the boxing match, the protagonist is forced to look at the skin of a "white" person close up, the face of the unconscious patron of his college, whom he had been asked to chauffeur around town in gratitude for his large donations. When the patron loses consciousness, the narrator drags him into an overcrowded bar. There, he is pushed against the man's body: "Suddenly a mass of whiteness was looming two inches from my eyes; it was only his face but I felt a shudder of nameless horror. I had never been so close to a white person before. In a panic I struggled to get away. With his eyes closed he seemed more threatening than with them open. He was like a formless white death, suddenly appeared before me" (1990, 86). The perception of light skin as a formless, lifeless, strange mass, as personified death, parodies the curious and up-close glance with which dark skin is usually grasped and described. Similar to what I noted in Kafka and Plath, the face—especially as soon as the eyes are closed—is not a human likeness but mere matter that is examined without empathy.

When the protagonist is pushed up against a woman in an overcrowded New York subway, he stares "with horror at a large mole that arose out of the oily whiteness of her skin." The protruding mole on the woman's oily-white cheek looks like a "black mountain sweeping out of a rainwet plain" (158). In contrast to such negative descriptions of light skin, dark skin is consistently depicted as attractive in Ellison's novel, though not without ironic stereotyping. For example, the protagonist's "white" lover—whom he himself had described as "a leathery old girl"—asks him to "lie back and let me look at you against that white sheet. You're so beautiful, I've always thought so. Like warm ebony against pure snow" (520). By contrasting the "black" skin and the white sheet, she turns the skin into a fetishized object of her erotic desire. The clichéd comparison of ebony and snow, a parody of the fairy tale of "Snow White," transforms the act of perceiving a real person into a mere aesthetic impression. Whiteness, on the other hand, declares the invisible man on the last page of the novel, "is not a color but the lack of one" (588).

John Edgar Wideman's novel *Sent for You Yesterday* (1983) picks up the idea of "white" skin as a "deficiency" by creating a character whose skin contains no pigments whatsoever. Brother Tate is an albino and thus in many respects a symbolic figure: in a society like the United States, where the word "color" has become a synonym for "race" (as, for example, in the positive in-group description "people of color"), the absence of any kind of color makes the body into something that is radically open to interpretation. Wideman raises the anthropological and ideological question of what "color" and "colorlessness" mean to the identity of their bearers by creating an African-American community in the midst of which lives the paradox of a "white" "black man." His lack of color makes him "less nigger and more nigger at the same time" (1988b, 17). Brother Tate is "more nigger" because he is an exemplary demonstration that membership to an ethnic group is not tied to skin tones but culturally determined. Although Brother Tate lacks the proper characteristic, he is unquestionably seen to belong. Wideman thus shows, more radically than color-line fiction does, the extent to which a concept of "races" that is based on the visibility and unambiguousness of skin tones is bound to fail from the start. In these novels, which were especially popular between the end of the century and the 1930s, a quadroon or octoroon (someone with a quarter or an eighth of "black blood") deliberately passes himself or herself off as "white" in order to enjoy a higher social status. The assumption of a different ethnic identity, which is employed as a plot motif in so-called mulatto fiction on the crossing of the color line, is called (racial) passing, which alludes to the double meaning of "to pass": to pass for someone else and to die.[2]

The so-called one-drop rule established during slavery times stated that any American with even a single drop of "black blood' would be legally considered "colored." Driven by fear of a contamination of the "white" gene pool, this dichotomous logic pretends to be based on distinguishable skin colors. But, in fact, it goes far beyond a visual epistemology, with the result that color, in the metaphor of the single drop, turns into a mere construct of difference. To this day, the law in the United States makes no provision for a dual racial identity. Depending on the state, children are automatically assigned to the race of the mother, or the father, or the African-American parent.[3] The constructs "black" and "white" thus establish in the United States an "epidermal hierarchy" that "equates the racial body with a perceptible blackness, while defining, in its absence, whiteness as whatever an African blackness is not" (Wiegman 1995, 8–9). One can almost say that the individual body schema is replaced, in the course of socialization, by a "racial epidermal schema" (Fanon 1967, 112).

It is therefore apparent that the place value and the multifarious functions of skin tones in African-American literature go far beyond a conventional schema of color symbolism or the conveyance of individual character traits. The question always revolves also around the unresolved identity of the characters and around the social hierarchies and values that are linked to skin tones. While the heroes and heroines in earlier texts were often very light skinned mulattos, a practice that Alice Walker called "colorism" and rightly criticized (1983, 290), notably dark-skinned main characters have appeared with increasing frequency in novels during the last few decades, especially in works by women writers. Blackness and African facial features are being consciously established as positive aesthetic and sensual categories.

Wideman repeatedly articulates the notion of being "stuck" in a specific colored skin as though in a bag. For example, we are told that the albino Brother Tate looks "dead in that bag of white skin" (1988b, 36), his son Junebug, is "traveling in a bag of skin" (145), and Junebug's siblings "run around black and shining in their skins" (141). In these body images, the skin envelops the self inescapably, imparting a determinative identity. Wideman articulates the moment of being imprisoned in the skin especially harshly in regard to skin tones, consciousness of which can become a deadly disease: "color can be a cage and color consciousness can become a terminal condition" (John Edgar Wideman, "The Divisible Man," *Life* (spring 1988), quoted in Riley 1993, 67). It is possible that Wideman is referring directly to the title of the novel *In the Castle of My Skin* (1953), by the Afro-Caribbean writer Georg Lamming, where dark skin, in the image of the "castle," is identified not only as a refuge but also as an inescapable prison. Skin is the primary agent that individualizes a human being and forms a closed world around him or her. For example, the narrator in *Sent for You Yesterday*, in his description of the street on which he grew up, emphasizes that skin (and its individual color) is the first and most fundamental world that separates human beings: "The life in Cassina Way was a world apart from Homewood and Homewood a world apart from Pittsburgh and Pittsburgh was the North, a world apart from the South, and all those people crowded in Cassina Way carried the seeds of these worlds inside their skins, black, brown and gold and ivory skin which was the first world setting them apart" (1988b, 21). In this community of golden, brown, and black tones, Brother Tate is a pariah, "ugly as sin," with a skin "wrinkled like a plucked chicken" or "colorless pie dough" (36).

Wideman falls back on a long tradition of exclusion to describe the defamation suffered by Brother Tate and his son Junebug, also an albino. Especially in African, South American, and Native American cultures—that is, in cultures in which a stark "color" deficiency is immediately apparent— albinos have traditionally been the object of special superstitions. In many religions, they were regarded as superhuman; normal social rules did not apply to them. For example, they were prohibited from marrying, were expelled from society, and oftentimes were even killed right after birth. The attitude toward them fluctuated among shame (especially on the part of the parents), indifference, and favored treatment, because people believed that they stood under special divine protection or were the dead come back to life (Robins 1991, 180ff.). Very early Western anthropology assumed that albinos were found only in non-European cultures. For a time, it was even believed that they constituted a separate race.[4] Observers failed for centuries to make the connection with individuals in their own cultures who did not have much pigmentation. Buffon's *Histoire naturelle* (1777) for the first time develops the idea that albinism is merely an individual variation within the species, a genetic biochemical deficiency, as one would call it today. Once observers realized that identical manifestations were found among Europeans, albinism disappeared from the discussion of "races" (Kutzer 1990, 205ff.)

In spite of this scientific understanding about the frequency and occurrence of albinos, the reasons for their lack of pigmentation, and the resultant demythicization, the fears and uncertainties that are triggered by the birth of such a child have not entirely disappeared even today. It is no coincidence that Brother Tate grows up with adoptive parents; his son Junebug is expelled from the community of his siblings and is even killed by them at the age of five. Junebug's mother, "a coal-black beautiful woman named Samantha" (1988b, 17), tries to understand the hatred her other children feel toward the outsider. But even she was traumatized by the birth of a child from whom, as she put it, the color had "drained." She explains the rejection by the siblings as the difficulty of actually seeing the albino—let alone recognizing him as related: "It's just children scared by something they ain't never seen. Junebug is a warm lump against her shoulder. A part of herself drained of color, strangely aglow. Her children don't understand yet. Perhaps they can't see him. Perhaps they look through his transparent skin and see only the pillow on which she's propped his head. She lowers her gaze to his pale, wrinkled skin, his pink eyes, then stares across him to their dark faces" (138). The first time Samantha had seen Brother, she thought it was a ghost who was standing in front of her door. Wideman is here explicitly hinting at the colloquial word "spook," a slang expression for "a black person" (Thorne 1991, 487). Describing a "white" "black" in this way turns the irony of calling a "black person" a (white) ghost upside down, which suddenly reestablishes the literal meaning of the word.

In spite of the lack of color, Samantha recognizes the unambiguous African features in Brother's face as he stands before her: "He was white, a color she hated, yet nigger, the blackest, purest kind stamped his features"

(1988b, 131). Although she actually and consciously picked only men with the darkest skin, "because in her ark she wanted pure African children" (134), Brother became her lover the same day. Touching his colorless skin becomes an ambivalent experience for Samantha, one not free of fear and disgust: "She could see through his skin. No organs inside, just a reddish kind of mist, a fog instead of heart and liver and lungs. She was afraid his white sweat would stain her body. . . . As soon as he left she inspected every square inch of her glossy, black skin in the piece of mirror hung on the bathroom door" (134). The irrational fear that Brother's "white" sweat would stick to her—an ironic reversal of the old, defamatory notion that the color of dark skin would rub off—impels Samantha to engage in this thorough inspection after he has left. The next morning, to reassure herself, she reads everything she can find in the public library on "melanin" and "disorders of melanin pigmentation." She learns that pigment-containing cells—melanocytes—are neuroectodermal in origin (i.e., they grow out of the outer layer of stem cells). Before the third month of pregnancy, these cells migrate into the skin, between the epidermis and the dermis, into the eyes, the intestinal tract, and the brain, where they accumulate. Samantha derives from this information a very original theory of "blackness":

> She read the words again, this time listening to their sound and dance and understood that melanocytes, the bearers of blackness, descended from royalty, from kings whose neural crest contains ostrich plumes, a lion's roar, the bright colors of jungle flowers. Even before birth, before the fetus was three months old, the wanderlust of blackness sent melanocytes migrating through the mysterious terrain of the body. Blackness seeking a resting place, a home in the transparent baby. Blackness journeying to exotic places with strange-sounding names. . . . Blackness would come to rest in the eyes; blackness a way of seeing and being seen. . . . Blackness something to do with long journeys, and eyes, and being at the vibrating edge of things."
>
> (135)

But Samantha arrives at this understanding that blackness is simply "a way of seeing and being seen" only after she has expelled from her mind everything she learned in school about biological-rationalistic models for explaining the "races" and reads the words out loud until they finally make sense to her. What Wideman implies, precisely by using as his basis the medical text as the paradigm of the twentieth century, is a specifically

African-American form of knowledge and understanding that deviates from the Western understanding of supposedly objective racial differences. While talk about "royalty," the "wanderlust of blackness," and the "journey to exotic places" is factually a misrepresentation of biological processes and their terminology, it is simultaneously, on a symbolic level, a reinterpretation of the status of African-American identity. It is a positive new definition, in which qualities such as mobility, activity, and vitality are identified as essentially "black" peculiarities, which, not coincidentally, happen to match the connotations of the word "colorful." When Samantha then reads about "disorders of melanin pigmentation," she is reassured to learn that Brother is the "healthy type" and that albinism generally is not contagious—that is, his lack of pigmentation was not a skin disease.[5] Despite his objective colorlessness, Brother had "enough blackness in his body" to counter his pale skin. Here, it becomes clear that what Samantha defines as "blackness" is an inner condition requiring no visual manifestation.

Another protagonist contemplates whether there is a primary, basic color over which all others are superimposed like added layers. As he is waiting for his colleagues in the gray of dawn, he looks first at the morning sky, then at his work boots blackened with shoe polish and covered with countless spots, and finally applies the question to Brother's skin. Implied in these musings—precisely because of their circuitous rhetorical path—is the question about the origin of humankind, the question of what constitutes the "first color":

> What was the right color of the sky? The first color? Did it start one color before it began going through all those changes? Was it one thing or the other? Blue or white or black or the fire colors of dawn and sunset the first day it was sky? You could use a chisel on his shoes and never get down to the first color. Carl's friend Brother was like somebody had used a chisel on him. A chisel then sandpaper to get down to the whiteness underneath the nigger. Because the little bugger looked chipped clean. Down to the first color or no color at all. Skin like waxed paper you could see through.
>
> (62–63)

He imagines that below the dark skin pigment lies a light dermal layer. Although this "whiteness underneath the nigger" is identified as "the first color," it should not be equated with the skin color of the so-called whites; instead, it possesses no real color qualities at all. In a non-albino, this form of "whiteness" as colorlessness, which Brother's transparent skin displays, must first be laid bare by "chipping" away the color pigments. In this poetic image, the color of the skin is applied over a base that is imagined as neutral.

Wideman thus refers to various cultural contexts: first, to the fact—known since the so-called polychromy debate of the nineteenth century—that Greek statues were originally painted, which means that the pure white marble sculptures we encounter in museums were covered in a layer of color in antiquity, a fact that considerably complicates the question of the "origin" of humankind. Second, Wideman's image implies in a sarcastic way the defamatory notion that the blackness of people of African descent was merely external dirt that could be washed off. In keeping with that idea, in the nineteenth and early twentieth century, a number of advertising illustrations for detergents and soaps featured a dark-skinned person being offered the cleaning products or a "white person" trying to wash or decolorize the dark-skinned person (Pieterse 1992, 195 ff.). By contrast, coloration in the analogy Wideman develops is not a form of degeneration or staining but is identified instead as a necessary layer for the existence of subjectivity. Brother, who lacks this subjectivizing layer, has no true core of identity. He is a surface onto which others project their desires and fears: it is therefore no coincidence that he lacks an individualizing name and is nearly mute. Brother lacks color, voice, and a name—a negative condensation of what Wideman defines as the "sense of identity": the fact that identity in general, and African-American identity in particular, is something that is "fragmentary, that is discontinuous, more and more so" (Coleman 1989, 158).

Central to the relationship between the albino and the other characters in the novel is the notion that it is the pigments alone that usually prevent the gaze from passing through the skin and into the body. Brother's "unsettling lack of color" (Wideman 1988b, 134) disturbs and frightens those around him; at the same time, the man with the transparent skin radiates an eerie fascination. The narrator also mentions his fear of looking through Brother—looking under his skin—and with it the difficulty of being able to get him into focus at all:

> If you looked closely Brother had no color. He was lighter than anybody else, so white was a word some people used to picture him, but he wasn't white, not white like snow or paper, not even white like the people who

called us black. Depending on the time of day, on how much light was in the room, on how you were feeling when you ran into Brother Tate, his color changed. I was already a little afraid of him, afraid I'd see through him, under his skin, because there was no color to stop my eyes, no color which said there's a black man or a white man in front of you. I was afraid I'd see through that transparent envelope of skin to the bones and the guts of whatever he was. To see Brother I'd have to look away from where he was standing, focus on something safe and solid near him so that Brother would hover like the height of a mountain at the skittish edges of my vision.

(15)

It is the pigments that would stop the gaze and categorize the person according to a dual scheme. But the presence of a colorless black man radicalizes the question about the location of "race" in the body, which cannot be the skin if Brother is considered an African-American even without the significant color. Categorizing him as "white" fails as well because his skin is "white" in a different way and his skin tone changes depending on the incidence of light and the angle from which one chooses to look at him.

On another level of meaning, the presence of pigmentation is equated with a psychological defense that protects a person from the gaze into the inner essence. Brother's lack of color, which causes those who look at him to see through his skin involuntarily, is thus also understood as a quality of fragility and lack of substance. No core is visible on the inside of the transparent man, merely an undefined mass. Brother himself, in one of the rare sequences in which his own thoughts are recorded, expresses his desire to conceal and protect his "nakedness," "the bare white" (174) from the gazes of others. As I have already noted on several occasions, a long physiognomic and literary tradition analogizes lightness and transparency of the skin with sensitivity and a positive transparency of emotions. Since dark skin is interpreted (from a "white" perspective) as impenetrable, changes less visibly, and is therefore not amenable to semiotic ascription, it is often seen as concealing—it becomes a "hide" in the literal sense of the word. And the fact that "color" has its etymological roots in the Latin verb "*celare*" (to hide) also points to the notion that color pigments are simultaneously the sheltering and concealing substances of the body surface.

Wideman picks up on such an interpretative pattern of the concealing "colored" skin and the involuntarily revealing light skin when he writes about a very light skinned African-American woman: "Her hand was brown as it ever got and that no browner than a cup of milk mixed with a tablespoon of coffee. Not even brown enough to hide the pink flush after it had been sloshing all morning in a sinkful of soap and dishes and pots and pans" (31). Freeda's skin, too light to conceal the "pink flush" of her hands after long immersion in dishwater, would qualify her for membership in a "blue-vein society." Between the late nineteenth and the middle of the twentieth century, these elite clubs of the African-American upper class, also called "bon ton societies," admitted only members whose skin was light enough to let the veins shine through. Admission was regulated by a variety of tests, for example, the so-called paper bag test (the skin had to be lighter than the color of a brown shopping bag) and the wooden door test (only those could enter the church or the meeting place through a certain door whose skin tone was lighter than the color of the wood) (Russell, Wilson, and Hall 1993, 24 ff.). Often this intraracial racism with its fixation on the lightness and transparency of the skin was also called "blue veinism," an allusion to the auditory double meaning of vein and vain.

When a character in Zora Neale Hurston's novel *Their Eyes Were Watching God* (1937) is called a "lucky man" because his wife is so light skinned that one can immediately see the traces on her skin when he hits her (1990, 140–141), this is another prejudice connected with the lightness of skin: in contrast to dark skin, one can leave on it traces that attest to the power one exercises over the object. In *Sent for You Yesterday*, by contrast, the "blue bruises showing through so plain on Junebug's skin" (1988b, 139), which attest to the abuse he suffers at the hands of his siblings, become for Samantha a painful symbol of her helplessness to reconcile her feelings for her albino son with those for her other children, who hate him.

Very early in its history, anthropology repeatedly put forth the thesis that "black" skin was thicker than "white" skin, a property that corresponded to an entire arsenal of negative interpretations (especially a lack of feeling and numbness) (Blankenburg 1996, 134; Gilman 1985, 114). Wideman turns this upside down by characterizing light skin—in its extreme form of albinism— as too thin and devoid of essence. It becomes clear that not only the attributed color but the entire interpretation of the skin is socially conditioned— even its thickness: in *Damballah*, one of the other parts of his *Homewood* trilogy, Wideman goes so far as to write this about an African abducted to the United States as a slave: "He could feel the air of this strange land wearing out his skin, rubbing it thinner and thinner" (Wideman 1988a, 18). Wideman's use of the skin motif is original and multilayered. He not only pursues Morrison's project of decoding the "denotative and connotative blackness that African peoples have come to signify" (1992, 6) but also probes, along complex paths, into conceptions of whiteness and albinism.

In many cultural traditions, there is a preference for light, milklike skin, especially in women, as is painfully clear in this passage from Paule Marshall's autobiographical story "Reena" (1983): "Because I was dark I was always being plastered with Vaseline so I wouldn't look so ashy. Whenever I had my picture taken they would pile a whitish powder on my face and make the lights so bright I always came out looking ghostly. My mother stopped speaking to any number of people because they said I would have been pretty if I hadn't been so dark. Like nearly every little black girl, I had my share of dreams of waking up to find myself with long, blond curls, blue eyes, and skin like milk" (Marshall 1983, 78–79). This preference for light skin also exists in cultures that assigned such priority to "white" before the colonization of the African and South American subcontinents (and the forced imposition of a hierarchy of lighter skin types)—for example, among the Aztecs, in early Japan, in India, and in many Arab cultures. Light skin is considered a sign of membership in higher social classes, evidence of youth and virginity. Attempts at rational explanations—as, for example, the contention that the skin of women becomes noticeably darker after pregnancy, which means that light skin signals virginity and therefore men are attracted to it "instinctively"—offer only partial answers to this phenomenon (Russell, Wilson, and Hall 1993, 71 ff.; Frost 1990). Likewise, the common claim that women are genetically endowed with lighter skin than men is biologically incorrect (Brownmiller 1984, 132).

In a multicultural society such as the United States, in which all conceivable skin tones appear side by side (and which is therefore especially revealing for the present study), the privileging of light skin types within ethnic groups has become a political problem, one that for the most part is not discussed, because of its explosive nature. In African-American culture, the gain in status that comes with lighter skin is perceived in an extremely ambivalent way. It is overshadowed by its subliminal legitimization of the rape of slave women, to this day the primary reason for the large number of individuals of mixed blood: it has been conclusively shown that miscegenation between "coloreds" and "whites" all but ceased after the Civil War and the abolition of slavery and did not start to increase again slowly until the twentieth century (Williamson 1980).

Beginning in the mid-nineteenth century, mulattos officially constituted for some time an additional group of "brown Americans" that was recorded separately in the census (and which, according to the 1915 census, accounted for three-quarters of all nonwhites). After 1920 this category was abolished, which meant that the old opposites of "white" and "colored" once again became the determinative scheme (113–114). Everyone not "white" was—and is—assigned to the category of "other." To this day, U.S. census forms have only a single category for "African American," whereas, by comparison, the category "Asian American" has nine subdivisions. In stark contrast to this legal homogenization of all African Americans, within the community itself the tone and consistency of skin down to the most minute shades are seen as markers of differentiation, indicated by the countless names for skin colors. While in "white" culture the color of the hair and eyes are usually the first characteristics used to sketch a person's appearance, in the African-American community, skin tone is paramount. A study from the 1940s, for example, found that 145 terms for skin tones were used among African-American high school students (Parrish 1946). Numerous other studies confirm this striking linguistic variety. Sociologists, like physicians, usually divide this variety into the three "basic tones" of yellow, brown, and black, which are then further differentiated in descriptions such as "dark brown," "plain brown," "light brown," "high yellow," "blue black," and "jet black" (Johnson 1973; Hughes and Hertel 1990; Hurston 1985).

In African-American literature, especially in works by women writers, the detailed, often playful and inventive descriptions of complexion fulfill a variety of functions: Brita Lindberg-Seyersted has argued that, apart from the most obvious one—that of painting a protagonist's physical appearance in the most individualistic and vivid manner possible—they also indicate the "gradual 'amalgamation' of the races" and a character's "social class." But the function that should be highlighted in the present context is the "aesthetic" one: Lindberg-Seyersted believes that the text, by means of the often highly sensual descriptions of skin, is infused with "an element of strong physical pleasure" (1992, 55). The metaphors and analogies used to describe the skin are often taken from the realm of food (sweets, spices, nuts, honey, or coffee) but also from the worlds of minerals (sand, earth, coal) and plants and animals. In the work of Morrison, who shall serve as my example, the field of association moves beyond even these areas of material culture.

In her novel *Tar Baby* (1981), one protagonist's skin is "as dark as a riverbed" (1982b, 113), one woman has "skin like tar" (45), another "midnight skin" (299), and the especially light skinned main character, Jadine, has a complexion the color of "a natural sponge" (131) and "raw silk thighs the color of natural honey" (272). In *Sula* (1973), there is a girl with skin "the color of wet sandpaper," while her girlfriend is described as "a heavy brown" (1982a, 52). One character in *Song of Solomon* (1977) is marked by "lemony skin" (1987, 14); a girl in *The Bluest Eye* has "something summery in her complexion" (1972, 53), and the skin of a man possesses "the pale, cheerless yellow of winter sun" (52). Descriptions like these, which make reference to nature, the sky, the seasons, precious cloth, and sandpaper, as well as fruits, honey, and much more, are consciously employed by Morrison and recur repeatedly throughout the novels. In contrast, for example, to the comparisons for the albino's skin in Wideman, what is at issue here are not—despite their plasticity—merely subjective impressions reflecting associations and projections. Rather, these are objective color qualities, which, though described with figurative language, are internally consistent. What Morrison is after are individualizing not typifying skin tones.

Morrison not only gives her protagonists telling, unusual, and ironic names (such as "Milkman Dead" or "Guitar"), whose origin is always part of the story she tells. She also lets the individual skin become a proper name, one that can even take the place of the real name, for example, when we hear about "the pale yellow woman" (1982a, 20), "this sponge-colored girl" (1982b, 213), "the chocolate eater" (289), "a high-yellow dream child" (1972, 52), or "this thin lemon-yellow woman" (1987, 137). Names evidently play an important role in African-American culture, since those who were dragged off to another continent as slaves often lost them together with their roots, something that Morrison, in an interview, called "a huge psychological scar" (Leclair 1993, 275). Slaves usually received their new names from plantation owners; at times, these were the owner's own names. In more recent African-American culture, many of these imposed slave names are being replaced by self-chosen names voluntarily adopted. Morrison has called this self-baptism, where the choice of the name usually refers to an individual's personal story or qualities, a way of regaining a part of one's identity, "because it reflects something about you or your own choices" (135). It is from this perspective that the many telling names in African-American literature in general, and in the work of Morrison in particular, take on their special significance. In Morrison, there is no description of "types" (as is the case in the realistic writers of the nineteenth century but also in early African-American literature), such that age, gender, and social class are coded by means of specific skin tones. Light and darker skin, a "summery" or a "wintery" complexion, does not a priori possess hierarchical value. The desire for as light a skin as possible as a way of attaining the privileges that brings—something Morrison has denounced as "color fetish" (1992, 23)—is subtly exposed in her novels.

In *Song of Solomon*, Macon Dead tells his son that his paternal grand-mother had been a light-skinned, beautiful woman: "Light-skinned, pret-ty. Looked like a white woman to me" (1987, 54). And he has this to say about Milkman's maternal grandfather, "a high-yellow nigger who loved ether and hated black skin" (77–78): "He delivered both your sisters him-self and each time all he was interested in was the color of their skin" (71). While Macon in this comment criticizes not only that his father-in-law personally delivered his own daughter's children (in his eyes, a moral fail-ing), but also and especially the man's color consciousness, he himself re-verts unreflectively to a light-skinned ideal of beauty in describing his own mother. Here is Morrison's description of one of the daughters (delivered by the father-in-law) as an adult woman: "High toned and high yellow she believed that what her mother was also convinced of: that she was a prize for a professional man of color" (188). Morrison goes on to deconstruct this belief: as the novel unfolds, the woman fails to find a husband at all, let alone a "professional man" to whom she could be a "prize" owing to her light skin. What Morrison alludes to here is the mating scheme postu-lated by sociologists in the first decades of the twentieth century: the ten-dency of upwardly mobile African-American men to marry primarily women with skin lighter than their own (Williamson 1980, 118). A wife's pale skin tone was (and is) instrumentalized as a status symbol indicating social advancement.

In *Tar Baby*, Jadine is also described as a "prize woman." One of her adoptive father's employees speaks of her as "a yalla," the pejorative name for particularly light skinned African-American women:

"Your first yalla?" he asked. "Look out. It's hard for them not to be white people. Hard. I'm telling you. Most never make it. Some try, but most don't make it."

"She's not yalla," said Son. "Just a little light." He didn't want any dis-cussion about shades of black folk.

"Don't fool yourself. You should have seen her two months ago. What you see is tanning from the sun. Yallas don't come to being black natural-like. They have to choose it and most don't choose it."

(1982b, 155)

Jadine "chooses" her dark skin; the tone becomes a conscious act—what Morrison in an essay described as the "acquisition of blackness."[6]

In several scenes of the novel, the model Jadine, who is constantly moving between African-American and European culture, finds herself unwittingly confronted with "blackness." Once, for example, freshly bathed and dressed in "Easter white cotton" (168), her foot sinks into a black, stinking swamp, and she is unable for several minutes to free herself (181 ff.). The black mud sticks to her skin and is difficult to remove once it has dried and hardened; Jadine's skin burns after her strenuous attempts to scrape it off. It is obvious that in this scene Morrison is inverting the forced whitening of the protagonist in *Invisible Man* by consciously reversing the configuration. In a different passage, Jadine lies down naked in the "dark luxury" of a black mink coat. She closes her eyes and "imagine[s] the blackness she was sinking into" (91). A little while later, after she has put her clothes back on, Son suddenly appears in her room: "As he stood looking at the coat she could not tell whether he or it was the blacker or the shinier, but she knew she did not want him to touch it" (114). The associative link between the fur coat and Son's black skin highlights once more the extent to which Jadine, because of her special status as a person of mixed blood, "chooses" her (erotically charged) "blackness," wearing it like an attractive coat. Son's black skin does strike her as enticing but at the same time also as contaminated; she does not want him to touch the coat, her artificial second skin.

In the course of the novel, Jadine, who does eventually become involved with Son in an amorous relationship, is increasingly confronted with the more primal "black" culture he represents. The real and at the same time metaphysically elevated blackness in his hometown ("the blackest nothing she had ever seen") seems menacing to her and gives her nightmares (251). Morrison alludes to the classic association of absence and eeriness with darkness when she has Jadine wake up at night in Eloe (again naked) and discover to her horror that there is not a single source of light—even the streets are not illuminated. In this scene, the blackness is consciously equated with the negation of reality, with evil and terror, as is common in Western aesthetics since the eighteenth century, at the latest.

In *Song of Solomon,* Pilate, in the face of this prejudice, emphasizes the rich variety and the special vitality of blackness. In contrast to color theory, in which black is seen as a monochrome color, she speaks of a "rainbow" of shadings of black (darknesses, skin tones):

And talking about dark! You think that dark is just one color, but it ain't. There're five or six kinds of black. Some silky, some woolly. Some just empty. Some like fingers. And it don't stay still. It moves and changes from one kind of black to another. Saying something is pitch black is like saying something is green. Green like my bottles? Green like a grasshopper? Green like a cucumber, lettuce, or green like the sky is just before it breaks loose to storm? Well, night black is the same way. May as well be a rainbow.

(40–41)

The fact that this description of the heterogeneous darknesses of the night uses the adjectives "silky" and "woolly," common attributes for the special quality of African-American skin and hair, indicates the degree to which Morrison is perfectly aware of the semantic ambiguity when she speaks of the night but implicitly means the complexion of her protagonists.

While blackness in Western thinking is traditionally seen not only as a monotonous deficiency but also as a mark or stigma,[7] *Tar Baby* has this to say about Margaret Street's unusually light and delicate skin: "It left its mark on her—being *that* pretty with *that* coloring" (1982b, 56). The extreme fragility of this transparent skin ("as delicate as the shell of a robin's egg and almost as blue" [55]), which does not allow Margaret to spend even a moment exposed to direct sunlight ("she was like a marshmallow warming but not toasting itself" [196]) is both an attribute of beauty and a stigma. The transparent skin tone singles her out but also makes her vulnerable. As we learn in the course of the novel, Margaret, as a young mother, had maltreated her young son's skin with needles and burning cigarettes. After the late confession of these sadistic acts, which were directed against the infant's "cream-colored" skin, her husband tries to come to terms with this shocking revelation: "Just a delicious pin-stab in sweet creamy flesh. That was her word 'delicious' " (231); " 'It's funny, but I would see the mark and see him cry but somehow I didn't believe it hurt all that much.' 'Mark' she called it. She saw the mark. Didn't think it hurt 'all that much.' Like a laboratory assistant removing the spleen of a cute but comatose mouse" (232). The ambivalent feelings that Margaret actually has toward her own skin are displaced by this destructive act onto the delicate skin of her baby. The "mark" that is Margaret's entire body surface (especially since she comes from an Italian family with an olive complexion) is violently inscribed into her infant son's skin. Her husband, who grasps the connection between Margaret's own skin and the abuse she inflicted on the son, thus refuses to beat her for what she did, as she demands that he do: "His shuddering finger went wild at the thought of touching her, making physical contact with that skin. His whole body recoiled" (239). His beautiful wife's skin, which Valerian originally admired, suddenly becomes a place from which he draws back in horror.

Two central female characters in Morrison's work—Sula in the novel of the same name, and Pilate Dead in *Song of Solomon*—possess skin that, despite their advancing ages and extreme lifestyles, shows no wrinkles, scars, or birthmarks of any kind. Both women have very dark, brown-black skin that, in an almost magical way, is spared from all the traces of life. These are protagonists whose skin egos appears invulnerable and unmarkable, while the unusually light skin of characters like Jadine or Margaret is exposed for its fetish character. At the same time, Morrison paints these latter figures as especially fragile, defenseless, and open to stigmatization.

This second chapter on the theme and motif of skin color has tried to show the extent to which recent African-American literature works through, reflects, and decodes what is considered the anthropology of physical differences. The associative field connected with the theories of skin color—"lightness" and "darkness," the "coloring" and "decoloring" of the skin, transparency and nontransparency, thickness and insensitivity—is deconstructed, not least by applying exoticizing strategies to "white" skin. The skin is not differentiated primarily by its degree of lightness—or, if it is, in order to reflect the master discourse—but with an entire spectrum of variables. I have examined the overarching question of the cultural interpretive strategies of skin color by looking at the example of the duality of "black" and "white," which to this day are considered the paradigmatic opposites.

10 hand and skin

Anthropology and Iconography of the Cutaneous Senses

Until now I have been dealing primarily with the perception and interpretation of the skin of others, of the other grasped by the gaze. I have examined the imagery and conceptual topoi of this skin, along with the awareness—depicted in literature and in other arts—that one's own skin is also visually perceived and might provide involuntary insights into hidden things. What has been left out is the perception of one's own body and the bodies of others by touching, being touched, and feeling one's own body. For that reason, I shall begin by looking at questions of etymology relating to "touch," "feeling," and "sensibility." I will also discuss the relationship of the cutaneous senses to the other senses as it has evolved in cultural history and aesthetics. Central to this examination will be the relationship between sight and touch—or, to use the terminology of the eighteenth century (where this juxtaposition was highly relevant), between "face" and "feeling." These two sensory complexes were often seen as complementary or contrary but at times also as analogous. The chapter concludes by raising the problem of the epistemological equating of skin and touch—or, to put it differently, by inquiring into the relationship between hand and skin, between active touching and the passive sensation of touch.

The subsequent chapter will introduce exemplary twentieth-century literary texts that, in very different ways, take as their theme the outstanding importance of cutaneous self-perception in the medium of literature. Because the material used in this and the following chapter to show the various aspects of meaning of touch and tactile perception is invariably diverse and heterogeneous, it will not be possible to plumb the individual discourses in all their complexity. I am merely interested in revealing a nexus of questions that has not been discussed until now but is indispensable for a cultural history of the skin: I am referring to the close relationship between perception and self-image, to the felt awareness of living in the body, of the boundaries of the body, and of ego identity. This question relates less to the history of a motif than to a basic anthropological issue, similar to that explored in the introductory chapter on skin in language.

In many of the European languages that are descended from Indo-Germanic, there is a striking semantic kinship between psychic feeling and the touching of the skin: whether the heart is touched or the skin is touched by a breeze, whether one speaks of being seized by something or seizing someone's hand, whether one feels cold toward something or something feels cold, whether one is moved by something or one moves a chair, the same verb is always used for both events. This correspondence of semantic fields—of inner feeling and external touching, moving, and feeling—which is found in other languages,[1] quite possibly points to what was originally a reciprocal relationship between emotions and touch. Older linguistic levels in the semantic field "to feel" should thus be seen as "indications of historical notions of feelings" (Böhme 1997a, 533).

In the period when the word "*Gefühl*" (feeling) first established itself in German—around the seventeenth century—it had "not yet been taken hold of by the strategy of psychologizing corporeal phenomena that was predominant since the era of 'sensibility' [*Empfindsamkeit*]"; instead, it was understood as the capacity for sensory perception and touch (522). Accordingly, "to feel" was likewise understood primarily in a corporeal sense until the eighteenth century, as sensory perception and the feeling of one's own body. Only gradually did there occur what Böhme calls the "*Verseelung*" of feelings, the process of infusing feelings with matters of the soul (534). This has led to the point where today we are forced to rely on context to recognize whether we are dealing with a physical or a psychological event when someone speaks about feeling (or being touched, or the like).

In Zedler's *Universal-Lexikon* (1753), the article "Fühlen, Gefühl" (to feel, feeling) does not discuss any inner emotions in the modern sense but only the "five external senses that are spread over the entire body" (1961, 9:col. 2225). By the time of the Grimm brothers' *Wörterbuch* (1826), there is a clear differentiation between a corporeal and an internal form of feeling: although the two forms are placed under the same entry in the dictionary, they are discussed in separate sections. The authors point out that "feeling" (*Fühlen*) traditionally had the same meaning as "emotion" (*Empfindung*) but was not distinct from it. As an example of the difference they offer the following sentence: "I feel [*fühle*] your hand and sense [*empfinde*] pleasure in caressing it" (1984, 3:col. 426). "*Fühlen*" is understood as more of a sensory experience; "*Empfinden*" as more of a mental-psychological one. Expanded senses of "*Begreifen*" (to comprehend, from the Latin *comprehendere*, to grasp) and "*Erfassen*" (to grasp) in German, as of "comprehension" in English, are derived concretely from the model of touching and the actions of the hand (Böhme 1996, 185 ff.). It is generally assumed (for example, in psychology and philosophy) that feelings gradually come to have merely a figurative connection with touching and contact. The corporeal feeling is proclaimed as a model, as a precursor on the level of individual history, of what are now inner feelings, as in Anzieu's psychoanalytical conception whereby skin sensations serve merely as analogies for psychic, unconscious processes. This postulated immateriality of feelings, however—its disconnect from its corporeal foundation—may possibly turn out to be a fallacy once it becomes clear that the emotional and the psychic dimensions quite simply cannot do without recourse to the tactile dimension.

The multifaceted and ambiguous nature of touch is reflected in allegorical depictions of the five senses, a genre that was popular from the Middle Ages to the eighteenth century. Pictorial representations of the senses are not known from antiquity and make their first appearance in the Middle Ages. From the outset, the assessment of the senses is based on two fundamental aspects reflected in the images: first, the question of the virtuousness of perception or the sinful abuse of the senses; second, the problem of the epistemological powers of the various perceptual tools (Nordenfalk 1976, 17).[2]

In a series designed by Frans Floris in 1561, the senses are allegorized by female figures placed in a coastal landscape and surrounded by characteristic animals. Each figure is associated with one specific animal: following tradition, sight has the eagle, hearing the stag, smell the dog, and taste the monkey. The sense of touch (*tactus*), however, has no fewer than three animals (figure 32). The spider in its web represents cautious groping and touching and artisanal skill; the parrot, who is biting the figure's hand, symbolizes pain; and the turtle, Aphrodite's animal, stands for sensual desire felt with the skin and also careful withdrawal in the face of danger (Putscher 1978, 153; Museo del Prado 1997, 108). The figure's raised index finger performs the tactile sense's typical gesture of pointing and warning. The depiction of two boats, a sailboat close to the horizon and a beached sloop in the right foreground, further points to the mediating function of the cutaneous senses, which possess the ability of actively spanning and abolishing distances. The net full of fish that is hanging out of the sloop corresponds to the spider's web: in both cases, the catcher perceives, through the indications of weight and movement (as qualities of touch), that something is in it. Moreover, weaving and fishing are both characterized as crafts.

The figure is looking at the bird biting her hand with a pained expression, while the other two animals get no attention at all: the skin sensation of pain overpowers all other perceptions, which is emphasized by the fact that the small inscription "Tactus" is placed directly above the parrot. Later, in the seventeenth century, there are a number of allegories of *tactus* itself as pain, in which the multiplicity of feeling is reduced entirely to this one sensation. Many of these allegories are scenes of surgery, which was still performed without anesthesia.

Thus the work of Floris still represents the complexity of the cutaneous senses, with the hand's localized sense of touch and the broader senses of the skin of the entire body still subsumed under the term "*tactus*"—not without reason does the caption read "tactus sensorium per totum corpus expansum est, ac proinde etiam eius organum" (the sense of touch is spread out over the entire body, and therefore it is also its organ). By contrast, in later works, the fifth sense is oftentimes reduced to the active hand and its haptic abilities. At times, these depictions show both a figure in the act of perception and the isolated organ.

Another pictorial type also appeared, one that did not show individual figures representing the various senses but a man and a woman in the process of sensory perception. In many cases, the woman is instructing the man in the respective sensory activity, for example, by holding up a mirror to him, playing a musical instrument, holding a blossom to his nose, or

figure 32
Frans Floris, *Touch* (1561)

handing him a piece of fruit. The emblematic tradition does not assign an object to the fifth sense as it does to the other four senses. But that is not the only reason why feeling is depicted in these scenes as direct skin contact, as an intimate, erotic embrace. The medium here is not an additional object but the concrete body of the other, something that becomes very clear in a series by Hendrick Goltzius (figure 33). The partially undressed man takes the woman, whose breasts are already bared, into his arms, while a turtle—as a negative symbol of sexual sin—is crawling across his lap. The location for this erotic tête-à-tête is an interior room concealed by curtains and drapes, a space that—in contrast to the preceding scenes, which often take place outside—points to intimacy and closeness.

In Abraham Bosse, on the other hand, *tactus* is the only sense that is confined to a pair of lovers (figure 34). To it alone is attributed intimate twosomeness, while hearing (*auditus*), for example, is defined as the sense of collective experience through the depiction of a group making music together. Once again *tactus* is interpreted as the sense of the erotic by illustrating it with an intimate rendezvous in a closed space. A nobleman and a lady are in a bedchamber. She is sitting on his lap; he has already taken off his hat; her stocking has slipped down, revealing her bare knee. The man is touching her décolleté, and she is lovingly running her fingers through his beard, while a chambermaid (with a disapproving expression unnoticed by them) is letting down the curtain on the bed. A warming fire in the fireplace hints not only at the expected shedding of the clothes and the lovemaking to come but also, in keeping with the iconographic tradition, at another quality of the tactile sense: the sensation of temperature.

It is quite obvious why such scenes representing *tactus* mark the conclusion of a series of the five senses (and in so doing simultaneously classify this sense as the lowest): whereas in the preceding scenes, which should also be understood as chronologically prior, the various senses are being sharpened and stimulated by having the body expose itself to the most diverse tastes and sensations, the scene in the fifth engraving—which is sensual in both meanings of the word—represents the goal and climax of this stimulation. The series can thus be read as the tableau of a seduction that is based on an Eve motif. That is why it always has to be the woman who is seducing the man into the so-called sinful pleasures (in Goltzius, this is especially clear in the allegory of *gustus*, where the woman is handing her companion a piece of fruit). In these series, not only touch specifically but perception as such tend to involve not an empirical discovery of the world

figure 33
Hendrick Goltzius, *Touch* (1595)

Quæ conspecta nocent, manibus contingere noli,
Ne mox peiori corripiare malo.

figure 34

Abraham Bosse, *Tactus/Le Toucher*
(seventeenth century)

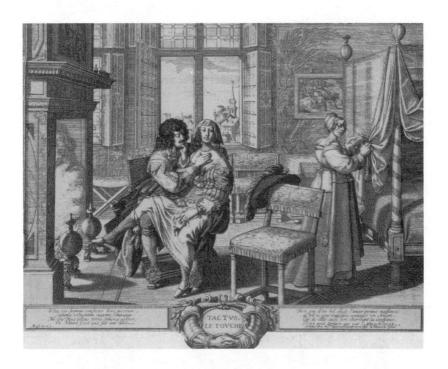

but an active and desired sensual pleasure. This second existential meaning of the senses, which had already become a theme in the Middle Ages in moralistic contexts, acquires here a new and primary rank—though with a contrary semantics.

Beginning in the Renaissance, the quarrel between the artistic genres (the so-called *paragone*) was no longer seen merely as a question regarding the hierarchical ranking of what had until then been discussed as the sister arts of painting and poetry, which is how the classical topos *ut pictura poesis* had framed the matter;[3] instead, it was increasingly seen also as a rivalry between sculpture and painting. This debate was about which could lay claim to primacy: sculpture, which is also accessible to the sense of touch, or painting, which can be perceived only visually. While the ability to mimic nature with ever greater perfection was discussed during the Renaissance, from the middle of the seventeenth century on it was the reception of art that stood at the center of attention. Thus the quarrel of the arts gradually became also a quarrel of the senses.

In the seventeenth century, this debate is then directly elevated into a theme in painting. José Ribera's *El éscultor ciego* (The blind sculptor), for example, shows an aged artist groping the head of a classical sculpture with his hands (figure 35). The work, painted in dark hues, illustrates the world of a blind person: cut off from the light, he experiences things exclusively through touch, though that experience is concentrated and interiorized, as it were. The motif of the blind sculptor goes back to the historical figure of the Italian artist Giovanni Francesco Gonnelli of Gambassi, who, after losing his sight, attained fame in the seventeenth century as a blind sculptor under the name "Il cieco di Gambassi" (Museo del Prado 1997, 180). During a stay in Rome, Ribera created a series of the five senses, in which the allegory of touch was likewise depicted as a blind man feeling the head of a sculpture. That is also the reason scholarship has given the work shown here, a creation independent of the series, the subtitle *El tacto*. It became the model for a whole host of works that dealt with this subject. In Ribera, the sense of touch is established as the sense of art, which is based not only on a specific perceptual aesthetics but also on a particularly sensitive aesthetics of production.[4]

Livio Mehus, in his painting *Il cieco di Gambassi* (The blind man of Gambassi, seventeenth century), shows an artist who is groping the head of an ancient sculpture with his right hand while his left hand is desperately trying to feel what is on the flat surface of a painting (figure 36). Apart from

figure 35

José Ribera, *El éscultor ciego*
(The blind sculptor) (1632)

the obvious motif of the quarrel of the arts, the depiction can also be read as the abstract allegory of mediality, in which the sensitive artist is connecting the three-dimensionality of the sculpture with the surface of the canvas—not through optical transference but by means of his inner eye, his empathy, and his hands. The artist in Mehus has bared shoulders and legs, an unusual depiction. It alludes to his lack of precious garments and points to his skin as the organ of sensibility. The nature of the exposure, reminiscent of female figures, feminizes the artist and assigns him to the world of interior space. The senses of the skin, Mehus seems to suggest, are not only organs for the active exploration of external objects via touch (as in Ribera) but also organs of self-awareness.

George Berkeley, in *An Essay Towards a New Theory of Vision* (1709), advances the thesis that seeing in perspective necessarily derives from original experiences of touch. The eye itself is capable only of detecting surfaces and colors; three-dimensionality and corporeality, on the other hand, can only be experienced through touch (Berkeley 1948). It is only the sense of touch that teaches the eyes "to see . . . outside themselves," as Étienne Bonnot de Condillac later paraphrased Berkeley (Condillac 1930, 171). While the visual only shows representations and can therefore be deceived, the sense of touch alone confirms the materiality of things and thus their real existence. Johann Gottfried Herder, in his 1788 treatise *Plastik: Einige Wahrnehmungen über Form und Gestalt aus Pygmalions bildendem Traume* (Sculpture: Some observations on form and shape from Pygmalion's creative dream), differentiates sight and touch by juxtaposing painting and sculpture (1994, 249). He privileges tactile perceptions, those "heavy *conceptions* [*Begriffe*] to which we slowly and with effort grope our way," over the quick "*ideas of the face*" (250), which grasp merely "dream" and "narrative magic" (259). Herder's thesis, following Berkeley, is "that *everything that has form is discerned only by the feeling of touch; the face discerns only surface*, more precisely, not corporeal surface but only *visible light surface*" (247). The face thus perceives only shapes, while touch is capable also of experiencing bodies.

The sensualists (Berkeley, Condillac, Herder) refer also to experiments with individuals blind from birth, which were popular in the eighteenth century. It was discovered that blind people who were given sight by surgical procedures were initially incapable of seeing three-dimensional shapes and spatial relationships and could only see two-dimensional surfaces, even though they had previously been perfectly able to perceive three-dimensionality by touch. The "groping, undistracted blind person,"

figure 36

Livio Mehus, *Il cieco di Gambassi* (The blind
man of Gambassi) (seventeenth century)

Herder believed, was able to gather "much more complete conceptions of corporeal qualities" than "the seeing person who glides over on a beam of sunlight" (1994, 249–250). Ribera's sculptor is a prototype of this ideal, concentrated haptic perception—personified in the figure of the "noble blind man" (Manthey 1983, 193)—as idealized in the aesthetic theory of the late eighteenth century.

Condillac, in his *Traité des sensations* (1754), emphasized that the model statue he was creating in imitation of the myth of Pygmalion and, by way of experimentation, endowed with the senses one by one, was able to say "I" only after it had received the sense of touch (1930, 75). Before that, when all it had was sight, smell, taste, and hearing, it did not yet know that it had a body (78). Only when the statue places its hands on itself is it able to finally discover its body as corporeal and spatial. And the existence of foreign objects is also something it realizes by means of touch, "when it touches things in which it does not find itself" (86). By contrast, if it places the hand on its own body, it "will find itself in each, because it will feel itself equally in both" (87). In this act of self-touching, "the same sentient being will reply from one to the other: this is myself, this is still myself" (88). Only in this way can it recognize itself as existent and unified. The human being acquires self-awareness through the active touching and tactile exploration of his or her own body surface.

"The object of touch is a force to which we are subject; the object of eye and ear a form we engender" (Schiller 1967, 195). This revealing quote from the letters published as *On the Aesthetic Education of Man* (1795) juxtaposes the proximal sense of touch—what Schiller calls "*Takt*"—with hearing and sight, which are defined as distal senses: while touch is something to which we are "subject" and therefore constitutes a "force," sensory perception with the eye and the ear is a willingly and actively engendered "form" and thus a kind of self-creation. In keeping with the Kantian approach, the topic of the senses is linked with the question of freedom; the ranking of the individual senses is undertaken in light of a postulated freedom or lack thereof on the part of the perceiving subject. But when Schiller says "*Takt*," is he speaking about the same sense of touch as the sensualist authors I mentioned earlier, who characterized *tactus* as the sense that revealed three-dimensionality and spatiality? The skin that Schiller is talking about here cannot turn away or close itself against stimuli. This sets it fundamentally apart from all other senses. Moreover, its sensory organs are not located exclusively on the head, the noblest part of man, as is the case with the other four senses, but are spread out over the surface of the entire body. Various epistemological strategies were devised to escape this problem of involuntariness and direct physicality—to achieve a liberation from what Schiller calls the touch to which we are "subject." The most important of these strategies were the reductionist equating of the sense of touch with the hand and the reduction of the multiplicity of the cutaneous senses to their tactile-haptic component. Both strategies are evident in the works on sensory aesthetics mentioned above, in which (as in more recent tracts on sensory physiology) the cutaneous senses are conceived of as active hand senses, with no real consideration given to their passive element, their being thrown into sensation.

Condillac makes an attempt at this differentiation between active and passive cutaneous senses by subdividing tactile perceptions into two kinds: "The one kind are extension, shape, space, solidity, fluidity, hardness, softness, movement, rest; the other kind are heat and cold and the different kinds of pleasures and pains. The relations of the latter are naturally indefinite. . . . But the relations of the former are known with more exactitude" (123).* This subdivision of the cutaneous senses into precise senses (designated for aesthetic perception) and imprecise senses (unsuitable for aesthetic perception) is determinative for the theory of art from the late eighteenth century on. Condillac differentiates clearly between what he classifies as the neutral and objective tactile perceptions of external form, surface composition, and movement and the highly subjective perceptions of heat, cold, pleasure, and pain, perceptions that determine a person's state of being. According to Condillac, only the tactile perceptions are capable of precise assessments of external objects and can therefore provide intersubjectively valid information, while the other skin sensations are imprecise. The former, moreover, are suitable for the reception (and production) of three-dimensional art, while the latter persist in a prereflective state.

Johann Jakob Engel, in his treatise "Über einige Eigenheiten des Gefühlsinnes" (On several characteristics of the sense of touch, 1793), likewise emphasizes that feeling, in contrast to the other senses, possessed not a single "tool" but a wide variety of them and specified furthermore that

* The English translation reads as follows in the original: "The relations of the former are naturally indefinite. . . . But the relations of the latter are known with more exactitude" (Condillac 1930, 123). This is clearly a mistranslation of the original, and I have therefore corrected it in the passage cited.—Trans.

those tools were different in "structure" (1805, 207). Entirely in keeping with tradition, Engel divides the human senses into coarser senses (taste and smell) and finer senses (face and hearing). He also draws on John Locke's differentiation between original and derived qualities of matter. The former are extent, shape, solidity, and movement, as physical qualities of things; the latter are, for example, colors, heat, and cold, as qualities accessible to human beings only via reception. Against the backdrop of these premises, he arrives at the following conclusion: "Feeling, to the extent that it is perceiving derived characteristics, is in this respect analogous to the coarser senses; to the extent that it perceives original qualities, it is analogous to the finer senses" (207). The finer senses make possible the "sensation of the beautiful" in the reception of art and supply "material for scientific understanding." The coarser senses, on the other hand, serve only "lust" and are therefore "merely animalistic" in nature (210–211)

Engel maintains that when it comes to the skin sensations of derived qualities (specifically, temperatures; he does not mention pleasure and pain explicitly, though they appear to be included), "the entire body is but a single organ." This accounts for the uniqueness of the sense of touch, which, in this respect, "does not possess a special tool all its own" (207–208). In contrast, when it comes to the "original qualities of extent and shape," feeling has "*two organs*," namely, both the hands as well as "every other part of our body that can more or less bend itself around an object; we can, as it were, feel with the tongue, between the lips, with the toes, which we do not at all train for this purpose, as well as with other movable parts of the body" (208–209). Because of this duality—the perception of both original and derived qualities—the resemblance between face, hearing, and feeling is always "imperfect" (209): it refers primarily to the tactility of the hands (and of the other "movable parts of the body") and leaves out the perception of derived qualities, which tend to be less precise, and the rest of the body's surface.

As Engel sees it, face, hearing, and the finer feeling have the advantage over smell, taste, and coarser feeling in that they are able to distinguish rapid series of successive impressions, are "better able to keep pace with the imagination," and are capable of "a *definiteness*, an *exactitude*" (271–272). Engel defines a finer sense as follows: "It is one that can distinguish a variety of impressions, unadulterated and pure, in very close proximity, and, because of the definiteness and exactitude of these impressions themselves, is capable of perceiving a precisely defined relationship between them. This definition of the finer sense makes that of the coarser sense obvious" (224). The internal differentiation of the cutaneous senses into fine and coarse eventually leads Engel to subdivide the *tactus* into two senses: the coarser "feeling" and the finer manual "touch" (*Getast*)—skin and hand, that is. The explanation he offers is "that the organ of feeling, since it is the entire outer body, does not coincide with that of touch any more than it does with all other organs" (227). The "touch" of the hand, as an independent sense, thus has as little in common with the cutaneous sensation of temperature and pain, or the touch perceptions and pleasurable sensations of the body surface, as it does with taste or sight, for example.

The differentiation introduced by Engel is continued, among other places, in Carl Gustav Carus's subclassification of a "cutaneous sense as feeling" and "a cutaneous sense as touch [*Getast*]," which he proposed in his work *Natur und Idee* (Nature and idea, 1861). In Carus's view, the former eventually develops "at the highest level, and by means of the element of movement, into the sense of touch," and as such it then brings "to awareness not only the spatial-external world that comes into contact with it, but at the same time also the location of its own body" (1975, 384). As the criteria for the distinction between "feeling" and "touch," Carus, unlike Engel and Condillac, therefore does not highlight the specific qualities of the object being perceived but the question of whether a perception is motorically active or passive. This kind of distinction between touch and the involuntary skin sensations seems useful, especially if it places the emphasis on the aspect of action and passivity—instead of applying, as Engel still did, more precise and more diffuse perceptual qualities as distinguishing criteria. The unreflected equating of the felt skin of one's own body and active touching, which together are supposed to make up the fifth sense, has led to a good deal of confusion and lack of clarity in the theory of perception, which has not necessarily done much for the skin as a tool of perception and a place of self-perception. But a separation of the two is only meaningful if it is no longer a question of establishing a hierarchy, a *paragone* of the cutaneous senses, but merely of acknowledging their plurality.

Hermann Schmitz, in his phenomenology of corporeality, places the emphasis on the difference between active and passive perceptions. He distinguishes perceptions that are "given *directly*" (are felt "in one's own body") and perceptions experienced "through mere looking and touching" (felt through sensory perceptions). The self-perception of one's own body through sight and touch here resembles the tactile perception of external objects. Schmitz describes it as "bodily" (*körperlich*), whereas he calls the phenomena conveyed directly "corporeal" (*leiblich*) (1982a, 11–12). Something is corporeal if its locality is "absolute" and "bodily" if its locality is "relative"—that is to say, related to the other places of one's own body (6). A locality is relative, according to Schmitz, if it is characterized by spatial orientation, meaning that it can be defined through a system of relationships of location and distance whereby several localities render one another mutually identifiable. The structure of these relative localities turns into the kind of habitual body schema we know from psychoanalysis (and which Merleau-Ponty introduced into philosophy). That schema also includes those body parts that cannot be experienced directly but only visually or tangibly, such as nails or hair (6 and 25). By contrast, Schmitz defines the "absolute-local certitude" such that it is identifiable even without a spatial orientation. Absolute localities form islands of perception in the sensation of one's own body (6 and 12).

What is significant for my purposes is that the body schema is not only created through external self-perception but also maintained by it, while the body islands are accessible to direct—that is, essentially passive—sensation. Touching and looking are in this sense elements of an active self-exploration, while the sensation of one's own body happens involuntarily. One's own touched (and visually examined) body possesses, on the outside, a sharp and flat boundary in the skin. The felt body, however, has no defined surfaces, even if it has mass (Schmitz 1992, 39–40). As Schmitz would have it, the touching self-perception that spreads over one's own body is thus, unlike the sensation of one's own body, a subject-object constellation in which one's own body is given the status of an object that is explored by means of the hand. To illustrate this split, Schmitz uses the example of a person with a fever, who perceives his forehead through his own-body sensation as hot but is surprised to find on touching it with his hand that it "actually feels quite cool" (1982a, 13). The distinction between the two perceptions arises from the fact that their self-reference is different, which can be encapsulated in the distinction between "I am warm" (own-body sensation) and "it feels warm."

Own-body sensation should not be seen as an additional sense that can be added to the other senses, like the *sensus communis* in medieval philosophy or Engel's "touch" as differentiated from "feeling." In the classic understanding, we are not dealing with a sense at all, since it is not about the exploration of the world but about a present becoming-aware of the self as a body in the world. But that is also what characterizes the cutaneous senses described as passive in this chapter; although Schmitz does not directly highlight these senses as own-body sensations, they do share the essential characteristics (directness, insular structure, absoluteness of locality). Schmitz shortchanges self-touching, however, by seeing one's own touched body merely as an object: after all, the body also feels the contact with its own hands, and in this way it attains awareness of itself—something physiology has called the phenomenon of "double sensation," with a touching and a touched component (Grosz 1994, 35–36).

Skin felt by way of one's own body as the place of self-consciousness often becomes a theme in literature, and it is, of course, even less amenable to codification than tactile gestures, for example.[5] Here, I should emphasize that in many instances where texts talk about feeling, it remains unclear whether this relates to psychic or corporeal sensation. In addition, according to Schmitz's theory of corporeality, feelings are not disembodied, hidden on the inside; instead, they are atmospheres poured out into undetermined expanses and often perceptible in a spatial direction. They represent "the keys of own-body sensation," of which one becomes aware only "when directly affected" (Böhme 1997a, 535). Merleau-Ponty has likewise emphasized the urgent need for us to abandon the notion of "the body as a transmitter of messages" (1962, 10), for perception is "defined as access to truth" (xvi). Accordingly, there is no being prior to perception; instead, bodily presence is experienced only in the moment of perception itself. The next chapter will show how this is to be understood through an examination of selected literary texts.

11 touchings

On the Analogous Nature of Erotic, Emotive,
and "Psychic" Skin Sensations

This chapter will draw on three literary texts to examine the connection between skin perceptions and bodily presence that I outlined in the last chapter. In addition, I will inquire to what extent it is at all possible to define perceptions of touch by the entire body surface as either erotic or neutral. I shall begin with two stories by Robert Musil, narratives that recount events narrowly from the subjective perspective of a single character. In these texts, as in Michael Ondaatje's novel *The English Patient*, the third selection, special significance is accorded to cutaneous sensations, or, as in Ondaatje, the painful loss of these sensations becomes the motif of the story.

Musil's story "Young Törless" (1906) concentrates on the inner conflict of the title character, whose psychological development is depicted as a process of individuation. Törless's perceptions, thoughts, and sensations form the filter of the radically subjective narrative. At the center are the feelings of the boarding school student Törless for his classmate Basini, who is caught stealing and is subsequently blackmailed, tortured, and sexually abused by Beineberg and Reiting, two students of the same cohort. At first Törless is only a passive observer of the dependency relationship between Basini and his tormenters, which stretches over months and becomes increasingly sadomasochistic. Eventually, Törless himself begins an erotic relationship with Basini, one that is marked by a constant ambivalence between "revulsion" and "urge" (1998, 118) or, as Musil puts it in a later passage, a "wavering between shame and desire" (145).

The inner sensations that draw Törless, despite his resistance, to Basini frequently find their corporeal expression on the skin of his entire body. The events evoke a specific body sensation, which Törless himself defines as a kind of "shudder"—as "a sensation of which the others knew nothing, but which must evidently be of great importance for his future life" (82). For Törless "realized that, with some extra faculty he had, he got more out of these happenings than his companions" (82). Whether Musil means by this extra faculty the cutaneous perceptions of the body surface with which Törless, figuratively speaking, lets himself be touched by the world or an inner sense (as a deeper understanding) is deliberately left open, because it is both. In this way the body "becomes the bearer and sensitive medium of feeling" (Frier 1976, 241).

When Törless, early in the story, is listening in the attic to the blows inflicted by Reiting and Beineberg and Basini's whimpering in response to them, he feels an urge to drop down from his squatting position: "It was an urge to press his body flat against the floorboards; and even now he could feel . . . how through the flesh and bones of his body his heart would slam against the wood" (1998, 80). The choice of the word "through" is revealing in that Musil in this passage, as in various others, is describing the skin as the felt boundary of a self "contained within it," as a phenomenal-felt space. This is one aspect that Schmitz neglected in his theory of corporeality: the perception of the body surface in contact with the materials surrounding it. The intense sensations that Törless feels in his skin then become erotic sensations: "An agreeable sensation went through Törless when he heard this whimpering. A tickling shudder, like thin spidery legs, ran up and down his spine, then contracted between his shoulder blades, pulling his scalp tight as though with faint claws. He was disconcerted to realise that he was in a state of sexual excitement" (81). The initially inexplicable "shudder," the indeterminate sensations on his back and the back of his head, eventually cause an erection. What begins as rather polymorphous sensations on the body surface culminates finally in genital arousal.

In a different passage, Musil describes Törless's sensations as similarly spread over the body. Here, they are not erotic but connected with self-awareness, with the state of wakefulness and the feeling of being alive: "Slowly the dream receded—slowly, like a silk cover slipping off the skin of a naked body, without ever coming to an end" (102). Wakefulness is compared with a state of undress, with a nakedness that is gradually freed from the cover of the dream. This envelopment by imagination and images is replaced by the cloth that is actually felt on the skin, which Törless suddenly becomes aware of: "But then again suddenly he became conscious of how his body was lapped by the mild, warm linen" (102). The fact that Musil emphasizes that Törless's skin was touched all over, "lapped," reveals once again the extent to which we are dealing with a passive, all-embracing cutaneous sensation. The sensual perception in turn becomes an "image"— that is, it becomes once again something rather imaginary:

> In his skin, all over his body, there awoke a sensation that suddenly turned into an image in his memory. When he was quite small . . . there had been times when he had a quite unspeakable longing to be a little girl. And this longing too had not been in his head—oh no—nor in his heart either—it had tingled all over his body and gone racing round under his skin. . . . Today, for the first time he felt something similar again—again that longing, that tingling under the skin.
> It was something that seemed to partake simultaneously of body and soul. It was a multifold racing and hurrying of something beating against his body, like the velvety antennae of butterflies.
>
> (102–103)

The childhood feelings of which Törless becomes aware in this transition stage from sleep to wakefulness, and that he simultaneously experiences again as though new, are dominated by the idea of possessing a female sexual identity. This longing "to be a little girl" is felt as a jubilant, arousing aliveness of the entire body surface, below which the sensation was racing, tingling. But at the same time we are told that this "something" is beating against his body, meaning that it evoked skin sensations everywhere from outside.

As in Musil's play *Die Schwärmer* (The visionaries, 1921), the young man's awakening sexuality is, by contrast, characterized by the fact that the sensations are located in the genitals and do not spread unbounded over the entire body. The latter state, which is depicted as an involuntary experience, occurs only in girls and in boys prior to puberty. In *Die Schwärmer*, one protagonist offers this description of the qualitative difference between "boy" and "man" and a woman: "As a boy, you see, as a naive child, I received, as soon as I saw you, a feeling of happiness diffused throughout my entire body, a feeling from which I had no way of saving myself. How much stronger it all is—in a man, where it becomes localized and erupts like an abscess!" (1957, 346). Törless feels the irritating difference between childhood and adulthood in much the same way in the scene in the attic and during the following night. With this juxtaposition, Musil comes remarkably close to Freud's conception of pregenital, infantile sexuality, the so-called polymorphously perverse feelings outlined in *Three Treatises on Sexual Theory* (1905) (Freud 1953, 125 ff.). Freud locates the transition from the polymorphous excitability of all skin zones to genital sexuality in puberty, the very phase of life that Törless is in. The passage quoted above describes the still childish sexuality, in contrast to later experiences, as an essentially more diffuse sensation that still arouses the entire body surface.

When Basini suddenly appears naked in front of Törless, the latter is at first blinded by the feminine-androgynous "image" of nakedness. He experiences a visual fascination, but that is immediately replaced by a skin sensation of warmth and burning:

> The sudden sight of this naked snow-white body, with the red of the walls dark as blood behind it, dazzled and bewildered him. Basini was beautifully built; his body, lacking almost any sign of male development, was of a chaste, slender willowyness, like that of a young girl. And Törless felt this nakedness lighting up in his nerves, like hot white flames. . . . There was an infatuating warm exhalation coming from the bare skin, a soft, lecherous cajolery. And yet there was something about it that was so solemn and compelling as to make one almost clap one's hands in awe.
>
> (1998, 119–120)

Törless, instead of giving in to the initially overwhelming sensations, forces Basini to get dressed and tell him what the others are doing to him. He discovers that they are sexually abusing him, tormenting and beating him, and that Beineberg pokes him with needles "to see if something doesn't manifest itself at some point or other on the body" (124). While Törless is dazzled and aroused by Basini's naked skin, Beineberg is penetrating this same body surface with needles in an attempt to extract perceptions forcefully. It is only later, when Törless is lying in his bed alone, that he is once again swept away by the "vision of Basini, of his bare, glimmering skin" (129).

Törless falls into a dreamless sleep, with "only an infinitely pleasant warmth spreading soft carpets under his body." After a while he awakens—to find Basini sitting on his bed. In an instant, Basini has "flung off his night-clothes and slid under the blankets and was pressing his naked, trembling body against Törless" (129). In anguish "Törless pushed his arms against Basini's shoulder, holding him off. But the hot proximity of the soft skin, this other person's skin, haunted him, enclosing him, suffocating him" (130), so that eventually he gives up his resistance. In this sequence, the skin is depicted as an organ of sensitivity that triggers an almost magnetic attraction. Musil describes the seduction scene as an "atmospheric field" (Schmitz 1982b, 314), as the involuntary attraction of skins and not (as so often in literature) of looks or other erotic-visual body signals.

Because Musil is interested in the transition from boyhood to manhood, he describes the impression that the feminine Basini makes on Törless against his will as one that sensitizes and arouses the latter's skin. In this phase of adolescence, desire is directed at an object in a manner that is still almost chaste. That is why Musil emphasizes on several occasions that this homoerotic urge is merely a passing passion, because Basini does not "arouse" in Törless a "desire that was—however fleetingly and perplexedly—a thorough-going and real one." Basini, we are told, with the "body of a little girl, a body still utterly sexless, merely beautiful," did not possess a defined male appearance (1998, 132). Musil describes a state that is not yet subject to the heterosexual matrix but only going to develop in that direction in due course. Significantly enough, Törless's attraction for Basini eventually ends when Basini's "bluish-tinged skin," covered with bruises and welts after months of torture in the attic, looks "like the skin of a leper" (152).

Culturally, the diffuse feeling spread over the entire body has been associated not only with infantile, prepuberty sexuality but also (and usually in a negative sense) with female sexuality. Freud, for example, speaks about children who, "under the influence of seduction . . . can become polymorphously perverse" and about the "average uncultivated woman in whom the same polymorphously perverse disposition persists" (1953, 191). In formulating this thesis, Freud was drawing on statements made by the paranoid Daniel Paul Schreber, who had said that "the feeling of sensual pleasure—whatever its physiological basis—occurs in the female to a higher degree than in the male, involves the whole body" (Schreber 1955, 205; Freud 1953). A 1954 quote from the psychologist Lawrence Frank reveals that this claim does not represent an outmoded way of thinking from the turn of the nineteenth century. Speaking about the development of tactile sensitivity in the sexes, Frank states that "the tactual-cutaneous sensitivity of the genitals at puberty becomes more acute and in the male becomes the major focus of his sexuality, while the female seems to retain more the larger overall tactuality of infancy" (Frank 1954, 137, quoted in Montagu 1971, 172). There is no need to comment further on the obvious value judgment this statement implies; nor do I wish to address Luce Irigaray's and Hélène Cixous's assertion that the female sex is superior precisely because of this plurality of feeling. I shall merely note that this way of thinking has evidently shaped the modern world down to our day.

Perhaps that explains why Musil's story "The Perfection of Love" (1911) describes sensations that are, in part, very similar to those experienced by young Törless, even though the focus of this story is on a woman who is already married. Using the stylistic device of the interior monologue, Musil employs a very rudimentary plot: Claudine, the main character, takes a journey by train to visit her illegitimate daughter at her boarding school. During her stay, she eventually—after long hesitation—allows herself to be seduced by a travel acquaintance. When it comes to the protagonist's feelings, all her emotions and perceptions are so deeply linked to skin metaphors and to notions of envelopment and touch that one can almost speak of a skin-soul. The kind of thinking that unites skin and soul was not foreign to Musil: in his notes to the novel *The Man Without Qualities*, we find the explicit term *"Hautich"* (skin ego) (1978, 2:1974)—which anticipates Anzieu's notion by half a century. In "The Perfection of Love," Musil completely dissolves the duality of psychic and corporeal feeling by rendering the two types of perception—even more radically than in Törless—phenomenologically and perceptually indistinguishable, with one continually merging into the other. Things that are felt, fantasized, and imagined are captured in the same perceptual modes—for example, those of cold and heat, of expansion and contraction.

Claudine's skin perceptions and imaginings—much like those of young Törless—are particularly intense when she is falling asleep or waking up, that is to say, during transitional phases in which the boundaries of the self are blurred. The first night she awakens, for "she knew at once that it was snowing," and runs barefoot to the window:

She felt a wave of sudden unreal heat and she almost began to scream, faintly, the way cats sometimes scream in fear and desire, as she stood there, wide awake in the night, while soundlessly the last shadow of her actions, strange even to herself, slipped back behind the walls of her inner being and these grew smooth again. . . . The room was chilly; the warmth of sleep slipped away from her skin, and vaguely, unresistingly, she swayed to and fro with it in the dark as in a cloud of faintness. . . . And yet she realised obscurely that it was not the stranger who tempted her, but simply this standing and waiting, a fine-toothed, savage, abandoned ecstasy in being herself, in being alive, awake here among the lifeless objects—ecstasy that had opened like a wound. And while she felt her heart beating, like some frenzied wild creature trapped within her breast, her body in its quiet swaying drew itself up, like a great exotic, nodding flower that suddenly shudders with the infinitely expanding rapture of mysterious union as it closes round its captive.

(1998, 197–198)

Temperatures, body warmth, and the chill of the room: these skin sensations are synesthetic, for they are associated both with impressions of light and soundlessness and with an inner faintness, that is, with impressions from quite disparate perceptual realms. The precision of the body perceptions in their transitory succession—of temperatures, the beating of the heart, and the felt "ecstasy" of being alive—stands in peculiar contrast to the vagueness of motions and thoughts: we hear of nebulousness, of the obscurity of realization, of the strangeness of her doings and emotions. What Musil describes is a transitional state, one in which the perceiving body is wide awake and aroused while reflective thinking is still suspended. In this mood, Claudine senses her body as a protective, sheltering space that is filled with a beating heart, though it can envelope that heart but imperfectly. To be a human being (or also a woman) is defined as an alive feeling of being "opened like a wound." The senses are imagined as this "wound." They are arrayed as the very thing that separates the human being from the world of objects, that by which he or she alone relates "to the world" (Merleau-Ponty 1962, 7).

When he says in the passage above that her body "closes round" her heart, Musil is locating the self in the interior of the body, though without equating it with the "heart," which she feels beating inside her like a strange "creature." Staying with the same image, Musil also observes that her past "had once been as close to her as her own body" (204) and that the body's "feelings and urges shut her in, closer than anything else" (213). Later, when she is on the way to her hotel room in the company of the stranger, "her body was trembling like an animal hunted down, deep in the forest" (221).

These passages, variations on the image of the body as a felt envelope, reveal a notion that conceives of the body as a "dwelling" and a "protective space" around the self, which the body firmly encloses—much like *Die Schwärmer* describes the human being as "wrapped in flesh" (1957, 316).

Contrasting with this secure feeling of corporeal "self-awareness" (1998, 210) is a scene in which Claudine is directly confronted by the stranger. Out on a walk together, she looks at her companion: "For a moment she felt as if thousands of crystals bound together to form her body were bristling and writhing. . . . A light rose within her, and the man on whom it fell all at once looked quite different in the glitter of it: his outlines shifted closer to her, twitching, jerking like her own heart, and she felt each of his movements inside her, passing through her body" (208). In this vision, Claudine's body is turned into a place of profane enlightenment. The light is a sensation of warmth and not primarily a visual experience. She feels the stranger from the inside *on* her body, the body *in* which she simultaneously senses herself. The skin becomes a kind of double interface between her and the world. Shortly afterward, this awareness of being in the body changes:

> She felt the man's eyes searching for hers, and all at once she was frightened and longed for the solid certainty of her own existence. She felt her clothes clinging to her, a husk enclosing the very last of the tenderness she knew to have been her own, and beneath that she felt her blood pulsing, and she could almost smell its quivering pungency. And all she had was this body that she was now to surrender, and this utterly other, spiritual feeling, this yearning beyond all reality—a sense of the soul that was now a sense of the body—ultimate bliss.
>
> (209)

Here, the body surface suddenly becomes the place of self-consciousness, which only establishes itself as such through a succession of various sensations: the "sense of the soul" is defined as a "spiritual feeling" and a "yearning beyond all reality" of the body, as the sensation of the clothes on her skin and of the throbbing blood beneath. The "husk" of the clothes enclosing her is the only certainty she finds in response to her longing for "her own existence"; even the skin does not appear to have a stabilizing function in this situation.

Following her body's state of supreme wakefulness in response to her companion's imagined touch, Claudine falls into the opposite state of insensitivity and numbness, which Musil once again relates to the skin's potential powers of perception: "She felt as if only some insensitive part of herself were present here among these people—her hair or nails, or a body that was all of horn" (210). In Musil, skins thus stands for the feeling or insensitive self as well as for the possibility of withdrawal and concealment—"one hides behind one's skin" (1957, 400), as it is explicitly expressed in *Die Schwärmer*. In *The Man Without Qualities*, Musil even goes so far as to say that all psychic-intellectual phenomena arise essentially from the all-embracing perceptions of the skin: "For in the last analysis, all thoughts come out of the joints, muscles, glands, eyes, and ears, and from the shadowy general impressions that the bag of skin to which they belong has of itself as a whole" (1995, 443).

This "displacement of the mind to the periphery" (443) is a concern that Musil explored in his literary works. It is striking how often he uses a comparative construct in which an inner state of awareness is defined more precisely through a skin analogy. A few illustrations: The state Claudine finds herself in is described as open "like a wound"; elsewhere she is tempted to yield herself to the stranger to feel "as though slashed open with knives" (1998, 213). She remembers her past, which "had once been as close to her as her own body" (204). Claudine is numb, as though she had "a body that was all of horn" (210); she shrinks from her feelings as though from "a delicate skin" (191). Inside of Törless is a certainty "like imperious knuckles rapping at a door," making him feel like "a woman who for the first time feels the assertive stirring of the growing child within her" (93). In *Die Schwärmer*, Anselm tells Regine that she is "nothing but a suppurating wound that will not heal" (1957, 342).

When self-awareness, the emotions, and the relationships of the protagonists are described in images of skin that is self-opened, forced open, closely enveloping, made of horn, suppurating, or "paper thin" (354), we realize yet again that Musil had already tested out his notion of the skin ego in the earlier works "Young Törless" and "The Perfection of Love," profoundly inner stories that explore subjective sensuousness. The skin metaphors and analogies thus not only function as ornamentation or graphic expressiveness but also express emotions and states of being that language is incapable of grasping directly. Figurative speech is therefore a necessary form of knowledge and expression. In it alone "becomes audible what both the speech of scientific reason and the speech of everyday life conceal" (Horn 1990, 87).

Musil's texts demonstrate the close connection of skin and self-awareness not only in relationship to present feeling and inner experience. He also uses skin metaphors when it comes to descriptions of emotional memory and the formation of character over time, as when we are told that all great passions leave their "brand-marks on the soul" (1998, 136) or that every hour of life leaves behind "only a very small pox mark" (1957, 349). In a draft letter to a lover in his adolescence, Musil defined "transplantation" as the process of giving a piece of one's own skin,

> so it can be applied to a wounded part of some other person. It then grows together with him and becomes a part of him and yet in the end it also remains a part of the body of the former. . . . For that is how it is with youthful friendships. People give each other some small, superficial piece of themselves—just a little flap of skin, a trifle, a little something, just the sort of thing one is capable of giving away at that time. But the other person then carries it with him unconsciously. And then if he is ever lonely, he suddenly remembers that he is actually carrying a piece of another loving person inside, and when he looks, it has grown and grown together with him, and it is with him in everything he does, and he is not at all alone.
>
> (1981, 55)

When Musil goes on to note that this process of the transplantation of the piece of skin is a *Magisterfrage* (a central question) for philosophers "who concern themselves with the problem of individuality" (55–56), it becomes clear that this is much more than a macabre analogy. What is at stake is the question of identity: to what extent is it possible at all to speak of individuality, or is every human being composed instead of a web of relationships, experiences, and memories, a web in which we can no longer identify the provenance of individual fragments? In Musil's reinterpretation, transplantation is not the insertion of a person's own tissue into an injured part of one's body; instead, the skin is grafted onto another person. At the same time, the notion of transplantation imparts something violent to the development of the self, in that—apart from physical pain—it emphasizes the necessity of intervention by an external agent. The process that Musil describes as "giving away" thus becomes an ambivalent sacrifice.

The complex interweaving of identity, memory, and skin that Musil defined in so exemplary a fashion in his transplantation metaphor is also central to Michael Ondaatje's *The English Patient* (1992). This novel is of interest in a number of ways to an examination of skin perceptions: not only because touching, feeling, tasting, and smelling—that is, perceptions of the lower senses—take up a good deal of space in the description of human interaction but also, and especially, because the main character is a man whose entire body is badly burned, whose skin sensations are profoundly reduced. What can we learn by examining this character about the connection of skin perceptions and self-awareness, in particular since his skin is all but gone?

In the frame story of the novel, a badly injured Count Lazlo de Almásy, the mysterious "English patient," whose identity has been destroyed beyond recognition and whose name is not known to anyone, finds himself toward the end of World War II in a bomb-shattered convent in Tuscany, where Hana, a young nurse, cares for him with selfless devotion. Only at the end of the novel do we discover that his burn wounds are directly related to her father's death, who was so badly burned in action that "the buttons of his shirt were part of his skin, part of his dear chest" (1996, 295).

Almásy, on the other hand, was not burned all over his body as the direct result of armed conflict (as the movie version hints at)[1] but through his fateful love for Katherine Clifton, the wife of a colleague who had supported Almásy's expedition into the North African desert. In a dramatic scene—of which we learn only through chronologically incoherent memory fragments as though from a feverish dream—Clifton, who has learned about the relationship between his wife and Almásy, crashes his plane in the desert of Uweinat in an attempt to kill Almásy on the ground, as well as himself and his wife, who is with him in the plane. His plan fails: Clifton dies, Katherine is seriously injured, Almásy escapes unharmed. He carries the dying Katherine into the "Cave of Swimmers," a cave decorated with prehistoric paintings, where they exchange some final words before Katherine loses consciousness.

When Almásy is pulling Katherine from the wreck, he sees that the crash, which has been fatal to her husband, has not left a single trace on the surface of her body: "There didn't seem to be a mark on her" (257). Her injuries are internal, not immediately apparent to the eyes, as a result of which Almásy does not know how serious they are. As he remembers it, before leaving her behind to look for help in the desert, he rubs her naked body with "sacred" color pigments that he scrapes from the walls of the cave with his hands—a desperate attempt to protect her body through a kind of magical ritual of touch: "He looked up to the one cave painting and stole the colours from it. The ochre went into her face, he daubed blue around her eyes. He walked across the cave, his hands thick with red, and combed his fingers through her hair. Then all of her skin, so her knee that had poked out of the plane that first day was saffron. The pubis. Hoops of colour around her legs so she would be immune to the human" (247). A little later, when the story has switched to a first-person narrative, Almásy describes the same scene this way: "When I turned her around, her whole body was covered in bright pigment. Herbs and stones and light and the ash of acacia to make her eternal. The body pressed against sacred colour" (260–261). This coloring of Katherine Clifton's body, which is transferred by touch, not only resembles a rite of immortality (or embalming), it is at the same time an act of tactile marking of zones, places, intensities, and touch points on the surface of her skin.

This scene is about making visible traces of touching and feeling, about the marking of "contingent singularities" (Serres 1985, 19), and thus about the establishment of the body surface as a place where individual and collective history meet. The skin, with its unique, "faithful, loyal tattooing," is more like a "bearer of traces" than a "bearer of banners" imitating icons or letters (21). In talking about the skin's bearing of traces—which he writes about, and not by accident, in connection with the impressionistic paintings of Pierre Bonnard—Serres uses the term "moiré," which describes a layered, restless, changing play of colors.

The coloring of Katherine's skin by the hands of her lover—which takes place, to be sure, when the female body has been rendered completely passive—is an act of touching that is not only contact with the surface but also imagined penetration. Thus Almásy's fantasies, reliving the farewell scene as he lies dying with burned skin, are marked by the penetrating merging with his lover's body: we are dealing with notions of merging, of receiving into oneself, of plunging into, and of sheltering oneself in somebody else. Ondaatje describes all this in images of an ecstatic experience of nature and with the archetypal forms of the tree, the river, and the cave. In death, sensual experiences and intense emotions are to find their mark on the skin:

> We die containing the richness of lovers and tribes, tastes we have swallowed, bodies we have plunged into and swum up as if rivers of wisdom, characters we have climbed into as if trees, fears we have hidden in as if caves. I wish for all this to be marked on my body when I am dead. I believe in such cartography—to be marked by nature, not just to label ourselves on a map like the names of rich men and women on buildings. We

are communal histories, communal books. We are not owned or monoga-
mous in our taste or experience. All I desired was to walk upon such an
earth that had no maps.

(1996, 261).

This passage revolves centrally around the difference between "marking"
and "labeling." Almásy understands this difference as that between the individual bearing of traces, on the one hand, and the marking with names—
as an integration into the symbolic order—on the other. The former is a
communal and communicative act, a leaving and taking on of traces, that
also permits additional markings by others and thus becomes a "communal
history." The latter, by contrast, is a conquering act of taking possession,
similar to the naming of geographic places or buildings after their discover-
ers or owners. The landscape of the skin that Almásy dreams of shortly before his death is thus not characterized by writing and names but by a plurality of memory traces. Although the body as a medium of memory is not
discursive, it is nevertheless historical. The tragic heart of the novel is the
fact that it is precisely a man who is so badly burned that he can hardly be
said still to have a skin of his own who fantasizes that his memories and sensations remain visible on his own skin and that of his lover in the form of
a tactile-erotic pattern. The protagonist's real slow death, which permeates
the entire novel, is that he himself neither bears memory traces nor is able
to retain them. The mention that Katherine, in the course of their relationship, inflicts a number of actual wounds on Almásy—bites, cuts, small
injuries (153–154)—reveals just how consciously Ondaatje interweaves the
bearing of epidermal traces and individual history.

The black encrustations on the surface of Almásy's body, the purple burns
on his shins, those skin surfaces that are the "colour of aubergine" (4), are
"volcanic flesh" (207), or simply "tarred black" (96) have erased everything
that was his history. In the course of the entire frame story, Almásy does not
utter his own name. It is not accident that Ondaatje leaves open the question
of whether he in fact no longer knows it as a result of the trauma or simply
refuses to say it because he is no longer the same person after the death of his
lover and the burning of his skin. "All identification consumed in a fire" (48)
is the word about him in the hospital, and this means that fire destroyed not
only that which formally identifies him as a person but also that which imparts identity. Almásy is nameless, like Wideman's albino Brother Tate. These
otherwise quite different literary characters share the connection between a
skin devoid of identity, the loss of a name, and the lack of social place.

To speak about "skinless perception" with respect to the "English patient," as Dietmar Kamper has suggested,[2] does not jibe with the phenomena that Ondaatje describes. For Almásy's body has retained all sense organs *except* for that of touch. Moreover, the notion of skinlessness tends to imply a phantasmal state devoid of covering that is not concerned with perception. Almásy, on the other hand, is *incapable* of perceiving anything with his skin, for he is "nonexistent except for a mouth, a vein in the arm, wolf-grey eyes" (247), as another character aptly remarks. That is also the outstanding impression in the film version: the paradox of a protagonist who, though constantly present under the gaze of the camera, is no longer present—because he lost his skin and with it not only the ability for mimic expression but also fundamentally the place where he could manifest himself visually. The novel describes him accordingly as a "ghost" (28) and a "bog-man of history" (96)—a terrifying specter of historical events.

Almásy's interactions with others are primarily verbal. The daily injection of morphine helps to suppress the pain that is ever present, even though most of the nerves of his skin were destroyed by the burns: "There is a face, but it is unrecognizable. The nerves all gone. You can pass a match across his face and there is no expression. The face is asleep" (28). The face, which is "asleep," stands metonymically for the death of the skin, for the slow dying of the injured man. The body's inability to move forces the patient to give himself over to his inner images, which are dominated by the loss of Katherine.

In the novel, unlike the film, Almásy returns to the Cave of Swimmers only three years later; he therefore knows for a certainty that Katherine is dead and her body should have long since decomposed. Still, he undresses outside the cave and approaches her remains naked, "as I would have done in our South Cairo room, wanting to undress her, still wanting to love her" (170). Remarkably enough the corpse appears to be intact. As he lifts it up and carries it out into the sunlight, the remnants of her clothes drop off "like cobweb," so that Katherine's body, too, is naked. Almásy marvels at the "airiness" (171) of her weight. He carries the body "as if it was the armour of a knight" (174)—an "armour" that is seemingly weightless. Ondaatje forgoes a description of what the corpse really looks like—that is unspeakable (and requires in the Hollywood version a shortening of the time period between the accident and Almásy's return to a few days). But the remark about "airiness" and the image of the naked corpse as "armour" suggests that Katherine's body, contrary to expectations, seems to consist only of skin, sheath, surface. As through some miracle, it decomposed from the inside; it is dried out and hollow.

We thus end up with a highly symbolic constellation, one that takes the use of the skin motif with respect to the lovers close to the realm of the mythical: while the only thing that remains of Katherine is her skin (which Almásy had impregnated by anointing it with sacred colors), Almásy survives his accident with all his body except for his skin. This configuration points to two things: first, it repeats the gender difference that I elaborated in the context of flaying, namely, the distinction between the (ideal) of male skinlessness and the reduction of the female to the skin as her essence and representation. The loss of the male skin is juxtaposed to a female inner loss (in the form of a lack of substance). Second, Ondaatje indicates in this way that on a symbolic level the two lovers would be whole only together—one body, in the Christological sense.

Almásy carries Katherine's hollowed-out skin-body through the desert to the airplane. He digs Clifton's plane out of the sand with his bare hands and manages to start it up. After placing the body in the plane, he sets out for the flight across the desert. Only in the air does he notice that the tank must have sprung a leak, oil is flowing into the cockpit. There is a short, the twigs that have become intertwined with Katherine's hair catch fire— ironically, they are acacia twigs, an old symbol of permanence and immortality. The plane crashes because Katherine's leaflike, dried skin, "the woman translated into leaves" (175), starts to burn. Eventually, Almásy himself is also on fire: "I fell burning into the desert. . . . I flew down and the sand itself caught fire. They saw me stand up naked out of it. The leather helmet on my head in flames" (5).

The nomads who see him emerging from the plane on fire and (more than) naked carry the badly injured Almásy on a stretcher to their camp. There, they soak large sheets in oil and cover his entire body until he is "anointed" (6)—in his recollection, he himself connects this treatment with this sacred rite. For weeks, the patient, who, surrounded by strangers, cannot communicate verbally, lies motionless, wrapped tightly in sheets. Only under the protective cover of darkness every night does one of the nomads carefully remove the sheets to check on his skin and refresh the tinctures. The raw flesh is never completely exposed: "Always there were ointments, or darkness, against his skin." At some point, a healer rubs his burned body with a greenish-black paste, "the most potent healer of skin" (9–10). These Eastern healing methods are interesting, because they stand out so sharply against the Western methods described later in the novel: while the Bedouins wrap Almásy every day in freshly soaked sheets, which give him a kind of oily, supple second skin, the doctors at the Italian hospital drip "tannic acid" on his raw flesh (48), a darkening acid solution that turns the skin into a hard, scabby crust, which is thereby able to tolerate contact with the air and "camouflages a burned man's rawness" (117).

With reference to Anzieu, it is possible to place the two treatments the helpless patient undergoes in context with the most extreme phantasms of skin ego disorders. In the Oriental method, the masochistic phantasm of flaying is reproduced over and over again: the protective (common) skin is peeled off the helpless burn victim, but he is then given a new one. The Western practice of encrusting the skin through chemicals evokes, on a symbolic level, the narcissistic phantasm of a "skin reinforced and invulnerable" (1989, 44–45). In connection with the fantasy of reinforced skin, Anzieu also speaks explicitly of a " 'crustacean' Ego" that replaces the skin's missing container and stimulus protection functions with a rigid armor (103). Both disorders of the skin ego are linked to the early childhood fantasy of a common skin with the mother:

> In the narcissistic phantasy, the mother does not share a common skin with her child, but gives her skin to him and he dresses himself in it triumphantly. . . .
>
> In the masochistic phantasy, the cruel mother only pretends to give her skin to the child. It is a poisoned gift, the underlying malevolent intention being to recapture the child's own Skin Ego which has become stuck to that skin, to strip it painfully from him in order to re-establish the phantasy of having a skin in common with him.
>
> (124)

The narcissistic personality wants to content itself with its own reinforced and thickened skin and does not wish to have a common skin with others, since that would reveal its dependency. The need to possess a skin ego armored to the extreme gives rise to an increasingly powerful fear of the decay of the rigidly sealed psychic container. What Anzieu interprets as the unconscious—and, in extremely fragile personality structures, at times necessary—supplementary achievement of the psyche, Ondaatje transforms, in his mythically transfigured images, into a painful physical reality.

Henceforth, the "English patient," whom the loss of skin has forced into the helpless regression of a (more than) naked infant, is existentially dependent on his caretakers. His situation among the Bedouins, in particular, resembles that of a premature baby, whose sole contact with the world comes through being swaddled and fed with prechewed food mixed with the saliva of another person. That the unwrapping of the sheets always takes place under the protective cover of darkness hints at an intuitive effort to avoid the shame that would result from the open display of this man whose entire skin has been disfigured. With regard to the care for patients with serious burns, Anzieu has noted that it poses a considerable psychological burden because of the extreme dependency it creates (202 ff.). One important defensive mechanism against this humiliating situation, according to Anzieu, is a (verbal) eroticizing of the relationship. In the novel, that occurs later between Hana and her patient, whom she cares for as a replacement for her deceased father but also like a lover:

> Every four days she washes his black body, beginning at the destroyed feet. She wets a washcloth and holding it above his ankles squeezes water onto him, looking up as he murmurs, seeing his smile. Above the shins the burns are the worst. Beyond purple. Bone.
>
> She has nursed him for months and she knows the body well, the penis sleeping like a sea horse, the thin tight hips. Hipbones of Christ, she thinks. He is her despairing saint. . . .
>
> She pours calamine in stripes across his chest where he is less burned, where she can touch him. She loves the hollow below the lowest rib, its cliff of skin. Reaching his shoulders she blows cool air onto his neck, and he mutters.
>
> (3–4)

This scene between Hana and the burned man, which alternates between maternal and erotic affection, is already described on the first page, and this moves touching in general and the skin injury in particular to the center of the theme. As the story unfolds, Hana's libidinous energy gradually shifts to the body of the Indian Kirpal Singh, called Kip, a pioneer in the English Army who takes up temporary quarters in the Tuscan convent and with whom she has a love affair. His brown skin with its multifarious shadings now becomes the object of her aesthetic-erotic desire. Kip's skin, a healthy (in both senses of the word) partial object, replaces the libidinous cathexis of her patient's injured skin. Thus the extensive, detailed skin descriptions in regard to Kip also have the function of showing how important the skin is for the perception of and desire for another person. Moreover, they also serve as a foil to the accounts of the patient's burned, insensitive, and unsightly skin.[3]

Essentially, what Ondaatje describes in *The English Patient* is a twofold interweaving: the female gaze at the male skin (Hana's perception of the patient and later of Kip) and the male gaze at the female skin (in Almásy's memories of Katherine). And the perceptions with the near senses are also extensive; we are given a depiction of how bodies are actually experienced: not primarily visually but essentially synesthetically. Perceiving a person means penetrating his or her aural closeness. And so we are told that Almásy and Katherine, during their love affair, were obsessed with penetrating the skin aura of their lover: "Their bodies had met in perfumes, in sweat, frantic to get under that thin film with a tongue or a tooth, as if they each could grip character there and during love pull it right off the body of the other" (173). The notion that character lies concealed in the body's smells, tastes, and fluids, and the desire to pull it off like a skin, makes clear the extent to which Ondaatje understands Almásy's loss of skin as an essential loss of identity and the extent to which the novel revolves concretely around this problem.

Using the figure of the burned Almásy and his failed relationship with Katherine Clifton, which ended by destroying both bodies, I have uncovered the extent to which sensual and emotive touches are understood as nondiscursive, invisible traces that, nevertheless, inscribe themselves on the skin. I mean this fully in the sense of Serres's image of a "skin dress" as a person's own "memory turned outward" (1985, 35–36). Remembrance is concretely tied to the presence of skin perceptions; the loss of these perceptions is tantamount to a loss of memory. The skin as a surface whose sensory-motoric tonus must be continuously maintained through external stimuli corresponds to the libidinous charging of the psyche, the maintenance of "inner tension" (Anzieu 1989, 139). The loss of that tension results in the fragmentation of the self, of memory, and of social relationships. Here, it becomes very clear that, in the final analysis, the skin ego cannot be an image ego at all: it is no visual image of the self (as psychoanalytical theory suggests) but instead a sensation ego that establishes and continuously sustains itself through tactile traces.

12 teletactility

The Skin in New Media

My excursion through the iconography and aesthetic of *tactus* and the meaning of skin in twentieth-century narrative texts has revealed the degree to which skin has been coded in Western thinking as a plural sense of closeness, intimacy, and eroticism. Contemporary attempts at interactive touch in new media follow the thread of this tradition: under the catchword "teletactility," the sensual experience of closeness and intimacy through touch is now being linked with anonymity and physical distance. In aesthetic theory, the skin as a sensory organ remained reduced, into the twentieth century, to the aspect Engel described as "*Getast*" (touching, groping), that is, primarily to the tactile exploration of objects with the hands (see Pinder 1948; Raphael 1989). Today, however, in the wake of proprioception and the integration of the body on the Internet, the aspect that was excluded in the late eighteenth century, subjective feeling, is starting to be given its due. It is important to emphasize this in view of the fact that even contemporary aesthetics speaks unreflectively about the sense of touch, which refers sometimes to the hand, sometimes to the entire skin with its multifarious sensors. Utopians today are less interested in the touch that was separated out in the eighteenth century than they are in subjective, inescapable feeling. It is precisely the parts of the cutaneous senses previously excluded from the aesthetic debate that are now being put to strategic use. The current trend toward the integration of the skin into the electronic network is conditioned by the (attributed) unfreedom, involuntariness, and eroticism of touch. It is all about the controlled creation of a loss of control, about a paradoxical interweaving of self-determination and exposure.

Beginning in the Renaissance, sight and touch in aesthetic discourse were usually juxtaposed as the highest and the lowest sense, respectively, with the negative quality of mere appearance attributed to sight and the positive ability to confirm materiality and real presence attributed to touch. The contemporary discussion picks up this tradition: the experience of authenticity through touch is supposed to generate the virtuality of the still missing dimensions of weight, mass, temperature, movement, and spatiality, so as to create a much more far-reaching simulation of real experience. The perceptual aesthetic theory of the eighteenth-century sensualists— what is seen or heard can be an illusion, while things explored by touch prove to be compellingly real—has been revived in cutting-edge discourses about immaterialization and virtuality. As a result, it is especially the cutaneous senses that have become the contact point of research and theorizing. The goal is no longer to have the body excluded from the electronic web (integrated merely via the eyes through eyephones, the ear through earphones, the hands through keyboards, data gloves, joysticks, or touchscreens) but to bring it into virtual reality as an entity with complete sensual perception.

The Australian performance artist Stelarc, who works with prosthetics, robotics, and tele-existence, has said that the body must "be situated out of the physical realm of biology and into the cyberzone of interface and expansion" (1995, 73), which would finally remedy what has hitherto been an "acute absence of physical presence . . . on the Internet" (1997, 156). Researchers are working on full bodysuits that turn the skin itself into an interface and support a complete immersion into data space, in this way making possible the communication across physical distances of not only sounds and images but in the future touch. The forms and functions of a conception of touch described as "teletactility" (Stenslie 1995, 180), although so far tested only in a few installations, not only demonstrate vividly the reductionism of current ideas of skin contact and intimacy but also provide insight into conceptions and phantasms of corporeality, sensory perception, and subjectivity at the end of the twentieth and the beginning of the twenty-first century.

The media theorist Derrick de Kerckhove has argued that the multi-sensory interactive systems of virtual reality are discovering the countless possibilities of the cutaneous senses in the first place. The issue is not only the technical simulation of touch but also new kinds of tactile experiences (1993, 152). Under the banner of printing, our culture, says de Kerckhove, has been dominated for centuries by the primacy of the visual (155); only through interactivity will it finally be able "to celebrate . . . the return of the sense of touch" (1996b, 335–336). De Kerckhove equates tactility with proprioception, which he defines as the "sense of one's own body, of being present with one's body" (1993, 139). Proprioceptive perception, which de Kerckhove claims is being "rediscovered" through new media, means to "feel" the relationship to one's environment instead of "visualizing" it, as we do now (139). In his view, proprioception serves to confirm virtual reality, as when he says: "The only sense we can really trust is touch, for it is where we also truly are" (167). This raises several questions: To what degree are the cutaneous senses actually attaining this prophesied new importance in the wake of the development of media and art? And is it possible that the distinction between near and far senses could become irrelevant in the future? Finally, I am interested in imparting the necessary historical context to contemporary concepts of touch and teletactile communication; in other words, I am interested in the genesis of the ideas that are active today.

Historically, as in the five senses series of the baroque, *tactus* was understood early on in the sense of intimacy, since—in contrast to sight, hearing, and smell—it essentially precludes a collective experience. In Abraham Bosse (figure 34), touch is the only sense that is confined to a couple; as such, it is today being purposefully applied in new media. The *subscriptio* on the right below the engraving could be translated as follows: even if it is sight that initiates love, merely looking at the desired object can never satisfy the lover, for whoever seeks pleasure can attain it only in touch, in the embrace. Though sight is defined as prior to touch, it is deficient when it comes to the fulfillment of desire. Likewise, the seventeenth-century epigram could be read as a kind of motto for contemporary trends in interactive art, where efforts are being made to compensate through touch for the sense of dissatisfaction left behind by the eye (and ear). The closing of distance promised by skin contact is intended as the remedy for the deficiency of sight, namely, its ontic distance. It is therefore no coincidence that cybersex installations were the first to experiment with the integration of skin.

To illustrate how tactility and skin are understood in new media, I shall look at a prominent example. In the *Cyber SM-Projekt* that Stahl Stenslie and Kirk Woolford installed at the Kölner Hochschule für Medien (Cologne College for Media) in 1993, as well as in Stenslie's subsequent *Inter-Skin-Projekt*, participants were hooked up to a "real-time, multisensory communications system for two users" (Stenslie 1995, 179). The participants wore " 'intelligent' Touch Suits" (figure 37), which turn the "body itself into the interface of communication" (184). Despite their spatial separation, the wired bodies can touch and stimulate each other—for example, one male participant in Paris was hooked up with a female participant in Cologne. In the *Cyber SM-Projekt*, this was still done via a visual interface: the users saw a body representation on the screen and by inputting data with a keyboard they imparted the sensations of pressure, cold, heat, and vibration to the body of the other person. However, what appeared on the screen was not the actual body of the person at the other end of the hookup but an arbitrary body shape selected from a large body bank. The intermediary visual interface was abolished in the *Inter-Skin-Projekt*: now participants touched their own bodies and transferred this touch via the Touch Suit directly to the skin of the other person. To quote Stenslie:

> The communications system places the emphasis on the conveyance and the reception of a sensual contact. If I touch my own body, I am at the same time also touching the other participant. . . . Above all, I have to do to myself what I want the other person to feel. This turns my own body into a self-referential object of communication. There is no possibility of forgetting oneself or of hiding behind the actions one is performing. If I touch my genitals, the other person will notice that I am touching them. Such a one-on-one transfer of stimuli creates a direct, immediate, almost intimate form of communication.
>
> (180)

Apart from the fact that it is highly questionable whether touch can in fact be adequately captured in the term "communication" (more on this below) and that the suit made up of individual sensors from the outset divides the body into sensual and nonsensual parts, what is striking is that the author is

figure 37
Stahl Stenslie and Kirk Woolford,
Cyber SM-Projekt (1993)

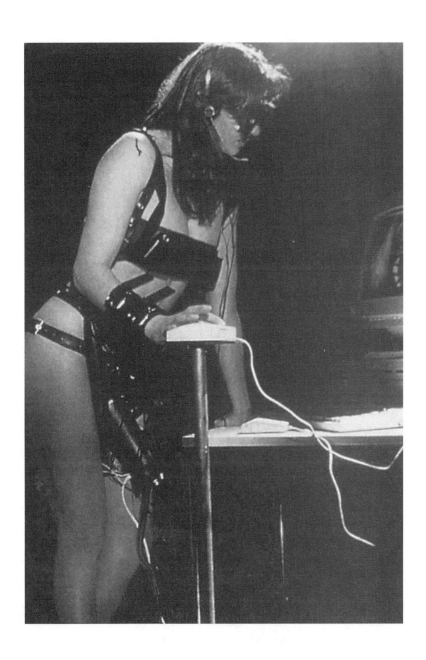

speaking about a "one-on-one transfer" of stimuli. This notion of an analogous transferability reduces touch to a mechanistic model, one that excludes both the dimension of atmospherics as well as every subjective element of any kind (an absence that is especially glaring in the case of erotic contact). Moreover, the entire setup rests on the idea of pushing a button or using a keyboard, except that now it is the body surface itself that is used in this way. Although the inventors admit that it will be many years before the sensors and stimulators "are as good as the skin" (Woolford 1995, 191), even with substantially more sophisticated technology, the questionable postulate that touch can be analogously transmitted remains. When Woolford, in the context of these cyberprojects, claims that "for human beings, a touch is usually sexual" (193), this represents precisely the kind of one-dimensional reduction of the cutaneous senses that I highlighted with regard to the five senses series.[1] In contrast to the necessary spatial proximity of the partner in the five senses series, the slogan for wired tactile eroticism is "intimate but anonymous" (Stenslie 1995, 182). Paul Virilio was therefore right when he spoke of a "paradoxical skin perspective," one in which the "electromagnetic prophylactic" replaces "the fragile protection of the condom" (1994, 195).

Incidentally, the characteristics of teletactile forms of touch that I have identified (intimacy without closeness, the intermediation of machines, contact under masks), show an astonishing convergence with current trends in the business of prostitution, which Cora Molloy (1996, 300) has encapsulated in the following formulas:

- Nudity is out. Sensual perception is heightened through a second skin. Automata pave the way to computer-directed cybersex.

- Sex is becoming more elaborate and thereby less spontaneous. Complex preparations require a so-called machine park and a well-stocked warehouse.

- The sexual experience of the future is autoerotic and narcissistic. It requires more of an organizer (male or female) than a partner. Over the medium term, self-productions will rationalize away even the organizer.

Teletactility revolves in a very similar way around the dialectic of self-determination and self-exposure, around the paradoxical linkage of intimacy and anonymity. But the inventors of teletactility keep talking about communication, not the gratification of lust.

In its broadest meaning, the concept of communication refers to messages and the transmission of information. The question is whether touch (in quotidian reality but also in the installations just examined) can even be adequately subsumed under this concept.[2] The skin as such is highly unsuitable as an interface, as it cannot guarantee an understandable coding or decoding.[3] To be sure, individual gestures of touch—for example, placing a hand on the shoulder or arm of another person—can carry a diversity of meanings; however, nonconventionalized gestures cannot be decoded like linguistic signs. Moreover, many kinds of touch do not *mean* something; they already *are* something (for instance, affection, desire, or anger). They do not directly stand for something else, representative like language, but are without reference. A touch thus possesses communicative character only if it is understood as such. What is questionable—for instance, with respect to the Inter-Skin system—is to what extent messages can or are supposed to be exchanged to begin with, especially since the participants do not know each other at all. Is this not instead a new variety of the erotic, one in which understanding, as opposed to experiencing, no longer plays any role at all? The concept of teletactile communication is therefore open to question: the fact is that it is not about coded and codable perceptions or information but about proprioception that is diffuse and as all-embracing as possible. Moreover, the goal is to blur the boundaries between what is perceived and what is performing the perception. This means, with respect to the classic model of communication, that it will no longer be possible to distinguish between sender and receiver.

Stelarc has also developed a system of distance touch. But his Stimbod system functions differently from Inter-Skin in that the receptive body is not passive and does not receive external stimuli by means of a data suit. Instead, the system of electronic muscle stimulation induces the body to touch itself and then to feel this touch. When Sandy Stone asked him about the "cyber-sexual implications," Stelarc, shown here wired with the necessary stimulators and sensors and also hooked up to an electronic third hand (figure 38), responded by saying: "If I was in Melbourne and Sandy was in NY, touching my chest would prompt her to caress her breast. Someone observing her would see it as an act of self-gratification, as a masturbatory act. She would know though that her hand was remotely and perhaps even divinely guided! Given tactile and force-feedback, I would feel my touch via another person from another place as a secondary and additional sensation. Or, by feeling my chest I can also feel her breast. An intimacy through interface, an intimacy without proximity" (Stelarc 1997,

figure 38
Stelarc, *The Third Hand* (1981)

153). The actuated touch is supposed to be feelable by the active partner via a feedback loop, specifically, together with the physiological reaction of the other person(s): thus (theoretically) one senses both oneself as well as the stimulus-receiving surface of the other body. This feeling-the-feeling-of-the-other-person is indeed an unheard-of utopianism: indeed, for centuries the tragedy of all lovers has been precisely that one's own sensations and feelings cannot be shared or conveyed—a situation that Niklas Luhmann has tried to grasp in the differentiation between "experiencing" and "acting" (1986). Even the boundaries of gender are to be transcended in the Stimbod experience when participants are able to experience male and female body sensations simultaneously: "chest" as "breasts."

Here, the skin, strictly speaking, is no longer an interface, the place that makes possible contact and perception while remaining a separating surface between the subjects; instead, the boundary of the skin is essentially abolished: "the sensation of the remote body sucked onto your skin and nerve endings, collapsing the psychological and spatial distance between bodies on the Net" (1997, 156), as Stelarc himself has described the (so far purely fictitious) synthesis of bodies. Both participants are to merge on the surface of their bodies; their skins are to "suck onto" each other, so that they are symbolically and sensorially given a common skin. The utopian designs of cyberspace thus seek once again to attain the phantasmal, primary-narcissistic nonseparation: the nearly total simultaneity of performed and experienced touch allows the distinction between the two to become blurred and in so doing abolishes the boundaries of the body. We are dealing with a paradoxical process: by intermediating a medial channel, the actual boundary is eliminated in favor of an amedial directness.

It is therefore no coincidence that it is Stelarc—the artist who, between 1976 and 1988, in twenty-five widely varied suspension performances, suspended himself by means of large hooks perforating his own skin (figure 39)—who repeatedly asserts that in cyberspace, finally, the body need not end where its own skin ends. The desire to transgress the utterly closed body-container is proclaimed, in that the transcending of the skin, which Stelarc demonstrated for decades on his own body, is now rhetorically stylized into an act of liberation: "Imagine: a body that is no longer tied to its skin. Until now the surface of the skin has been the place where the world begins and the self simultaneously ends. . . . But now it is expanded and rendered permeable by technology. . . . Skin no longer means closure. If surface and skin rupture, it is as though the inner and the outer dissolve" (1996, 319).

figure 39
Stelarc, *Tilted/Twisting: Event for Cone
Configuration* (1980)

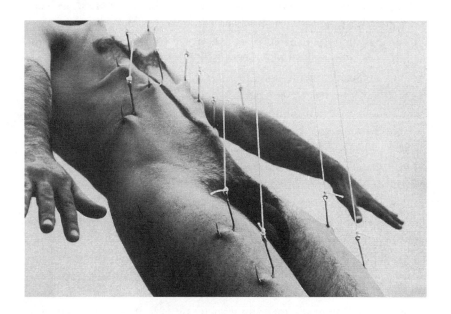

The extension of the skin described here, which at the same time entails its penetration through the implantation of nanotechnology,[4] is a grandiose, narcissistic fantasy. It is a fantasy which de Kerckhove, another leading thinker of teletactility, has made his theme when he says that "the computer-aided body transcends its traditional boundaries organically embedded in the skin" and that in the future the "earth atmosphere sensitized by its satellites" will become "our new skin" (1996b, 333). What is in question at the moment "is the boundary that is represented by our skin; a limit that is the decisive pillar of our standard equipment of individual psychology. Through interactive media the boundaries between what is happening outside and what is inside our consciousness become fluid, and soon we will no longer be entirely sure where our body begins and where it ends" (1993, 166).

There are two reasons that it is precisely the skin that is used to illustrate this dissolution of the inner and the outer: first, historically the skin was defined as the final boundary of the self; second, it was also defined as the sensory organ that was most strongly corporeal and the one we are least able to escape from. But the other senses, too, have been drawn into this process of dissolution, with the result that they can no longer be understood as distance senses. The eyes, which are surrounded by tight-fitting eyephones, are no more able to avoid the impressions impinging on them than is the skin, which as a whole is encased in a data suit. De Kerckhove is therefore right when he says "that all interface technologies are variations on the expressive forms of touch" (1996b, 335) when it comes to exposing the body directly and inescapably to virtual environments. In euphoric language, he talks about how "every interactive system between body and machine is a variation of the ability to touch and let oneself be touched" (334). The cutaneous senses are becoming the new guiding sense, in that henceforth all senses are to function through the interfaces directly connected with the body and more or less on the model of tactile contact.

Stelarc, no doubt more radically than any other body artist of the seventies, recognized early on the preeminent importance of the skin as a problematic boundary and wiring surface. His skin suspensions, initially conceived as private happenings in small galleries (figure 40) and later also as public spectacles, were intended for him to attain a condition of weightlessness—or at least to depict it by means of the stretched skin: "To me it is part of the manifestation of the gravitational pull, of overcoming it, or of at least resisting it. The stretched skin is a kind of gravitational landscape. . . . The

figure 40
Stelarc, *Pull Out/Pull Up: Event for
Self-Suspension* (1980)

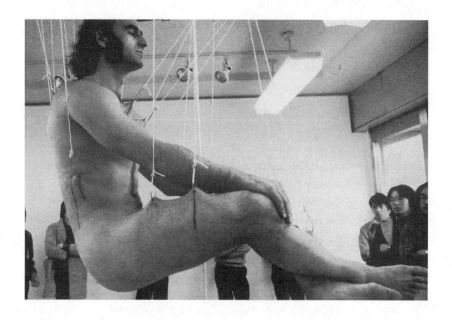

stretched skin in fact authenticates the suspension in a planetary gravitational field. It is the physical penalty you pay for suspending your body" (1984, 16).

As is evident from his words, the suspensions were about the (symbolic) overcoming of gravity and thus also about a state of disembodiment, of nonworldliness. Here, the skin stands metonymically for the heaviness of the entire body. Again and again Stelarc compares the pain and danger the artist must go through to attain this state with what a woman suffers during pregnancy and childbirth: labor and birth pains are unavoidable side effects but not the real purpose of pregnancy. An artist, by analogy, strives to give birth, not to children but to "new ideas," and he must accept the pain and the risk as the price for this desire (16–17). Stelarc is here assuming a twofold position, for he is both the one giving birth and the embryo. This double function becomes clear in the spatial conception that underlies many of the early suspensions: as he still does in performances today, Stelarc externalizes the inside of his body with sensors—for example, by means of tones or sounds that acoustically amplify the beating of the heart or the circulation of the blood and convey them to the outside.[5] But in this way the space in which the event is taking place becomes an expanded body—or, in an obvious interpretation, a kind of womb. The "sound aura" (16) creates around the naked, helplessly suspended body an acoustic sheath that seems to come quite close to the actual sounds in the uterus: in a sense, Stelarc creates his own uterus by externalizing his body interior. He himself experiences the suspended body as weightless, but the audience, too, describes it as "flowing" and "gliding," which likewise points to this uterine state of being. In his suspensions, Stelarc repeatedly gives birth to himself; thus they have less a cathartic and more a generative function. And it is only in this context that it becomes disquieting that he describes the pain of his skin as a "physical penalty" for his desire, since the word "penalty" implies that this embodied fantasy is inappropriate (or excessive).

On the one hand, we can read the desire for the abolition of gravity as the phenomenon of disembodiment and as such as the early precursor to a phenomenon repeatedly diagnosed in new media, namely, the disappearance of the body (which Stelarc anyhow keeps describing as obsolete). The penetration of the body surface stands for what Stelarc continuously proclaims as the elimination of the skin as a "meaningful site" and "a barrier between public space and the physiological realm" (1995, 73).

On the other hand, today it is precisely a reflexive return to the body, to is materiality and heaviness, that is becoming necessary as a way of counteracting the implicit weightlessness of virtuality. As de Kerckhove has said, the body is currently being proclaimed and rediscovered as the fundamental "point of being" (1996b, 344) of the global, networked human being. And so a comparison of the early and later works of Stelarc reveals a double contradiction: the suspensions as truly radical physical acts serve to disembody and overcome the skin, while the later performances, using virtual reality and the Internet, are intended to serve a new corpo-reality and sensory perception: "Technology, which shatters the body's subjective totality of reality, now returns to reintegrate its fragmented experience. It literally brings the body back to its senses (sensors)" (Stelarc 1984, 52). Already in his skin suspensions, Stelarc consciously addressed and displayed the kind of information overkill that awaits us today.[6] In this scenario, the broadly penetrated skin, which is exposed to a flood of extreme stimuli, corresponds to the immense, unbearable mass of data of the networks. The ropes in the performances that lift the artist's body into the air and hold him there with his surface tensed and stretched to the extreme and that often run off every which way represent an illustration of the very world-spanning web that media prophets today are calling the "new skin" of humanity: "The world as an extension of the skin is much more interesting than the world as an extension of the image" (Kerckhove 1996b, 345). For now, however, it remains an open question whether humankind will be able to endure—psychologically and emotionally—this phantasm of the grandiosely expanded skin.

13 conclusion

All the sources and theories I have examined in this book relate to the phenomenon of the skin itself across an unbridgeable distance. They are images or language, scientific or artistic discourse. Certain aspects can be captured by these specific mediations and expressive forms, while others are necessarily absent. Even a synthesis of the various discourses does not close the distance—it can never be more than an approximation by degrees. That is why my analysis probed into the most diverse forms of knowledge and representational strategies. I looked at figurative expressions and idiomatic sayings, at skin in language. I analyzed tendencies to physiologize the skin, as well as attempts to turn the surface of the body and face into a semiotic—a meaning-bearing—surface. Finally, I examined processes of visualization, not least with respect to the dimensions that resist representation or are excluded from it.

My hope in grappling with skin in such a wide-ranging and contrasting manner was to avoid the kind of reductionism that would result from too narrow a perspective, for example, by looking exclusively at the question of the literary coding of facial skin tones. Allowing this kind of plurality of discourse proved to be necessary in that the various levels I have discussed are closely interrelated. Still, it is not possible to summarize the study here. Formulating final results would mean that the complex configurations I have presented are reducible to individual core theses. That is obviously not the case. Skin is subjective and singular, a "discrete diversity" (Serres 1985, 62). It resists both overarching statements and unambiguous semiotic coding. And yet, in these concluding remarks, I would like to identify a few central aspects and relate them to each other.

Every reader will have thought of other examples—images, texts, sayings—that I did not consider in this study. This shows how present skin is in the individual and collective understanding of the world, and it makes it all the more remarkable that is has received so little attention in the study of cultural history. One is therefore justified in speaking of cultural repression mechanisms that until now have largely excluded skin from discourse, precisely because it proves to be so inescapable and close. And the humanities are no exception, either. My study has shown, however, that narrative literature has retained an awareness of skin, giving it considerable space not only as a means of characterizing individuals physiognomically and pathognomically but also as a place of subjectivity and connection to the world. Literature functions as a mouthpiece of the unconscious by addressing skin as the surface for the question of identity and as a primary "medium of elementary contact" (Tellenbach 1968).[1] The presence of skin in literary texts (and in works of art in general) is therefore usually latent, lying below the general threshold of awareness. But it needs to be emphasized in this context that skin, as understood here, is represented as more than a literary (or painterly) motif, for that requires not only content that is typical, general, and capable of being conventionalized but also semantic unity and definability. Some of the individual aspects I have discussed, such as flaying, the birthmark, or the armored skin, are perfectly capable of taking on the character of a motif, but nevertheless they have remained largely undiscussed as independent motifs, the interpretation of which has an established tradition in literary studies.

The present book has probed into the contribution of the so-called lower senses with respect to the structure and formation of the human being, for the historical-anthropological significance of skin is not limited to its physiological functions. Moreover, it is also not the case that these physiological functions become psychologized and interiorized during the course of ego formation and are thereby turned into the mere model of contact and psychic coherence. Rather, the skin continuously retains both the physiological tasks and the constitutive aspects it contributes to the psychic self. It is significant to what extent psychological, psychoanalytical, psychosomatic, and in part also medical treatises, as soon as they address skin diseases and their supposed psychic causes, invariably fall back on legends, fairy tales, idiomatic expressions, and literary examples.[2] This act of invoking the aid of the poetic within scientific discourse reveals the extent to which it is poets, in particular, who keep alive or develop in language specific possibilities of experience that would otherwise find no expression.

At the outset, I formulated the guiding thesis that figurative speech about skin reveals a duality between thinking about the self as in the skin and the self as the skin. I further noted that the notion of the self as in the skin has undergone a highly problematic development right up to the present day: human beings feel increasingly less sheltered in the skin and more concealed and hidden—less protected and more imprisoned. Medicine was late in recognizing that the skin itself exhibits autonomous functions, namely, that it is permeable and also forms a closure against the environment. At a time when the body surface was still thought of as porous and open, the human being was, on a symbolic level, more connected to the world and therefore dependent on supplementary envelopments. Nakedness, in the full sense of the word, thus became possible only late. Today, the skin is experienced as something that, while individualizing the person, primarily creates separation. Hence it is only the autonomy of the self that leads to the discovery of the tragedy of isolation and disconnectedness from the world. Norbert Elias identified the *Homo clausus* as a general structure of the modern individual: the increasingly rigid separation between inner and outer and with it the increasing unrecognizability of the other. The present study adds specificity to this notion by recognizing the separating function of the skin as one central motif.

It is only the experience of the body as a monad—concretized in the image of the skin as a wall—that then gives rise to the ecstasy of stepping out of the dermis. It is revealing for the history of gender, however, that fantasies of leaving and overcoming one's own skin are positive only in male poets, philosophers, and artists. Female writers and "dark-skinned" authors (both male and female), by contrast, tend to speak of a passive captivity in one's own skin, which is often experienced as stigmatized. Fantasies of overcoming and modifying the body surface by the protagonists in these works are marked by violence, pain, and anxieties over identity.

Moreover, the texts of Sylvia Plath demonstrate to what extent poetic images of the flaying and skinlessness of the female body must work against a centuries-old taboo that has defined the skin as the existential attribute of the feminine. On the one hand, the removal and lifting up of the gender-neutral (meaning, male) skin becomes the emblem of knowledge, whose fundamental idea rests on the notion of uncovering. On the other hand, a number of male thinkers from Swift to Nietzsche use the removal of female body skin repeatedly as a negative image for a form of penetrating understanding that is seen as deleterious to the preservation of the self. It is therefore only the skinning of males that functions as a model of knowledge as well as a metaphor of transformation. At the same time, it is usually the naked body of the woman that serves in the philosophical tradition of allegory as a representation of unconcealed knowledge and the truth.

It is striking that the motif of the worn facial skin—for instance, in Rilke, Kafka, and Jahnn—is likewise tied to the feminine. Jahnn's pathological protagonist is looking for the face behind the female mask and peels off the skin, after having killed the woman, only to find raw, bloody flesh. In Rilke, a scare causes the face of an unnamed female protagonist to pull away from the underlying layers and remain behind in the woman's hands. The first-person narrator does not dare to look into the skinless face. When Kafka addressed a problem he presents as a *conditio humana*—namely, that we always place the same face into the same hands and are never able to change this dress—he is likewise using "girls" as an example. As I have shown, the topos of skin as a concealing mask is generally imagined—picking up the Lady World motif—in connection with the female sex. At the same time, the removal of the skin—as in Rilke—triggers fantastic fears. It therefore comes as no surprise when Plath, for instance, picks up the compulsive attachment to an identity-bestowing mask as a motif in her poetry and prose. Here, alienation from the self is cast in terms of alienation from one's skin.

Although male flaying ceased to be taboo and came to be glorified at the beginning of modern anatomy, there is also a masculine body image of armored, thickened skin. In the myth of Achilles and the legend of armored Siegfried, this skin possesses a single vulnerable spot as a *signum humani*, a sign of the character's humanness. The counterpart of this armored skin is the female birthmark, which in literature (for example, in Hawthorne) stands for sinfulness and mortality but also potential identification. Although it seems somewhat risky to formulate overarching hypotheses given the limited number of sources examined, two general observations are possible: the problem of male skin in the arts has a tendency to concern itself with its thickness and strength (or with the firmness and solidity of shape of what lies underneath), while the problem of female skin revolves more around the smoothness of the surface and the space-creating function of the sheath but also around the dialectic of transparency and concealment.

Physiological experiments between the seventeenth and the nineteenth century that sought to work out the anthropological difference between African and European skin types touched essentially on three areas: the varying thickness of skin, the differing degrees of transparency, and the question of discoloration caused by the alleged presence of additional color substances in darker skin. What is remarkable is that these attributions—which African-American writers today are trying to deconstruct—show a remarkable convergence with other central questions of this study: the claim that darker skin is thicker in the final analysis also means that it is seen as firmer and thus as more masculine. Parallel to that, the postulated nontransparency of African skin types is placed into the same context as the question of gender, for in literary and philosophical texts, it is usually the woman in whom emotions become visible as blushing and blanching. The implication is that women and children are less able to conceal their emotions, which show themselves involuntarily on and in their diaphanous epidermis. With respect to the ethnic skin, this means that the European skin, in contrast to the African skin, once again shows a tendency to be thought of as more feminine since it is less concealing. Fears of the rubbing off of darker skin pick up on the problem of containment. The body image that is thus created is porous, a body from which something leaks out involuntarily.

In the late eighteenth century this kind of open body surface became a problem, as evidenced in the changes in cosmetic, hygienic, physiotherapeutic, and dermatological practices between the seventeenth and the early nineteenth century. Only the bourgeois body comes to possess a symbolically flat, two-dimensional surface. But it is only this kind of surface that can be coded and given semiotic meaning. Physiognomy and pathognomy emerge at this time as leading disciplines, in which—to put it in simplified terms—the skin, on the one hand, was supposed to be closed and unwounded and, on the other hand (in noble circles), had to be far less made up and more natural than a mere century earlier. The dictate that arises from these attitudes states that skin should reveal a person's essence. Nineteenth-century literature would subsequently project onto this surface distinctive personalities and states of being.

The potential recognizability of an individual's being on the skin was not questioned again until much later, as in the work of Kafka and Plath. Central to both authors is the enigma of face and body skin. Grotesque elements in their descriptive writing but also a medical-objective gaze can be read as a strategy of letting the person disappear as a human counterpart, casting him or her as a foreign body, a mere objectified thing. The described details (scars, spots, skin blemishes) are not infused with psychological meaning but exist as purely material phenomena. Tendencies to render the skin and the body surface enigmatic are used primarily to fend off the object. But this hostility toward the other skin also reveals itself in imagined or real scenes in which racist aggressions are directed concretely against the dark skin of African or African-American protagonists.

Attraction to and aggression against the skin of another person are always closely related with the problem of the desire for and the warding off of contact. Drawing on literary texts by Musil and Ondaatje, I have shown to what extent skin perceptions (and the memory of them) constitute a skin ego, which is not an image ego but more like a sensation ego. The English patient's lack of skin turns him not only into someone who is bodily absent but also into a person with a disappearing memory. Both authors use identical perceptual and descriptive modes to depict what is felt with the skin, what is fantasized and imagined. This points to the semantic proximity between internal and external feeling, a proximity that eighteenth-century aesthetics (Herder, Condillac) had already tried to make use of.

The theme of the senses in literature, philosophy, and the fine arts was traditionally linked to two aspects: the question of exploring and discovering the world and the question of the virtuous or sinful-pleasurable use of the senses. Historically, no sense complex was more deeply affected by this duality than the skin. The opposition of hand and skin as perceptual organs presented an epistemological problem, one that made touch into a special case of sensory aesthetics and sensory theory. The *paragone* of the senses, which compared the individual sensory organs with one another, had a coarsening effect on the cutaneous senses by reducing their functional differentiation and abilities and limiting them to a few dimensions. The radical differentiation between touch (*Getast*, active exploration by the hands) and feeling (*Gefühl*, the passive cutaneous senses of the body surface) established a rift or split within the cutaneous sensations. The tactile aesthetic of the "noble blind person," from Ribera to Herder, who explores by touch external objects inwardly, has substantially less to do with the skin as discussed in this study than it does with passive suffering, as described, for example, by Schiller. Literary writers, in particular, repeatedly take up the theme of this latter aspect of being in the skin as a suffered, passive, and at times stigmatizing feeling. In so doing, they are concerned with the entire surface of the face and the body as something that is worn and felt. In aesthetic discourses, on the other hand, from the quarrel of the arts in the Renaissance right up to medical physiology, the skin is usually reduced to its active, haptic component. This is the case because feeling with the entire body surface can disempower the subject, since it often shifts ominously from a neutral to an erotic, polymorphous-sensual feeling. Only new media are trying to come to terms once again with this plurality.

In his novel *The Man Without Qualities*, Musil described skin as "life's traveling bag" (1995, 2:736). My hope is that skin has also proved to be a durable, form-giving, and at the same time permeable "traveling bag" of these studies, all of which are an attempt at groping toward understanding of a topic as complex as it is fragile.

notes

1. The Depth of the Surface: Introduction

1. A number of studies have appeared on the psychosomatic aspect of skin diseases; see, for example, Lévy 1997; Rechenberger 1976; Gieler and Bosse 1996; Maguire 1991; Condrau and Schipperges 1993.

2. The cycle by Jenny Holzer is in the Gallery Monika Sprüht (Cologne) and was reproduced in the *Süddeutsche Zeitung Magazin*, no. 46 (November 19, 1993): 4–43.

3. Paul Valéry, "L'idée fixe; ou, Deux hommes à la mer," in *Oeuvres complètes* (Paris: Gallimard, Pléiade, 1957), 2:215–216, quoted in Anzieu 1989, 60.

4. This is how Freud put it in an authorized footnote that was added to the 1927 English edition of "The Ego and the Id" (no German version of the footnote is extant): "I.e. the ego is ultimately derived from bodily sensations, chiefly from those springing from the surface of the body. It may thus be regarded as a mental projection of the surface of the body, besides, as we have seen above, representing the superficies of the mental apparatus" (1961, 26). See also Anzieu 1989, 85.

5. I will briefly list the eight functions here. I will also mention the underlying unconscious phantasma when these functions fail or are overactive, since these anxiety structures illustrate very well what Anzieu is talking about. It

needs to be emphasized that, in keeping with psychoanalytical theory, we are fundamentally dealing with unconscious notions, that is, with processes that cannot be perceived, guided, or controlled. (1) Anzieu begins by referring to a *maintenance* function: "In the same way that the skin functions as a support for the skeleton and the muscles, the Skin Ego fulfills a function of *maintaining* the psyche." The psychical function develops through the interiorization of maternal "holding," the way the mother holds the baby and supports it against her own body. The anxiety that is structurally associated with this function is that of an unsupported and formless psyche. (2) The skin ego acts as a *container:* "To the skin as a covering for the entire surface of the body and into which the external sense organs are inserted, corresponds the *containing* function of the Skin Ego." This function rests on the sensation and the image of the skin as a bag. The analogous anxiety structure is that of the psychical or physical emptying of the inside—conceptualized in the image of the skin broken by holes, the skin ego as a colander. (3) The function of providing a *protective shield against stimulation* parallels the function of the epidermis in shielding "the organism in general against physical attack, some forms of radiation, and an excess of stimuli." The paranoid anxiety associated with this function is that something is intruding into the psyche. It takes two forms: "(a) they are stealing my thoughts . . . ; (b) they are putting thoughts into my head." (4) Just as the surface of the human skin differs from one person to the next, the skin ego takes on an *individuation* function: parallel to the narcissistic and social meaning of individual skin characteristics, the individuation function of the skin ego "gives the Self a sense of its own uniqueness." It thus serves to protect and distinguish oneself from the other and helps to sustain the consciousness of one's own identity. (5) Next, the skin ego has the function of *intersensoriality*, that is, it "connects up sensations of various sorts." This function is based on the fact that the surface of the skin contains all other sense organs. The skin ego is, correspondingly, seen as a psychic surface that interconnects sensations of the most diverse kind. "A defect in this function gives rise to the anxiety of the body fragmented, or more precisely of it being dismantled, that is, of an anarchic, independent functioning of the various sense organs." (6) Another function of the skin ego is that of *supporting sexual excitation*: "the baby's skin is the object of libidinal cathexis on the part of the mother." Care, nursing, and feeding are accompanied by pleasurable skin contact. The skin ego thus constitutes the foundation of any sexual excitation, which is prepared and initiated by skin pleasure. Erogenous zones appear on the surface of the skin, which is also where the difference between the sexes is perceived. If the cathexis of the skin is more narcissistic than erotic, "the envelope of excitation may be replaced by a gleaming narcissistic envelope, supposedly rendering its owner invulnerable" but also insensitive. (7) Anzieu follows this with the skin ego's function of *libidinal recharging*: he notes a congruence between the skin as a surface whose sensorimotor tonus is permanently maintained by external stimulation and the skin ego with its function of libidinal recharging of the psyche, the "maintenance of internal energetic tension." "The failure of this function produces one of two types of antagonistic anxiety: anxiety that the mental apparatus will explode under the pressure of an overload of excitation . . . , or Nirvana anxiety, i.e., that one might fulfill the desire of reducing tension to zero." (8) The eighth function is that of *registering tactile sensory traces*. Through its sensory organs, the skin provides direct information about the external world. Membership in a social group is also shown on the skin: for example, through incisions, skin color, piercing, tattooing, or makeup. Anxiety related to this function can be expressed, first, in the fear of being branded by shameful and indelible marks such as eczema or rashes and, second, in the fear of losing the capacity to retain traces. On all of these functions, see Anzieu 1989, 98–105.

2. Boundary Metaphors: Skin in Language

1. To improve readability, I have corrected the convention in Grimm of writing all German nouns in small letters.

2. The saying *povera la tua pella* in Italian also replaces the name of the person with "skin"—a skin that deserves pity, is poor. In Italian, *"pelle"* is sometimes used for a person all by itself; in this case it generally has the negative connotation "dishonest" or "unscrupulous," which is intensified by the ironic addition of *"buona"*(good).

3. This means the person is by nature saucy and inclined to joking (Ersch and Gruber 1828, 203).

4. "Die neunerley heud einer bösen frawen, sambt ihren neun eygenschaften" (The nine kinds of skin of an evil woman along with their characteristics) is the title of one of Hans Sachs's poems (1870, 232 ff). Or consider the following:"Die weiber haben neun Häute und in jede ist ein eigen Schelmenstückchen eingewickelt" (Women have nine skins, and in each is wrapped its own kind of little mischief) (*Der viesierliche Exorcist*, quoted in Grimm and Grimm 1984, 10:col. 701).

5. On the theory of "nonconceptuability," see Blumenberg 1993b, 75 ff.

6. See *Körper und Bauwerk, Daidalos* 45 (September 1992); Reudenbach 1980, 651 ff.; Evers 1995.

7. This connection has long been imagined across cultures, as evidenced, for example, in the similarity in the ornamentation and coloring with which the Maori of Polynesia tattoo their bodies and decorate their houses and in the transfer of body paintings to house walls in the ritual of women's art in West Africa. Both references come from exhibits in the Hamburg Museum of Ethnology: "Bemalte Häuser—Bemalte Körper: Frauenkunst aus Westafrika" (Painted houses—Painted bodies: Women's art from West Africa, 1995) and "Maori Haus" (permanent exhibit, with documentation).

8. The close connection between skin (*Haut*) and house (*Haus*) in the German language is already indicated by their etymological kinship: "*Haut*" comes from the

Middle High German "*hus*," which is considered a close relative of "*hut*" (Middle High German "skin") with a different suffix. The root common to both words appears in German with the simple initial consonant *h*, which evolved from the older *k*, which in turn can be traced back to the stronger anlaut *sk* in the cognate languages. *Sku*—as the original root of both house and skin—means "to cover" and "protect" (Grimm and Grimm 1984, 10:col. 640).

9. In Augustine, the corpse is the spent house of a person, whose spirit once inhabited it. Adorning the dead body therefore amounts to decorating the walls in the house of an exile. The soulless body, even when adorned, is worthless (Klauser et al. 1986, col. 968).

10. As in the pre-Socratic philosopher Empedocles (Böhme 1988). Böhme speaks of a body experience that is marked by penetrability: "All perceptions, even thought, previously followed a model of a person being filled with material streams, moving atmospheres, breathy streams of images, flowing incorporations" (217). In Neoplatonic thought, the eyes are "sluice-gates" through which perceptions reach the inside like a stream and there injure the "soul" or the "heart" (Burton 1989–2000).

11. On the history of this topos in philosophy, see Blumenberg 1988, 207 ff.

12. A thorough analysis of Plath's texts, in particular, and of the question of whether the experience of the skin as a wall in general is gender-bound can be found in chapter 6.

3. Penetrations: Body Boundaries and the Production of Knowledge in Medicine and Cultural Practices

1. An exemplary case of the intermingling of the inside of the body and the outside world is one scene in Rabelais where, at a feast of cattle slaughtering, the entrails of the animal body are externalized and then immediately consumed by the human body. Structurally, this symbolic process of ingestion and excretion, of opening and closing, is never ending, for the grotesque body "swallows the world and is itself swallowed by the world" (317).

2. On the classical notion of the transubstantiation of various body fluids into each other and on the analogies between fluids today differentiated as male and female, see also Laqueur 1990, 35 ff.

3. "The skin itself seems made to be permeable from the inside: it has 'sweat holes' which heat could open to allow the discharge of humidity, bloody matter, and impurities. A swelling, a boil on the skin, was a sign for some matter that was pushing toward the periphery in search of an outlet. . . . Other phenomena on the skin were also considered as exits: varicose veins showed throbbing blood pushing toward the outside; 'redness on the skin,' facial burns, Saint Anthony's fire, was caused by peccant matter breaking out; a rash was an issue; scabies seemed a salutary discharge; liver spots were impure stuff brought to the outside" (Duden 1991a, 121–122).

4. "Même lorsque l'idéologique médicale s'inverse lentement, . . . une thérapeutique d'extractions (le mal est un surcroît—quelque chose de plus ou de trop—qu'il faut enlever du corps par la saignée, la purge, etc.) est remplacée par une thérapeutique d'adjonctions (le mal est un manque, un déficit, qu'il faut suppléer par des drogues, des soutiens, etc.)" (De Certeau 1979, 7).

5. The opposite trend can be found in the flesh sculptures of the human preparator Honoré Fragonard, who in the years before the French Revolution perfected the technique of preserving flayed corpses as timeless sculptures. Fragonard's real specimens can still be seen today in the Maison d'Alfort near Paris. See the illustrations in Lemire 1990, 167ff.; Pilet 1981.

6. A plaster mold was made of the clay model and filled with wax; the wax cast was then colored by using the model as a constant guide (Lesky 1971, 366–367).

7. Thus the title of a large exhibition in Paris in 1993. See Jean Clair, ed., *L'âme au corps: Arts et sciences, 1793–1993*, catalog of the Grand Palais, Paris (Paris: Gallimard, 1993).

8. Under National Socialism, for example, the claim was circulated that the disreputable field of dermatology and syphilis research, in particular, were dominated by Jewish scientists, a charge that was intended to underscore the infectious and unclean status of the Jews (Gilman 1992, 287).

9. A reproduction of this family tree can be found in Stafford 1993, 303.

10. Incidentally, this contradicts Foucault's thesis about decreasing disease localization from the late eighteenth century on. Foucault argued that with the rise of clinical-pathological anatomy it is not knowledge itself that changed but merely the form of knowledge about the inside of the body: previously, intracorporeal lesions were locally identified, in that one organ inside the body space of the dead was identified as the cause of the preceding illness. By contrast, what characterizes the new forms of perception is that an epistemological privilege is accorded to the anatomical surface gaze. The space of the disease is defined by means of the thin layers of the internal tissue. The intracorporeal membranes—individual tissues frequently of extreme delicacy—envelop the organs, pervade them, connect them with each other, and form large systems over and above them (Foucault 1973, 124ff.).

11. Reproductions can be found in Lemire 1990, Stafford 1993, de Bersaques 1994, Tilles and Wallach 1996, and Walther, Hahn, and Scholz 1993. In addition to the largest collection of moulages in Paris, other important collections are in the German Hygiene Museum (Dresden) and the Karolinum (Prague).

12. Compare, for example, the identifications in the historical collection of real specimens in the pathology department of the Charité in Berlin.

13. The collections of moulages in the German Hygiene Museum, to give another example, were used from the beginning of this century not only to document medical conditions and train doctors but also to educate the public. The authorities were counting on the terrifying and deterrent effect of the moulages, especially with regard to venereal diseases (Walther, Hahn, and Scholz 1993, 9–10).

4. Flayings: Exposure, Torture, Metamorphoses

1. The engraving reproduced here was first published in Gaetano Petrioli's *Tabulae anatomicae a celeberrimo pictore Petro Berretino Cortonesi delineatae* (1741), although it goes back to a drawing by Pietro Berretini da Cortona dating from as early as 1618. I have chosen to show the later engraving, since the illusion of the hollow body is even more pronounced in this illustration. For a comparison of the two illustrations, see Roberts and Tomlinson 1992, 275.

2. This tractate is essentially an imitation of the collection of plates by Vesalius, whose assistant Valverde had been on occasion. But the *écorché* shown here is among the independent designs by Gaspar Becerras for Valverde's atlas (Poseq 1994, 6).

3. Bonansone, drawing on the famous series of *écorchés* from Vesalius's *Fabrica*, also fashioned a series of fourteen anatomical studies in which men flay themselves or are already skinless. The dating is unclear; scholars place it between 1560 and 1570 (Massari 1983, 109).

4. For an interpretation of this painting within the context of the cultural history of anatomy, see also Böhme 1992, 134 ff.

5. The myth tells us that Marsyas played on his flute (which was later sometimes understood as a Pan flute, though originally it was a narrow, single-reed flute). Apollo played on the kithara, although even in antiquity this instrument was not clearly differentiated from the lyre. In the Renaissance, Apollo was then increasingly depicted with a Lira da Braccio, as is the case in this painting.

6. Midas had been asked to judge another musical contest, that between Apollo and Pan, and he had declared Pan the winner. As punishment, Apollo had him grow donkey ears, which are clearly visible in the engraving. Combining the two musical contexts in one image was Meier's idea (Rapp 1985, 69 n. 5).

7. In his treatise *Plastik* (Sculpture, 1788), Johann Gottfried Herder, referring to the "terribly natural unnaturalness" of Marco D'Agrate's marble sculpture of Bartholomew in the Cathedral of Milan (1562), which is considered an especially realistic work, notes that no Greek sculptor would have been able to "flay out" a sculpture in this manner (1994, 272).

8. The corporeal aspect of punishment becomes a secondary aspect that should be avoided if possible; henceforth punishment should be directed exclusively at the criminal's "soul" (Foucault 1979).

9. Compare the mention of flayings in Joel Chandler Harris's *Uncle Remus: His Songs and Sayings* (1881), and Charles W. Chesnutt's *The Conjure Woman* (1899). These texts are classic examples of African-American vernacular culture.

10. Goethe quotes this saying, which refers to a fragment by the Attic comedian Menander, in Greek (1974, vol. I). [In John Oxenford's English translation, the passage from Menander reads: "Man does not learn unless he is thrashed." Since one of the meanings of the Greek word is "flaying," which is the meaning of interest to the author, I have chosen the more literal translation.—Trans.]

11. Rousseau's motto is a reference to a satire by the Roman writer Aulus Persius Flaccus (34–62 C.E.), where it is said: "Ego te intus et in cute novi" (I knew you, inside out, Satire III, l. 30). With this motto, Rousseau thus expresses the certainty that he knows himself and will portray his character without reservations. The motto is repeated at the beginning of the second part of the *Confessions*.

12. For a contextualization of the skinning metaphor with the idea of *Bildung* in Goethe, see Dane 1994, 141 ff.

13. The author of the Deuteronomic history may have been familiar with the Marsyas myth. In the texts that have handed down, this myth, that of Hygin (60 B.C.E.–10 C.E.) is the only one that mentions the Scythian as the flayer, a figure that classical sculpture took over. The Second Book of the Maccabees war written earlier, presumably in the period after 160 B.C.E.

14. The only exception of which I am aware are three anatomical depictions by Jacques Fabian Gautier d'Agoty (1710–1786): his *Anatomie des parties de la génération* (1773) features the side view of a highly pregnant, skinless woman, whose muscles seem wound around her body like tight, striated wraps of cloth—or even look like some kind of armor. The opened uterus, too, is depicted like a web of layers (see the illustration in Stafford 1998, 176). The *Anatomie générale* (1774) shows a woman's torso with a skinned right side. Gautier d'Agoty also fashioned the "anatomical angel," a turned female figure whose back muscles are exposed in such a way that the skin flaps look like wings (see the illustration in Lemire 1993, 83). All three images are extremely stylized, artificial, and highly theatrical; they therefore skirt the phantasm of the skinned woman, even though they show it.

15. Directed by Jonathan Demme, based on a novel by Thomas Harris (Columbia Tri-Star, 1990).

16. What is created in this way is a "posthuman sex" (Halberstam 1991, 37 ff.). From a mythological perspective, the taking of the (originally necessarily intact) skin of an enemy and the act of clothing oneself in it result in a strengthening of one's own protection, the belief being that the power of the other person is transferred to the new owner through the skin (Anzieu 1989, 50).

5. Mirror of the Soul: The Epidermis as Canvas

1. Goethe's comments from his autobiographical work *Dichtung und Wahrheit* refer to a letter from Herder in which the latter had engaged in a play on words with the name Goethe and the words "*Götter*" (gods), "*Goten*" (Goths), and "*Kot*" (excrement).

2. It remains unclear whether the existence of Michelangelo's features on the skin of the flayed apostle was an open secret in his day or whether his contemporaries in fact did not recognize this (Steinberg 1980, 426).

3. Steinberg argues that Michelangelo knew Job 19:25–26 in the version of Thomas Aquinas (which differs from standard modern translations): "I know that my Redeemer liveth, and in the last day I shall rise out of the earth. And I shall be clothed

again with my skin and in my flesh I shall see God." He supposedly saw it on a popular medal of the Last Judgment that Bertoldo di Giovanni had created for the Medici family. On this medal, as well, the Last Judgment is understood as an individual's hope of resurrection. The inscription on the medal reads "Et in carne mea videbo deum salvatorem meum" (Steinberg 1980, 434, 450 n. 34).

4. Steinberg points to a verse by Michelangelo that says the human soul is still clothed in mortal flesh during a person's lifetime—"l'anima della carne ancor vestita"—this flesh changes over the years, and eventually, in an act of transformation, detaches itself again from the soul in death—"or che'l tempo la scorza cangia e muda la morte" (Michelangelo 1863, 216, 349).

5. "O fussi sol le mie l'irsuta pelle . . . / che con ventura stringe si bel seno" (Michelangelo 1863, 179).

6. Oliver König has advanced the thesis that with the rise of the nudity culture (since the beginning of the twentieth century) nakedness has been losing its connotations of frailty and vulnerable exposure (1990, 71). The present study shows that this thesis cannot be sustained; rather, there appears to be merely a predominant desire to suppress these associations.

7. Various Greek myths, like those recounting the fates of Actaeon, Medusa, and Medea, revolve around this problem of blinding, loss of self, or destruction. See Benthien 1994b; Böhme 1988 and 1997b; Caillois 1959; Rank 1913.

8. The root *"skam"/"skem,"* like "skin" and "house," goes back to the Indo-Germanic stem *"kam"/"kem"* (cover, veil, conceal).

9. Wurmser believes that these self-judgments are even more real than those of the traditional psychoanalytical notion of shame, according to which shame is tied to the castration complex (the woman's shame because of her "genital defect," the man's shame because he is vulnerable to castration anxiety) (1981, 92).

10. Dane quotes these terms from Goethe's tale "Der Mann von fünfzig Jahren" (The man of fifty, 1818); they are characterized by the fact that they were "used both for medicinal remedies and as cleansing and nourishing agents" (1994, 52).

11. It is clear that this is based on a specific ideal of beauty. "The sole constant that existed in the most varied definitions of bodily beauty over the centuries was light skin, especially in women; this changed only in the course of the twentieth century. In paintings of the time, as well, one can see that women are generally depicted with lighter skin than men and that women of higher social standing always have a lighter skin than their female servants" (Dane 1994, 69–70).

6. Mystification: The Strangeness of the Skin

1. "Often when I see clothes with manifold pleats, frills, and appendages which fit so smoothly onto lovely bodies I think they won't keep that smoothness long, but will get creases that can't be ironed out, dust lying so thick in the embroidery that it can't be brushed away, and that no one would want to be so unhappy and so

foolish as to wear the same valuable gown every day from early morning till night. And yet I see girls who are lovely enough and display attractive muscles and small bones and smooth skin and masses of delicate hair, and nonetheless they appear day in, day out, in this same natural fancy dress, always propping the same face on the same palms and letting it be reflected from the looking glass. Only sometimes at night, on coming home late from a party, it seems in the looking glass to be worn out, puffy, dusty, already seen by too many people, and hardly wearable any longer" (Kafka 1976, 382–383).

2. In Kafka's story *The Metamorphosis*, the surface of the body's getting dusty even becomes a mark of the isolation and lack of contact suffered by Gregor Samsa, who has been transformed into a bug. This is the result of his bodily ugliness, because of which no family member wants to come close to him, let alone clean him.

3. In a similar vein, Kafka writes about a lady at the theater that she had a "coarse nose" and a "face smudged with soot" (1976, 719).

4. Von Matt's notion of portrait, however, seems too narrow in the sense that Kafka explicitly describes bodies as well, not only faces. And even when he is talking about faces, these are frequently corporeal. As *pars pro toto*, they stand for the surface of the entire body, which means they are not exclusively a matter of portraits in the art historical sense.

5. Compare the examples already cited or Kafka's remarks about Frau Klug: "She looked at me, especially when she was silent up there in the window of the compartment, with a mouth rapturously contorted by embarrassment and slyness and with twinkling eyes that swam on the wrinkles spreading from her mouth" (1976, 652). Here are two examples of leatherlike skin: "At noon the departure of Frau von W., the Swedish widow who resembles a leather strap" (903); "this thin face with yellowish, leathery, bony cheeks and black wrinkles spreading over all of it at every movement of his jaws" (771).

6. See the overview in Kittler 1990, 116–117.

7. First published under the pseudonym Victoria Lucas a few months before Plath's death, *The Bell Jar* did not appear under her own name until 1971.

8. An example of the taste of skin: "Teeth gouged. And held. Salt, warm salt, laving the tastebuds of her tongue" (1979, 184). This comes from a description of how a female protagonist bites a man on his cheek (see also n. 10, below). Of the sound of skin: "I heard the scissors close on the woman's skin like cloth and the blood began to run down—a fierce, bright red" (1971, 53). Here the narrator in *The Bell Jar* is present at a birth in a hospital where a Caesarean section is performed. Of the smell of skin: "These cadavers were so unhuman-looking they didn't bother me a bit. The had stiff, leathery, purple-black skin and they smelt like old pickle jars" (51).

9. During a mental crisis at the age of twenty, Plath took sleeping pills at her mother's home and lay down in a hidden, narrow crawlspace under the porch whose opening she blocked with stacked firewood. (I will only mention here the symbolism of

the place she chose, which is simultaneously tomb and womb *and* a reinforcing support skin.) After several days, however, she was found and saved, her face injured
and badly infected. A deep abrasion left behind a scar under her left eye (Stevenson
1989, 45–46).

10. The story "Stoneboy with Dolphin" describes how, at a Cambridge party, the
protagonist Dody Ventura bites the cheek of Leonard, a poet she admires—a scene
that makes reference to the real first encounter between Plath and her future husband, the poet Ted Hughes. As the text unfolds, the protagonist reflects on this
oral-sadistic act, "which would mark her by tomorrow like the browned scar on
her cheek" (1979, 186). Through the bite wound, which will leave a scar on
Leonard's cheek, she likens Leonard to herself, turns him into a symbolic ally who
is marked like she is. By referring to the scar in "Tongues of Stone" as a "scarlet
letter," she is assimilating herself to a literary model: Nathaniel Hawthorne's guilt-
ridden and outcast protagonist Hester Prynne.

11. Compare the exemplary case description in Wurmser 1981, p. 115–116.

12. "Mutilation of the skin by cutting with razors, glass and knives is a more dramatic means by which an individual endeavours to maintain body boundaries and self-
cohesion" (Biven 1982, 224).

7. Armored Skin and Birthmarks: The Imagology of a Gender Difference

1. This is the version in Homer; elsewhere it is Paris who strikes Achilles in his vulnerable spot.

2. Becoming mortal through love—which is what happens to Siegfried in a figurative sense—is an old tragedy motif, one that Jahnn, for example, invokes in his re-
working of the Medea myth (Benthien 1994a). Siegfried is described as sexually
inexperienced in Hebbel (Ehrismann 1981, 27); this makes it possible to interpret
the revelation of his vulnerability as part of his surrender.

3. Social information is characterized by the fact that it is "reflexive and embodied;
that is, it is conveyed by the very person it is about, and conveyed through bodily expression in the immediate presence of those who receive the expression."
According to Goffman, "discredited individuals" are those whose stigmas are
known or can be directly perceived; "discreditable individuals," by contrast, poss-
es a (still) unknown stigma (1963, 43, 44).

4. See *Meyers Konversationslexikon* 1909, 14:333–334.

5. This becomes clear especially if we place it into the context of Hawthorne's novel
The Scarlet Letter: the mark of disgrace sewn onto the dress of the adulteress Hester Prynne, the scarlet letter "A," makes unmistakably clear that this woman is depraved because she has been touched. It is only later, as the story unfolds, that the
stigma changes into a protective sign of untouchability, so that Hester, precisely
because of her stigma, need not fear any sexual violence toward her.

6. For a detailed interpretation, especially of the character of Undine, see Stephan 1988, 249 ff.

8. *Different Skin: Skin Colors in Literature and the History of Science*

1. In the discussion that follows, I will place the terms "race," "white," and "black" in quotation marks to indicate that I am referring to the concepts and conceptions these words entail, which I have made the subject of my critical inquiry. After 1945 the word "race" could no longer be used without quotation marks in Germany, and even auxiliary terms such as "ethnic group" don't always work. I have also enclosed "black" and "white" within quotations marks to highlight that I am not talking about actual color tones but about ascriptions.
2. In the eighteenth century alone, more than forty studies were written on this topic (Mazzolini 1990).
3. For an exhaustive decoding of blushing in Kleist, see Skrotzi 1971.
4. On this as it relates to the eighteenth century, see Gilman 1982.
5. Particularly so in the drama *Straßenecke* (Street corner, 1931), which follows the Brechtian didactic theater, and in the tragedy *Medea* (1924), in which the title character is reinterpreted as an African woman.
6. In the present discussion, which is concerned with the semantics of dark skin, I am not able to examine in detail the very complex sequence that follows this scene: Horn takes the mutilated (and castrated) corpse of the diver to a doctor, who is to perform a dissection on the body. Before the dissection takes place, Horn, driven by an overpowering emotion, plunges his hand into a wound at the hip and tears out a piece of bone, which in the course of the novel takes on the character of a relic. A similar sequence of penetration into the (male) wound occurs in the story "Die Nacht aus Blei" (Night of lead, 1956). On the fantasy of the opening and penetration into the body of others as a pregenital-archaic desire in Jahnn, see also Reemtsma 1996.
7. The analogy between skin and the surface of the sea crops up again in the second part of "Niederschrift." Here, Horn is saying that in the human being it is only the "seeming sea smoothness of the skin" that conceals the gaze from that which lies behind it: arteries, nerves, organs—and at times "the roots of drives, the chambers of the secret desires" (1986b, 393).

9. *Blackness: Skin Color in African-American Discourse*

1. On the tabooing of this issue, see Russell, Wilson, and Hall 1993.
2. Famous examples of this genre are Charles W. Chesnutt's *The House Behind the Cedars* (1900), James Weldon Johnson's *The Autobiography of an Ex–Colored Man* (1912), Nella Larsen's *Quicksand* (1928) and *Passing* (1929), and Jessie Fauset's *Plum Bun* (1929).

3. "Although a few states . . . do not adhere strictly to the one-drop rule, no state takes into consideration an infant's physical appearance, and none gives adults the right to change their original race designation, even if they feel they have been categorized incorrectly" (Russell, Wilson, and Hall 1993, 78–79). Compare Williamson 1980, 1 ff.; Gatewood 1996, 2444 ff.

4. Voltaire, for example, has this to say about albinos: "As far as bodily strength and mental powers are concerned, they rank below the Negroes, and nature has presumably assigned them a place between the Negroes and the Hottentots above them and the apes below them as one of the steps leading from humans down to the animals" (Voltaire 1878, 367–368).

5. "Enough blackness in his body to counteract the runaway evil affecting his skin. Nothing in Brother to rub off on her, to transform her into one of those pinto-pony-looking people with white patches on their faces and arms, the vitiligo and phenylketonuria which were sicknesses, wars in the body between the forces of light and darkness" (Wideman 1988b, 136).

6. In her analysis of Hemingway's *The Garden of Eden*, Morrison notes that the "white" protagonist, Catherine Bourne, and her lover constantly sun themselves to obtain a dark skin: "Catherine well understands the association of blackness with strangeness, with taboo—understands also that blackness is something one can 'have' or appropriate; it's the one thing they lack, she tells him. Whiteness is here a deficiency. She comprehends how this acquisition of blackness 'others' them and creates and ineffable bond between them—unifying them with estrangement" (1992, 87).

7. This thinking arose in the wake of the thesis that dark-skinned people are the descendants of Cain or Ham, who were cursed and also externally stigmatized by their dark skin color. The interpretation of racial difference as a mark of punishment on the skin led not only to the legitimization of slavery through the Bible but also influenced theories later called monogenetic: it was only through recourse to the Book of Genesis that the question of how the physical differences between nations could develop from a single ancestral pair became acute (Mazzolini 1990, 179–180). See also Musgrave (1986, 8–9).

10. Hand and Skin: Anthropology and Iconography of the Cutaneous Senses

1. Ann Jessie van Sant, in her study *Eighteenth-Century Sensibility and the Novel* (1993), is exemplary in showing for the English-language context the extent to which the literature of sensibility—which, in this regard, can be largely equated with the literature of *Empfindsamkeit* that appears in German-speaking lands—is forced to borrow the vocabulary of physical touching and contact to describe experiences understood as being inward. "To touch the heart," "to move the passions," "to be impressed," or "to agitate the mind" are all descriptive expressions that—much like similar expressions in German—draw on tactile experiences (93–94).

2. On the later iconography, see also Kaufmann 1943.

3. On this, see Lee 1967, 3. The debate was based in particular on Horace's simile "ut pictura poesis" from his *Ars poetica* (which states that poetry is like painting), as well as on Aristotle's *Poetica*.

4. See Museo del Prado 1997, 180.

5. Barbara Korte has formulated the reductionist thesis that all touching in literature can be subsumed under the concept of coding (1996, 125 ff).

11. Touchings: On the Analogous Nature of Erotic, Emotive, and "Psychic" Skin Sensations

1. *The English Patient* (1996), dir. Anthony Minghella, screenplay by Anthony Minghella and Michael Ondaatje.

2. "Körper auf Zeit: Die Narbenschrift einer hautlosen Wahrnehmung," lecture presented on April 17, 1997, as part of the symposium *Hautlabor* at the Hochschule für Bildende Künste in Hamburg.

3. To speak again about the fetishizing of dark skin at this point would be repetitive. However, the fact that a male dark skin is given this erotic charge in a woman's consciousness—what is more, from the perspective of a "white" Canadian and against the background of a Tamil-Singhalese-Dutch author—points to a post-colonial, positive recoding of dark hues, similar to what I noted in the work of Morrison. Here is an example from the perspective of Hana: "She learns all the varieties of his darkness. The colour of his forearm against the colour of his neck. The colour of his palms, his cheek, the skin under the turban. The darkness of fingers separating red and black wires, or against bread he picks up off the gunmetal plate he still uses for food. . . . She loves most the wet colours of his neck when he bathes. And his chest with its sweat which her fingers grip when he is over her, and the dark, tough arms in the darkness of his tent, or one time in her room when light from the valley's city, finally free of curfew, rose among them like twilight and lit the colour of his body" (1998, 127).

12. Teletactility: The Skin in New Media

1. The fact that more than half of the eighteen illustrations accompanying the two essays by Stenslie and Woolford show naked women's bodies, and that we find only images of young women dressed in nothing but data suits and none of naked, wired male bodies, speaks to the projective background of these most recent male fantasies.

2. Incidentally, this subsumation is also occurring in the behavioral sciences. See Grammer 1996, 95.

3. "A mediating instance is required to make possible interaction with a medium, one that guarantees not only the mutuality of the information exchange but also adequate—i.e., understandable for the linked systems—coding and decoding, so

that 'meaning' can be attributed. This 'mediating' instance is called 'interface' "
(Halbach 1994, 13–14).

4. "If my earlier performances can be characterized as exploring and piercing the
body (the three films about the inside of the stomach, the lung, and the intestine;
the twenty-five suspensions), in that they showed the physical parameters and normal capacities of the body, the new performances visually and auditorily expand
and reinforce the body. Expanded body processes encompass brain waves (EEG),
muscles (EMG), pulse (plethysmogram), and blood circulation. . . . The idea is to
introduce a work of art into the body, to erect the sculpture in an internal space.
The body becomes hollow, the distinction among *public, private*, and *physiological*
spaces becomes meaningless" (Stelarc 1995, 76–77).

5. Later, he also added optical impulses, for example, laser beams from the eyes that
visualize and externalize the cardiac rhythm.

6. "The body must burst from its biological, cultural and planetary containment. De-
synchronize and depart. Once the body attains planetary escape velocity it will be
launched into new evolutionary trajectories" (Stelarc 1984, 24).

13. Conclusion

1. Tellenbach, however, does not examine the skin as one of the "media of elementary contact" (which he completely overlooks in this context); instead, his
topic is "taste and atmosphere" (1968).

2. Gieler and Bosse 1996; Rechenberger 1976; Maguire 1991; Lévy 1997; Anzieu
1989; Montagu 1971; Séchaud 1996; Biven 1982.

bibliography

Ableman, Paul. 1982. *Anatomy of Nakedness*. London: Orbis.

Abraham, Ulf. 1990. "Rechtspruch und Machtwort: Zum Verhältnis von Rechtsordnung und Ordnungsmacht bei Kafka." In Wolf Kittler and Gerhard Neumann, eds., *Franz Kafka: Schriftverkehr*, 248–278. Freiburg: Rombach.

Anderson, Mark M. 1994. *Kafka's Clothes: Ornament and Asceticism in the Habsburg Fin de Siècle*. Oxford: Oxford University Press, Clarendon.

Anzieu, Didier. 1984. "La peau de l'autre: Marque du destin." *Nouvelle Revue de Psychanalyse* 30:55–68.

———. 1989. *The Skin Ego: A Psychoanalytic Approach to the Self*. Trans. Chris Turner. New Haven and London: Yale University Press.

———. 1994. *Le penser: Du Moi-peau au Moi-pensant*. Paris: Dunod.

Axelrod, Steven Gould. 1990. *Sylvia Plath: The Wound and the Cure of Wounds*. Baltimore: John Hopkins University Press.

Bachelard, Gaston. 1964. *The Poetics of Space*. Trans. Maria Jolas. Boston: Beacon.

Bachmann-Medick, Doris. 1996. "Einleitung." In Doris Bachmann-Medick, ed., *Kultur als Text: Die anthropologische Wende in der Literaturwissenschaft*, 7–66. Frankfurt: Fischer.

Bakhtin, Mikhail. 1984. *Rabelais and His World*. Trans. Helene Iswolsky. Blooming-ton: Indiana University Press.

Balint, Michael. 1987. *Regression: Therapeutische Aspekte und die Theorie der Grundstörung*. Stuttgart: Klett-Cotta, 1987.

Balzac, Honoré de. 1909. *A Woman of Thirty*. Trans. George Burnham Ives. Boston: Little, Brown.

Barruzi, Arno. 1993. "Vom Tastsinn des animal rationale." In Michael Großheim and Hans-Joachim Waschkies, eds., *Rehabilitierung des Subjektiven: Festschrift für Hermann Schmitz*, 111–128. Bonn: Bouvier.

Barta Fliedl, Ilsebill and Christoph Geissmar, eds. 1992. *Die Beredsamkeit des Leibes: Zur Körpersprache in der Kunst*. Salzburg: Residenz.

Barthel, Christian. 1989. *Medizinische Polizey und medizinische Aufklärung: Aspekte des öffentlichen Gesundheitsdiskurses im 18. Jahrhundert*. Frankfurt: Campus.

Barthes, Roland. 1978. *A Lover's Discourse: Fragments*. Trans. Richard Howard. New York: Hill and Wang.

Bastian, Till and Micha Hilgers. 1990. "Kain: Die Trennung von Scham und Schuld am Beispiel der Genesis." *Psyche* 44:1100–1112.

Baumstark, Reinhold and Peter Volk, eds. 1995. *Apoll schindet Marsyas: Über das Schreckliche in der Kunst*. Catalog of the Bavarian National Museum. Passau: Passavia.

Beier, Rosemarie and Martin Roth, eds. 1990. *Der Gläserne Mensch—Eine Sensation: Zur Kulturgeschichte eines Ausstellungsobjekts*. Catalog of the German Historical Museum, Berlin. Stuttgart: Hatje.

Békésy, Georg von. 1959. "Similarities Between Hearing and Skin Sensation." *Psychological Review* 66, no. 1 (January): 1–23.

Benninghoff, Alfred, Kurt Goerttler, and Kurt Fleischhauer, eds. 1985. *Makroskopische und mikroskopische Anatomie des Menschen*. 3 vols. 13th/14th eds. Munich: Urban und Schwarzenberg.

Benthien, Claudia. 1994a. "Das Feste, das Fließende und das Fragmentarische: Grundstrukturen in Jahnns Tragödie *Medea*." *Forum: Homosexualität und Literatur* 22 (November): 63–81.

———. 1994b. "Meiner Augen Sehnsucht: Blick, Blendung und Begehren in Hans Henry Jahnns Tragödie 'Medea.'" M.A. diss., Washington University, St. Louis.

———. 1996. "Im Leibe wohen: Zur Kulturgeschichte und Metaphorik des Hauses und der Grenze im Diskurs über die Haut." In *Tasten*, 143–163. Kunst- und Ausstellungshalle der BRD, Schriftenreihe Forum 7. Göttingen: Steidl.

———. 1997a. " 'The Whiteness Underneath the Nigger': Albinism and Blackness in John Edgar Wideman's *Sent for You Yesterday*." *Utah Foreign Language Review* 1:3–13.

———. 1997b. "Häutungen: Folter—Enthüllung—Gestaltwandel. Zur Kulturgeschichte einer 'Entdeckung.'" *Paragrana* 6, no. 1: 197–217.

———. 1998. "Hand und Haut: Zur historischen Anthropologie von Tasten und Berührung." *Zeitschrift für Germanistik*, n.s., 8, no. 2: 335–348.

Berg, Eberhard and Martin Fuchs, eds. 1993. *Kultur, soziale Praxis, Text: Die Krise der ethnographischen Repräsentation.* Frankfurt: Suhrkamp.

Bergmann, Anna. 1997. "Töten, Opfern, Zergliedern und Reinigen in der Konstitutionsgeschichte des modernen Körpermodells." *Metis* 6, no. 11: 45–64.

Berkeley, George. 1948. "A New Theory on Vision." In *The Works of George Berkeley.* Ed. A. A. Luce and T. E. Jessop. Vol. 1. London: Nelson.

de Bersaques, J. 1994. *L'art de regarder: Histoire visuelle de la dermatologie et de la mycologie.* Beerse, Belgium: Janssen-Lilag.

Bick, Ester. 1968. "The Experience of the Skin in Early Object-Relations." *International Journal of Psycho-Analysis* 49:484–486.

Biven, Barrie M. 1982. "The Role of the Skin in Normal and Abnormal Development with a Note on the Poet Sylvia Plath." *International Review of Psycho-Analysis* 63, no. 9: 205–258.

Blankenburg, Martin. 1996. "Rassistische Physiognomik: Beiträge zu ihrer Geschichte und Struktur." In Claudia Schmölders, ed., *Der exzentrische Blick: Gespräche über Physiognomik,* 133–161. Berlin: Akademie.

Blumenberg, Hans. 1960. "Paradigmen zu einer Metaphorologie." In *Archiv für Begriffsgeschichte* 6, 7–142. Bonn: Bouvier.

———. 1988. *Höhlenausgänge.* Frankfurt: Suhrkamp.

———. 1993a. *Die Lesbarkeit der Welt.* 3d ed. Frankfurt: Suhrkamp.

———. 1993b. "Ausblick auf eine Theorie der Unbegrifflichkeit." In *Schiffbruch mit Zuschauer. Paradigma einer Daseinsmetapher,* 75–93. Frankfurt: Suhrkamp.

Böhme, Gernot. 1989. "Der offene Leib: Interpretationen der Mikrokosmos Makrokosmos Beziehung bei Paracelsus." In Dietmar Kamper and Christoph Wulff, eds., *Transfigurationen des Körpers: Spuren der Gewalt in der Geschichte,* 44–59. Berlin: Reimer.

Böhme, Gernot and Hartmut Böhme. 1996. *Feuer, Wasser, Erde, Luft: Eine Kulturgeschichte der Elemente.* Munich: Beck.

Böhme, Hartmut. 1988. "Sinne und Blick: Zur mythopoetischen Konstitution des Subjekts." In *Natur und Subjekt,* 215–255. Frankfurt: Suhrkamp.

———. 1992. *Hubert Fichte: Riten des Autors und Leben der Literatur.* Stuttgart: Metzler.

———. 1996. "Der Tastsinn im Gefüge der Sinne: Anthropologische und historische Ansichten vorsprachlicher Aisthesis." In *Tasten,* 185–210. Kunst- und Ausstellungshalle der BRD, Schriftenreihe Forum 7. Göttingen: Steidl.

———. 1997a. "Gefühl." In Christoph Wulf, ed., *Vom Menschen: Handbuch Historische Anthropologie,* 525–548. Weinheim: Beltz.

———. 1997b. "Enthüllen und Verhüllen des Körpers: Biblische, mythische und künstlerische Deutungen des Nackten." *Paragrana* 6, no. 1: 218–246.

Böhme, Hartmut and Klaus Scherpe. 1996. "Zur Einführung." In Hartmut Böhme and Klaus Scherpe, eds., *Literatur und Kulturwissenschaften: Positionen, Theorien, Modelle,* 7–24. Reinbek: Rowohlt.

Bolte, Otto. 1964. "Dermatologie und Kunst: Über die malerische Darstellung menschlicher Haut and menschlicher Kopfbehaarung als Ausdruck stilistischer und kunstgeschichtlicher Wandlung." *Der Hautarzt* 15:442–448.

Braun, Christina von. 1997. "Zum Begriff der Reinheit." *Metis* 6, no. 11: 7–25.

Brownmiller, Susan, 1984. *Femininity*. New York: Linden.

Buchborn, E. 1988. "Beziehungen zwischen innerer Medizin und Dermatologie." In Günter Burg, ed., *Dermatologie: Entwicklung und Beziehungen zu anderen Fachbereichen*, 349–355. Munich: Urban und Schwarzenberg.

Büchner, Georg. 1986. *Complete Works and Letters*. Trans. Henry J. Schmidt. New York: Continuum.

Buffon, Georges-Louis Leclerc de. 1861. "Variétés dans l'espèce humaine." In *Oeuvres choisies de Buffon*. Vol. 1. Paris: Firmin Didot.

Burton, Robert. 1989–2000. *The Anatomy of Melancholy*. Intro. J. B. Bamborough. 6 vols. Oxford: Oxford University Press, Clarendon.

Caillois, Roger. 1959. "Der Komplex Medusa." *Antaios* 1:527–555.

Cameron, Deborah and Elizabeth Frazer. 1987. *The Lust to Kill: A Feminist Investigation of Sexual Murder*. New York: New York University Press.

Carus, Carl Gustav. 1975. *Natur und Idee oder Das Werdende und sein Gesetz: Eine philosophische Grundlage für die Naturwissenschaften*. Hildesheim: Olms.

De Certeau, Michel. 1979. "Des outils pour écrire le corps." *Traverses* 14/15:3–14.

Charbon, Rémy. 1996. "Der 'weiße' Blick: Über Kleists *Verlobung in St. Domingo*." In Hans Joachim Kreutzer, ed., *Heinrich von Kleists Erzählung 'Die Verlobung in St. Domingo.'* Kleist Jahrbuch 1996, 77–88. Stuttgart: Metzler.

Clair, Jean, ed. 1993. *L'âme au corps: Arts et sciences, 1793–1993*. Catalog of the Grand Palais. Paris: Gallimard.

Coleman, James W. 1989. "Interview with John Edgar Wideman." *Blackness and Modernism: The Literary Career of John Edgar Wideman*, 145–162. Jackson: Mississippi University Press.

Condillac, Étienne Bonnot de. 1930. *Condillac's Treatise on the Sensations*. Trans. Geraldine Carr. Los Angeles: School of Philosophy, University of Southern California.

Condrau, Gion and Heinrich Schipperges. 1993. *Unsere Haut: Spiegel der Seele, Verbindung zur Welt*. Zurich: Kreuz.

Dagognet, François. 1982. *Faces, surfaces, interfaces*. Paris: Vrin.

———. 1993. *La peau découverte*. Paris: Les empêcheurs de penser en rond.

Dane, Gesa. 1994. *Die heilsame Toilette: Kosmetik und Bildung in Goethes "Der Mann von fünfzig Jahren."* Göttingen: Wallstein.

Delestre, Jean Bernard. 1866. *De la physiognomie: Teste-dessin-gravures*. Paris: Renouard.

Diderot, Denis. 1995. *Diderot on Art*. Ed. and trans. John Goodman. Vol. 1, *The Salon of 1765 and Notes on Painting*. Intro. Thomas Crow. New Haven: Yale University Press.

Didi-Huberman, Georges. 1987. "The Figurative Incarnation of the Sentence (Notes on the Autographic Skin)." *Journal: A Contemporary Art Magazine* (spring): 67–70.

Diggory, Terence. 1979. "Armored Women, Naked Men: Dickinson, Whitman, and Their Successors." In Sandra M. Gilbert and Susan Gubar, eds., *Shakespeare's Sisters: Feminist Essays on Women Poets*, 135–150. Bloomington: Indiana University Press.

Dorfles, Gillo. 1974. " 'Innen' et 'Aussen' en architecture et en psychanalyse." *Nouvelle Revue de Psychanalyse* 9:229–238.

Duden, Barbara. 1991a. *The Woman Beneath the Skin: A Doctor's Patients in Eighteenth-Century Germany*. Trans. Thomas Dunlap. Cambridge: Harvard University Press.

———. 1991b. *Der Frauenleib als öffentlicher Ort: Vom Mißbrauch des Begriffs Leben*. Hamburg: Luchterhand.

Duerr, Hans Peter. 1988. *Nacktheit und Scham*. Der Mythos vom Zivilisationsprozeß 1. 2d ed. Frankfurt: Suhrkamp.

———. 1993. *Obszönität und Gewalt*. Der Mythos vom Zivilisationsprozeß 3. Frankfurt: Suhrkamp.

Eder, M. 1988. "Pathologie und Dermatologie." In Günter Burg, ed., *Dermatologie: Entwicklungen und Beziehungen zu anderen Fachbereichen*, 375–381. Munich: Urban und Schwarzenberg.

Ehring, Franz. 1989. *Hautkrankheiten: 5 Jahrhunderte wissenschaftlicher Illustration*. Stuttgart: Fischer.

Ehrismann, Otfrid. 1981. "Siegfried. Studie über Heldentum, Liebe und Tod: Mittelalterliche Nibelungen, Hebbel, Wagner." In Detlef Colln, ed., *Hebbel-Jahrbuch*, 11–48. Heide: Boyens.

Eiblmayr, Sylvia. 1993. *Die Frau als Bild: Der weibliche Körper in der Kunst des 20. Jahrhunderts*. Berlin: Reimer.

Elias, Nobert. 1978. *The Civilizing Process*. 2 vols. Trans. Edmund Jephcott. New York: Urizen.

Ellison, Ralph. 1990. *Invisible Man*. New York: Vintage.

———. 1994. *Shadow and Act*. New York: Quality.

Engel, Johann Jakob. 1805. "Über einige Eigenheiten des Gefühlssinnes." In *J. J. Engels Schriften* 9:201–228. Berlin: Mylius.

Ersch, J. G. and J. G. Gruber, eds. 1828. *Allgemeine Encyklopädie der Wissenschaften und Künste*, vol. 3, part 2. Leipzig: F. A. Brockhaus.

Evers, Bernd, ed. 1995. *Architekturmodelle der Renaissance: Die Harmonie des Bauens von Alberti bis Michelangelo*. Catalog of the Altes Museum, Berlin. Munich: Prestel.

Ewing, Willam A. 1994. *The Body: Photoworks of the Human Form*. London: Thames and Hudson.

Export, Valie. 1995. "Kausalgie." In Christoph Geissmar-Brandi and Eleonora Louis, eds., *Glaube Hoffnung Liebe Tod*, 468–469. Catalog of the Kunsthalle, Wien. Klagenfurt: Ritter.

Fanon, Frantz. 1967. *Black Skin, White Masks*. New York: Grove.

Feher, Michael. 1989. Introduction to Michael Feher, Ramona Naddaff, and Nadia Tazi, eds., *Fragments for a History of the Human Body*, 1:11–17. New York: Zone.

Fehl, Philipp. 1995. "Über das Schreckliche in der Kunst; 'Die Schindung des Marsyas' als Aufgabe." *Apoll schindet Marsyas: Über das Schreckliche in der Kunst*, exhibition catalog, Bayerisches Nationalmuseum. Passau: Passavia.

Fischer-Homburger, Esther. 1998. "Die Haut retten." *Du* 4:76–77.

Flügel, J. C. 1986. "Psychologie der Kleidung." In Silvia Bovenschen, ed., *Die Listen der Mode*, 208–263. Frankfurt: Suhrkamp.

Foucault, Michel. 1973. *The Birth of the Clinic*. Trans. A. M. Sheridan Smith. New York: Pantheon.

———. 1979. *Discipline and Punish: The Birth of the Prison*. Trans. Alan Sheridan. New York: Vintage.

Fouqué, Friedrich de la Motte. 2000. *Romantic Fairy Tales*. Trans. Carol Tully. London: Penguin.

Frank, Lawrence K. 1954. "The Psychological Approach to Sex Research." *Social Problems* 1:137.

Freud, Sigmund. 1953. "Three Essays on Sexuality and Other Works." In *The Standard Edition of the Complete Psychological Works of Sigmund Freud*, trans. James Strachey, in collaboration with Anna Freud, assisted by Alix Strachey and Alan Tyson. Vol. 7. London: Hogarth.

———. 1961. "The Ego and the Id and Other Works." *The Standard Edition of the Complete Psychological Works of Sigmund Freud*, trans. James Strachey. Vol. 19. London: Hogarth.

———. 1963. "Introductory Lectures on Psycho-analysis." *The Standard Edition of the Complete Psychological Works of Sigmund Freud*, trans. James Strachey. Vol. 15. London: Hogarth.

Frier, Wolfgang. 1976. *Die Sprache der Emotionalität in den "Verwirrungen des Zöglings Törleß" von Robert Musil*. Bonn: Bouvier.

Fritsch, Peter. 1985. "Die Haut." In Alfred Benninghoff, Kurt Goerttler, and Kurt Fleischhauer, eds., *Makroskopische und mikroskopische Anatomie des Menschen*, 2:565–586. 13th/14th eds. Munich: Urban und Schwarzenberg.

Frost, Peter. 1990. "Fair Women, Dark Men: The Forgotten Roots of Colour Prejudice." *History of European Ideas* 12, no. 5: 669–79.

Gatewood, Willard B. 1996. "Skin Color." In Jack Salzmann, David Lionel Smith, and Cornel West, eds., *Encyclopedia of African-American Culture and History*, 5:2444–2449. New York: Macmillan.

Gay, Peter. 1973. *The Enlightenment: A Comprehensive Anthology*. New York: Simon and Schuster.

Geissmar-Brandi, Christoph and Eleonora Louis, eds. 1995. *Glaube Hoffnung Liebe Tod*. Catalog of the Kunsthalle, Wien. Klagenfurt: Ritter.

Geitner, Ursula. 1992. *Die Sprache der Verstellung: Studien zum rhetorischen und anthropologischen Wissen im 17. und 18. Jahrhundert.* Tübingen: Niemeyer.

Gergen, Kenneth J. 1967. "The Significance of Skin Color in Human Relations." *Daedalus* 96:390–406.

Gieler, Uwe. 1986. "Haut und Körpererleben." In Elmar Brähler, ed., *Körpererleben: Ein subjektiver Ausdruck von Leib und Seele. Beiträge zur psychosomatischen Medizin.* Berlin: Springer.

Gieler, Uwe and Klaus Andreas Bosse, eds. 1996. *Seelische Faktoren bei Hautkrankheiten.* Berne: Hans Huber.

Giersch, Ulrich and Ulrich Raulff. 1979. "Gesicht, Gefühl, Gehäut." *Tumult* 2:70–85.

Gilman, Sander L. 1982. *On Blackness Without Blacks: Essays on the Image of the Black in Germany.* Boston: Hall.

———. 1985. "Black Bodies, White Bodies: Toward an Iconography of Female Sexuality in Late Nineteenth-Century Art, Medicine, and Literature." *Critical Inquiry* 12, no. 1: 204–242.

———. 1986. "Black Sexuality and Modern Consciousness." In Reinhold Grimm and Jost Hermand, eds., *Blacks and German Culture,* 35–53. Madison: University of Wisconsin Press.

———. 1992. *Rasse, Sexualität und Seuche: Stereotype aus der Innenwelt der westlichen Kultur.* Reinbek: Rowohlt.

Goethe, Johann Wolfgang. 1974. *The Autobiography of Johann Wolfgang von Goethe.* Trans. John Oxenford. 2 vols. Chicago: University of Chicago Press.

———. 1982. *Wilhelm Meister's Years of Travel.* Trans H. M. Waidson. 3 vols. London: Calder.

———. 1984. *Faust I and II.* Ed. and trans. Stuart Atkins. Cambridge, Mass.: Suhrkamp/Insel.

———. 1988a. "Götz von Berlichingen." In *Early Verse Drama and Prose Plays.* Ed. and trans. Cyrus Hamlis and Frank Ryder. New York: Suhrkamp.

———. 1988b. *Scientific Studies.* Trans. Douglas Miller. New York: Suhrkamp.

———. 1988c. *Dramen, 1765–1775.* Ed. Dieter Borchmeyer, with collaboration from Peter Huber. Sämtliche Werke: Briefe, Tagebücher und Gespräche, part 1, vol. 4. Frankfurt: Klassiker.

———. 1988d. *Dramen, 1765–1775.* Ed. Dieter Borchmeyer, with collaboration from Peter Huber. Sämtliche Werke: Briefe, Tagebücher und Gespräche, part 1, vol. 4. Frankfurt: Klassiker.

———. 1988e. *Gedichte, 1800–1832.* Ed. Karl Eibl. Sämtliche Werke: Briefe, Tagebücher und Gespräche, part 1, vol. 2. Frankfurt: Klassiker.

———. 1997. *Das erste Weimarer Jahrzehnt: Briefe, Tagebücher und Gespräche.* Sämtliche Werke: Briefe, Tagebücher und Gespräche, part 2, vol. 2. Ed. Hartmut Reinhardt. Frankfurt: Klassiker.

Goffman, Erving. 1959. *The Presentation of Self in Everyday Life.* Garden City, N.Y.: Doubleday.

———. 1963. *Stigma: Notes on the Management of Spoiled Identity.* Englewood Cliffs, N.J.: Prentice-Hall.

Grammers, Karl. 1996. "Berühren und Verführen: Die Logik der taktilen Kommunikation." *Tasten*, 91–109. Kunst- und Ausstellungshalle der BRD, Schriftenreihe Forum 7. Göttingen: Steidl.

Grant, Michael and John Hazel. 1993. *Who's Who in Classical Mythology.* London: Dent.

Graves, Robert. 1960. *The Greek Myths.* 2 vols. New York: Penguin.

Graves, Robert and Raphael Patai. 1964. *Hebrew Myths: The Books of Genesis.* New York: Doubleday.

Grimm, Jacob and Wilhelm Grimm. 1984. *Deutsches Wörterbuch.* Ed. Moritz Heyne. 33 vols. Reprint. Munich: dtv.

Gröning, Karl. 1997. *Geschmückte Haut: Eine Kulturgeschichte der Körperkunst.* Munich: Frederking und Thaler.

Grosz, Elisabeth. 1994. *Volatile Bodies: Toward a Corporeal Feminism.* Bloomington: Indiana University Press.

Hahn, Susanne and Dimitrios Ambatielos, eds. 1994. *Wachs-Moulagen und Modelle.* Wissenschaft im Deutschen Hygiene-Museum, 1. Dresden: DHM.

Halbach, Wulf R. 1994. *Interfaces: Medien- und kommunikationstheoretische Elemente einer Interface-Theorie.* Munich: Fink.

Halberstam, Judith. 1991. "Skinflick: Posthuman Gender in Jonathan Demme's 'The Silence of the Lambs.' " *Camera Obscura* 27:37–52.

———. 1995. *Skin Shows: Gothic Horror and the Technology of Monsters.* London: Duke University Press.

Hamann, Frauke and Regula Venske, eds. 1994. *Weiberjahnn: Eine Polemik zu Hans Henny Jahnn.* Hamburg: eva.

Harather, Karin. 1995. *Haus-Kleider: Zum Phänomen der Bekleidung in der Architektur.* Vienna: Böhlau.

Hauskeller, Michael. 1995. *Atmosphären erleben: Philosophische Untersuchungen zur Sinneswahrnehmung.* Berlin: Akademie.

Hawthorne, Nathaniel. 1982. "The Birthmark." In Roy Harvey Pearce, ed., *Tales and Sketches*, 764–780. New York: Literary Classics.

———. 1986. *The Scarlett Letter.* Ed. Nina Baym. New York: Penguin.

Hebbel, Friedrich. 1963–1964. *Werke.* 2 vols. Ed. Gerhard Fricke, Werner Keller, and Karl Pornbacher. Darmstadt: Wissenschaftiche Buchgesellschaft.

Heiligenthal, Peter and Reinhard Volk, eds. 1972. *Bürgerliche Wahnwelt um Neunzehnhunder: Denkwürdigkeiten eines Nervenkranken von Daniel Paul Schreber.* Wiesbaden: Focus.

Hensel, Herbert. 1966. *Allgemeine Sinnesphysiologie: Hautsinne, Geschmack, Geruch.* Berlin: Springer.

Henseler, Heinz. 1974. *Narzißtische Krisen: Zur Psychodynamik des Selbstmords*. Reinbek: Rowohlt.

Herder, Johann Gottfried. 1966. *Outlines of a Philosophy of the History of Man*. Trans. T. Churchill. New York: Bergman.

———. 1985–1997. *Werke in 10 Bänden*. Ed. Martin Bollacher et al. Frankfurt: Klassiker.

———. 1994. *Schriften zu Philosophie, Literatur, Kunst und Altertum, 1774–1787*. Ed. Jürgen Brummack and Martin Bollacher. Vol. 4 of *Werke in 10 Bänden*. Frankfurt: Klassiker.

Herrlinger, Robert. 1968. "Die geschundene Haut im barocken anatomischen Titelkupfer." In Heinz Goerke and Heinz Müller-Dietz, eds., *Verhandlungen des XX. internationalen Kongresses für Geschichte der Medizin*, 474–496. Hildesheim: Ohlms.

Höfer, Werner and W. Prankl. 1968. *Die vierte Haut: Leitbild einer Stadt*. Vienna: Ranner.

Hoffmann, Detlef. 1989. "Der nackte Mensch: Zur aktuellen Diskussion über ein altes Thema." In Detlef Hoffmann, ed., *Der nackte Mensch*, 7–29. Marburg: Jonas.

Hofmann, Werner. 1973. "Marsyas und Apoll." *Merkur* 27, nos. 4/5: 403–417.

Hohnemser, Richard. 1911. "Wendet sich die Philosophie an den Tastsinn?" *Zeitschrift für Ästhetik und allgemeine Kunstwissenschaft* 6:405–419.

Hollander, Anne. 1993. *Seeing through Clothes*. Berkeley: University of California Press.

Holubar, Karl, Cathrin Schmidt, and Klaus Wolff. 1993. *Challenge Dermatology: Vienna, 1841–1992*. Vienna: Österr. Akademie der Wissenschaften.

Holzegel, K. 1995. "Zur ärztlichen Führung Neurodermitiskranker." *Dermatologie* 43:995.

Horn, Katalin. 1995. "Die Identität des Helden und der Heldin: Leib, Kleid und Tierhaut im Volksmärchen." In Paul Michael, ed., *Symbolik des menschlichen Leibes*, 191–207. Schriften zur Symbolforschung, 10. Bern: Lang.

Horn, Peter. 1990. " 'Man verkriecht sich hinter seiner Haut': Zu Robert Musils 'Die Schwärmer.' " In *Acta Germanica: Jahrbuch des Germanistenverbandes im Südlichen Afrika*, 79–105. Frankfurt: Lang.

Hughes, Michael and Bradley R. Hertel. 1990. "The Significance of Color Remains: A Study of Life Chances, Mate Selections, and Ethnic Consciousness Among Black Americans." *Social Forces* 69:1105–1119.

Hurston, Zora Neale. 1981. "Characteristics of Negro Expression." In *The Sanctified Church: The Folklore Writings of Zora Neal Hurston*, 49–68. Berkeley: Turtle Island.

———. 1985. "Glossary of Harlem Slang." In *Spunk: The Selected Stories of Zora Neale Hurston*, 91–96. Berkeley: Turtle Island Foundation.

———. 1990. *Their Eyes Were Watching God*. New York: Harper.

Jager, Bernd. 1984. "Body, House, City; or, The Intertwinings of Embodiment, Inhabitation and Civilisation." In Dreyer Kruger, ed., *The Changing Reality of Modern Man: Essays in Honor of Jan Hendrik van den Berg*, 51–61. Juta, Capetown: Juta.

Jahnn, Hans Henny. 1985. *Perrudja*. Ed. Gerd Rupprecht. Hamburg: Hoffmann und Campe.

————. 1986a. *Fluß ohne Ufer I: Das Holzschiff; Die Niederschrift des Gustav Anias Horn I.* Ed. Uwe Schweikert. Hamburg: Hoffmann und Campe.

————. 1986b. *Fluß ohne Ufer II: Die Niederschrift des Gustav Anias Horn II.* Ed. Uwe Schweikert. Hamburg: Hoffmann und Campe.

————. 1988. *Dramen I, 1917–1929.* Ed. Ulrich Bitz. Hamburg: Hoffmann und Campe.

————. 1993. *Dramen II, 1930–1959.* Ed. Uwe Schweikert and Ulrich Bitz. Hamburg: Hoffmann und Campe.

Jardner, Herbert W. 1995. "Kleidung als Wohnung des Leibes: Ikonographische Betrachtun gen zur textilen Metaphorik der Atoin Meto in West-Timor." In Michael Großheim, ed., *Leib und Gefühl: Beiträge zur Anthropologie,* 169–192. Berlin: Akademie.

Johnson, Kenneth R. 1973. "Words Used for Skin Color in the Black Culture." *Florida Foreign Language Reporter* 11:15–40.

Joraschky, Peter. 1986. "Das Körperschema und das Körper-Selbst." In Elmar Brähler, ed., *Körpererleben: Ein subjektiver Ausdruck von Leib und Seele. Beiträge zur psychosomatischen Medizin,* 34–49. Berlin: Springer.

Kafka, Franz. 1976. *Selected Writings.* Trans. Willa Muir, Edwin Muir, and others. London: Secker and Warburg, Octopus.

————. 1983. *The Complete Stories.* Ed. Nahum N. Glatzer. New York: Schocken.

————. 1990. *Tagebücher.* Schriften, Tagebücher, Briefe: Kritische Ausgabe, vol. 3. Ed. Hans-Gerd Koch, Michael Müller, and Malcolm Pasley. Frankfurt: Fischer.

————. 1994a. *Drucke zu Lebzeiten.* Schriften, Tagebücher, Briefe: Kritische Ausgabe, vol. 7. Ed. Hans-Gerd Koch, Wolf Kittler, and Gerhard Neumann. Frankfurt: Fischer.

————. 1994b. *Tagebücher.* Ed. Wolf Kittler, Hans-Gerd Koch, and Gerhard Neumann. Frankfurt: Suhrkamp.

Kamper, Dietmar and Christoph Wulf. 1982. "Die Parabel der Wiederkehr: Zur Einführung." In Dietmar Kamper and Christoph Wulf, eds., *Die Wiederkehr des Körpers,* 9–19. Frankfurt: Suhrkamp.

————. 1984. "Blickwende: Die Sinne des Körpers im Konkurs der Geschichte." In Dietmar Kamper and Christoph Wulf, eds., *Das Schwinden der Sinne,* 9–17. Frankfurt: Suhrkamp.

————. 1989. "Lektüre einer Narbenschrift: Der menschliche Körper als Gegenstand und Gedächtnis von historischer Gewalt." In Dietmar Kamper and Christoph Wulf, eds., *Transfigurationen des Körpers: Spuren der Gewalt in der Geschichte,* 1–7. Berlin: Reimer.

Kant, Immanuel. 1977. *Schriften zur Anthropologie, Geschichtsphilosophie, Politik und Pädagogik.* Vol. 11 of *Werkausgabe.* Ed. Wilhelm Weischedel. Frankfurt: Suhrkamp.

———. 1978. *Anthropology from a Pragmatic Point of View*. Trans. Victor Lyle Dowdell. Rev. and ed. Hans H. Rudnick. Carbondale and Edwardsville: Southern Illinois University Press.

Kaufmann, Hans. 1943. "Die Fünf Sinne in der niederländischen Malerei des 17. Jahrhunderts." In Hans Tintelnot, ed., *Kunstgeschichtliche Studien: Festschrift für Dagobert Frey*, 133–157. Breslau: Schmidt.

Kerckhove, Derrick de. 1993. "Touch versus Vision: Ästhetik neuer Technologien." In Wolfgang Welsch et al., eds., *Die Aktualität des Ästhetischen*, 137–168. Munich: Fink.

———. 1996a. "Täuschung der Eigenwahrnehmung und Automatisierung." *Die Zukunft des Körpers II, Kunstforum* 133:121–125.

———. 1996b. "Propriozeption und Autonomation." In *Tasten*, 330–345. Kunst- und Ausstellungshalle der BRD, Schriftenreihe Forum 7. Göttingen: Steidl.

Kittler, Wolf. 1990. "Schreibmaschinen, Sprechmaschinen: Effekte technischer Medien im Werk Franz Kafkas." In Wolf Kittler and Gerhard Neumann, eds., *Franz Kafka: Schriftverkehr*, 75–163. Freiburg: Rombach.

Klauser, Theodor et al., eds. 1976. *Reallexikon für Antike und Christentum*. Vol. 4. Stuttgart: Hiersemann.

———. 1978. *Reallexikon für Antike und Christentum*. Vol. 10. Stuttgart: Hiersemann.

———. 1986. *Reallexikon für Antike und Christentum*. Vol. 13. Stuttgart: Hiersemann.

Kleine-Natrop, Heinz Egon. 1961. "Vom Schinden und den Geschundenen." *Ästhetische Medizin* 10, no. 8: 237–252.

Kleist, Heinrich von. 1961. *Sämtliche Werke und Briefe in zwei Bänden*. Ed. Helmut Sembdner. 3 vols. Munich: Hanser.

———. 1997. *Selected Writings*. Ed. and trans. David Constantine. London: Dent.

Klimpel, Manfred. 1980. *Ferdinand von Hebra, Atlas der Hauterkrankungen (1856–1876)*. Cologne: Forschungsstelle des Instituts für Geschichte der Medizin der Universität zu Köln.

Knigge, Volkhard. 1989. "Die Nackten—das Nackte—der Akt: Psychoanalytische Bemerkungen über Imaginäres und Symbolisches am Nackten." In Detlef Hoffmann, ed., *Der nackte Mensch*, 102–116. Marburg: Jonas.

Kohl, Karl-Heinz. 1986. *Entzauberter Blick: Das Bild vom Guten Wilden*. Frankfurt: Suhrkamp.

König, Oliver. 1990. *Nacktheit: Soziale Normen und Moral*. Opladen: Westdeutscher.

———. 1997. "Haut." In Christoph Wulf, ed., *Vom Menschen: Handbuch Historische Anthropologie*, 436–445. Weinheim: Beltz.

Korte, Barbara. 1996. "Berührung durch Text: Zur Semiotik der Berührung in der Literatur." *Tasten*, 125–142. Kunst- und Ausstellungshalle der BRD, Schriftenreihe Forum 7. Göttingen: Steidl.

Kremer, Detlef. 1989. *Kafka, die Erotik des Schreibens: Schreiben als Lebensentzug*. Frankfurt: Athenäum.

Kristeva, Julia. 1982. *Powers of Horror: An Essay on Abjection.* Trans. Leon Roudiez. New York: Columbia University Press.

———. 1987. *Tales of Love.* Trans. Leon S. Roudiez. New York: Columbia University Press.

Krüger-Fürhoff, Irmela Marei. 1998. "Der vervollständigte Torso und die verstümmelte Venus: Zur Rezeption antiker Plastik und plastischer Anatomie in Ästhetik und Reiseliteratur des 18. Jahrhunderts." *Historische Anthropologie, Zeitschrift für Germanistik,* n.s., 3, no. 2: 61–74.

Kuryluk, Ewa. 1991. "The Flaying of Marsyas." *Arts Magazine* 65 (April): 44–47.

Kutzer, Michael. 1990. "Kakerlaken: Rasse oder Kranke? Die Diskussion des Albinismus in der Anthropologie der zweiten Hälfte des 18. Jahrhunderts." In Gunter Mann and Franz Dumont, eds., *Die Natur des Menschen: Probleme der Physischen Anthropologie und Rassenkunde (1750–1850),* 189–220. Stuttgart: Fischer.

Lacan, Jacques. 1977. "The Mirror Stage as Formative of the Function of the I." Trans. Alan Sheridan. In *Selections.* New York: Norton.

Lacombe, P. 1959. "Du rôle de la peau dans l'attachement mère-enfant." *Revue française de Psychanalyse* 23, no. 1: 83–102.

Lant, Kathleen Margaret. 1993. "The Big Strip Tease: Female Bodies and Male Power in the Poetry of Sylvia Plath." *Contemporary Literature* 34, no. 4: 620–669.

Laplanche, J. and J.-B. Pontalis. 1994. *Das Vokabular der Psychoanalyse.* Trans. Emma Moersch. 12th ed. Frankfurt: Suhrkamp.

Laqueur, Thomas. 1990. *Making Sex: Body and Gender from the Greeks to Freud.* Cambridge: Harvard University Press.

Larsen, Nella. 1995. *Quicksand/Passing.* Ed. Deborah E. McDowell. New Brunswick, N.J.: Rutgers.

LeCat, Claude-Nicolas. 1765. *Traité de la couleur de la peau humaine en générale, de celle des Negres en particulier, et de la métamorphose d'une de ces couleurs en l'autre, soit de naissance, soit accidentellement.* Amsterdam: n.p.

Leclair, Thomas. 1993. " 'The Language Must Not Sweat': A Conversation with Toni Morrison." In Henry Louis Gates Jr. and K. Anthony Appiah, eds., *Toni Morrison: Critical Perspectives Past and Present,* 369–377. New York: Amistad.

Lee, Rensselaer W. 1967. *Ut Pictora Poesis: The Humanistic Theory of Painting.* New York: Norton.

Lehmann, Hans-Thies. 1991. "Das Welttheater der Scham: Dreißig Annäherungen an den Entzug der Darstellung." *Merkur* 45, nos. 9/10 (September/October): 824–838.

Lemire, Michel. 1990. *Artistes et morteles.* Paris: Chabaud.

———. 1993. "Fortunes et infortunes de l'anatomie et des preparations anatomiques, naturelles et artificielles." In *L'âme au corps: Arts et sciences, 1793–1993,* 70–101. Catalog of the Grand Palais. Ed. Jean Clair. Paris: Gallimard.

Lesky, Erna. 1971. "Anatomia Plastica im Wiener Josephinum." *Du* 5 (May): 366–377.

Lévinas, Emmanuel. 1987. *Totalität und Unendlichkeit: Versuch über die Exteriorität*. Freiburg: Alber.

Lévy, Alfred. 1997. *Haut und Seele: Auf dem Weg zu einer psychosomatischen Dermatologie*. Würzburg: Könighausen und Neumann.

Lichtenberg, Georg Christoph. 1983. "Über Physiognomik; wider die Physiognomen. Zu Beförderung der Menschenliebe und Menschenkenntnis." In Franz H. Mautner, ed., *Aufsätze, Satirische Schriften: Schriften und Briefe*, 2:78–116. Frankfurt: Insel.

Lindberg-Seyersted, Brita. 1992. "The Color of Black: Skin Color as Social, Ethical, and Esthetic Sign in Writings by Black American Women." *English Studies* 73, no. 1: 51–67.

Linke, Detlef B. 1998. "Aus der Haut fahren." *Du* 4:74–75.

Logau, Friedrich von. 1872. *Sämmtliche Sinngedichte*. 4 vols. Ed. Gustav Eitner. Tübingen: Literarischer Verein in Stuttgart.

de Loisy, D. 1981. "Enveloppes pathologiques, enveloppements thérapeutiques." *L'Evolution Psychiatrique* 46:857–872.

Luhmann, Niklas. 1986. *Love as Passion: The Codification of Intimacy*. Trans. Jeremy Gaines and Doris L. Jone. Cambridge: Harvard University Press.

Lyotard, Jean-François. 1993. *Libidinal Economy*. Trans. Iain Hamilton Grant. Bloomington: Indiana University Press.

Mach, Ernst. 1959. *The Analysis of Sensations and the Relation of the Physical to the Psychical*. Trans. C. M. Williams. Rev. and supp. from the 5th German ed. by Sydney Waterlow. New York: Dover.

Maguire, Anne. 1991. *Hauterkrankungen als Botschaften der Seele*. Trans. Dieter Kuhaupt. Olten: Walter.

Mahler, Margaret S., Fred Pine, and Anni Bergman. 1975. *The Psychological Birth of the Human Infant: Symbiosis and Individuation*. New York: Basic.

Manthey, Jürgen. 1983. *Wenn Blicke zeugen könnten: Eine psychohistorische Studie über das Sehen in Literatur und Philosophie*. Munich: Hanser.

Marples, Mary. 1973. "The Human Skin as an Eco-System." In Jonathan Benthall, ed., *Ecology in Theory and Practice*. New York: Viking.

Marshall, Paule. 1983. "Reena." In *Reena and Other Stories*. Old Westbury, New York: Feminist.

Massari, Stefania. 1983. *Giulio Bonasone*. 2 vols. Rome: Qusar.

Matt, Peter von. 1989. *"Fertig ist das Angesicht": Zur Literaturgeschichte des menschlichen Gesichts*. Frankfurt: Suhrkamp.

Mattenklott, Gert. 1982. *Der übersinnliche Leib: Beiträge zur Metaphysik des Körpers*. Reinbek: Rowohlt.

———. 1991. "Das tastende Auge." *Provokation der Sinne, Daidalos* 41 (September): 106–114.

Mazzolini, Renato G. 1990. "Anatomische Untersuchungen über die Haut der Schwarzen (1700–1800)." In Gunter Mann and Franz Dumont, eds., *Die Natur*

des Menschen: Probleme der Physischen Anthropologie und Rassenkunde (1750–1850),
169–187. Stuttgart: Fischer, 1990.

McMaster, Juliet. 1992. "The Body Inside the Skin: The Medical Model of Character in the Eighteenth-Century Novel." *Eighteenth Century Fiction* 4, no. 4 (July): 277–300.

Meisel, Gerhard. 1990. "Transplantation und Metamorphose: Das Motiv der Haut bei Musil und Kafka." In Josef Strutz and Endre Kiss, eds., *Genauigkeit und Seele: Zur Österreichischen Literatur seit dem Fin de Siècle,* 171–190. Musil Studien, 18. Munich: Fink.

Meisenheimer, Wolfgang. 1991. "Eine Sache der Haut." *Provokation der Sinne, Daidalos* 41 (September): 114–118.

Mercer, Kobena. 1994. *Welcome to the Jungle: New Positions on Black Cultural Studies.* New York, London: Routledge.

Merkel, Friedrich. 1917. *Haut, Sinnesorgane und nervöse Zentralorgane.* Die Anatomie des Menschen, 5. Wiesbaden: Bergmann.

Merleau-Ponty, Maurice. 1962. *Phenomenology of Perception.* Trans. Colin Smith. New York: Humanities.

Meyers Konversationslexikon. 1907–1909. 20 vols. 6th ed. Leipzig: Bibliographisches Institut.

Michelangelo. 1863. *Le Rime di Michelangelo Buonarotti cavate degli autografi.* Ed. Cesare Guasti. Florence: F. Le Monnier.

Mollenhauer, Klaus. 1989. "Der Körper im Augenschein: Rembrandts Anatomie-Bilder und einige Folgeprobleme." In Dietmar Kamper and Christoph Wulf, eds., *Der Schein des Schönen,* 177–203. Göttingen: Steidl.

Molloy Cora. 1996. "Fünf Thesen zu Liebestechniken." In *Tasten,* 300–302. Kunst- und Ausstellungshalle der BRD, Schriftenreihe Forum 7. Göttingen: Steidl.

Montagu, Ashley. 1971. *Touching: The Human Significance of the Skin.* New York: Columbia University Press.

———. 1984. "Die Haut." In Dietmar Kamper and Christoph Wulf, eds., *Das Schwinden der Sinne,* 210–225. Frankfurt: Suhrkamp.

Montesquieu, Charles-Louis de Secondat de la Brède. 1958. *De l'esprit des lois.*" In *Oeuvres complètes.* Ed. Roger Caillois. Vol. 2. Paris: Gallimard.

Morris, David B. 1991. *The Culture of Pain.* Berkeley: University of California Press.

Morrison, Toni. 1972. *The Bluest Eye.* New York: Washington Square.

———. 1982a. *Sula.* New York: Plume.

———. 1982b. *Tar Baby.* New York: Plume.

———. 1987. *Song of Solomon.* New York: Plume.

———. 1992. *Playing in the Dark: Whiteness and the Literary Imagination.* New York: Vintage.

Müller-Seidel, Walter. 1987. *Die Deportation des Menschen: Kafkas Erzählung "In der Strafkolonie" im europäischen Kontext.* Frankfurt: Fischer.

Museo del Prado, ed. 1997. *Los Cinco Sentidos y el Arte*. Madrid: Electa.

Musgrave, Marian E. 1986. "Literary Justifications of Slavery." In Reinhold Grimm and Jost Hermand, eds., *Blacks and German Culture*. University of Wisconsin Press.

Musil, Robert. 1957. *Prosa, Dramen, Späte Briefe*. Ed. Adolf Frisé. Reinbek: Rowohlt.

———. 1981. *Briefe, 1901–1942*. Ed. Adolf Frisé. Reinbek: Rowohlt.

———. 1995. *The Man Without Qualities*. Trans. Sophie Wilkins. 2 vols. New York: Knopf.

———. 1998. *Selected Writings*. Ed. Burton Pike. New York: Continuum.

The Nibelungenlied. 1969. Trans. A. T. Hatto. New York: Penguin.

Nietzsche, Friedrich Wilhelm. 1966. *Basic Writings of Nietzsche*. Trans. Walter Kaufmann. New York: Modern Library.

———. 1974. *The Gay Science*. Trans. Walter Kaufmann. New York: Random House.

———. 1986. *Human All-Too-Human*. Trans. R. J. Hollingdale. Part 1. Cambridge: Cambridge University Press.

Nordenfalk, Carl. 1976. "Les cinq sens dans l'art du Moyen Age." *Revue de l'Art* 34:17–28.

Nunberg, Herbert and Ernst Federn, eds. 1976. *Protokolle der Wiener Psychoanalytischen Vereinigung*. Vol. 1. Frankfurt: Fischer.

Oettermann, Stephan. 1994. *Zeichen auf der Haut: Die Geschichte der Tätowierung in Europa*. Hamburg: Europäische Verlagsanstalt.

Oken, Lorenz. 1811. *Lehrbuch der Naturphilosophie*. Vol. 3. Jena: Frommann.

Ondaatje, Michael. 1996. *The English Patient*. New York: Vintage.

Ovid. 1955. *Metamorphoses*. Trans. Mary M. Innes. New York: Penguin.

Pankow, Gisela. 1982. "Körperbild, Übergangsobjekt und Narzißmus." *Jahrbuch der Psychoanalyse* 14:216–228.

Parrish, Charles H. 1946. "Color Names and Color Notions." *Journal of Negro Education* 15:13–20.

Perniola, Mario. 1989. "Erotik des Schleiers und Erotik der Bekleidung." In Dietmar Kamper and Christoph Wulf, eds., *Der Schein des Schönen*, 427–451. Göttingen: Steidl.

Pieterse, Jan Nederveen. 1992. *White on Black: Images of African and Blacks in Western Popular Culture*. New Haven: Yale University Press.

Pilet, Charles, ed., 1981. *L'autre Fragonard*. Paris: Jupilles.

Pinder, Wilhelm. 1948. "Unser Tastsinn und die Kunst." In *Von den Künsten und der Kunst*, 23–32. Berlin: Deutscher Kunstverlag.

Pitzen, Marianne, Mako, K. Ursula Otto, and Annelene Bantzer, eds., 1983. *Haut*. Catalog of the FrauenMuseum Bonn. Bonn: Tempelhoff.

Plath, Sylvia. 1971. *The Bell Jar*. New York: Harper and Row.

———. 1979. *Johnny Panic and the Bible of Dreams: Short Stories, Prose, and Diary Excerpts*. New York: Harper and Row.

————. 1981. *Collected Poems*. Ed. Ted Hughes. London: Faber and Faber.

————. 1983. *The Journals of Sylvia Plath*. Ed. Ted Hughes and Frances McCullough. New York: Ballantine.

Plessner, Helmut. 1980. *Anthropologie der Sinne*. Gesammelte Schriften, vol. 3. Ed. Günter Dux, Odo Marquard, and Elsabeth Stroker. Frankfurt: Suhrkamp.

Poseq, Avigdor W. G. 1994. "Michelangelo's Self-Portrait on the Flayed Skin of St. Bartholomew." *Gazette des Beaux Arts* 124 (July/August): 1–13.

Pouchelle, Marie-Christine. 1981. "Des peaux des bêtes et des fourruses: Histoire médiévale d'une fascination." *Les temps de la réflexion* 2:403–438.

Proppe, A. 1964. "Der Krankheitsbegriff in der Dermatologie." *Studium Generale* 17, no. 8: 545–554.

Pusey, William Allan. 1933. *The History of Dermatology*. Springfield, Ill., and Baltimore: C. C. Thomas.

Putscher, Marielene. 1972. *Geschichte der medizinischen Abbildung*. Vol. 2, *Von 1600 bis zur Gegenwart*. 2d ed. Munich: Moos.

————. 1978. "Das Gefühl: Sinnengebrauch und Geschichte." In Marielene Putscher, ed., *Die fünf Sinne: Beiträge zu einer medizinischen Psychologie*, 147–158. Munich: Moos.

Rank, Otto. 1913. "Die Nacktheit in Sage und Dichtung: Eine psychoanalytische Studie." *Imago* 2:409–446.

Raphael, Max. 1989. "Der Tastsinn in der Kunst." In *Aufbruch in die Gegenwart: Begegnung mit der Kunst und den Künstlern des 20. Jahrhunderts*, 121–130. Ed. Hans-Jürgen Heinrichs. Frankfurt: Suhrkamp.

Rapp, Jürgen. 1985. "Ein Meisterstich der Florentiner Spätrenaissance entsteht: Bemerkungen zum Probedruck mit Vorzeichnungen für Melchior Meiers Kupferstich 'Apollo mit dem geschundenen Marsyas und das Urteil des Midas' in den Uffizien." *Pantheon* 43:61–70.

Rechenberger, Ilse. 1976. *Tiefenpsychologisch ausgerichtete Diagnostik und Behandlung von Hautkrankheiten*. Göttingen: Verlag für medizinische Psychologie.

Reemtsma, Jan Philipp. 1996. "Die Blutkur oder Die Angst vor den Ansprüchen der Oberfläche und warum alles immer wieder auf den Mord hinausläuft." In Hartmut Böhme and Uwe Schweikert, eds., *Archaische Moderne: Der Dichter, Architekt und Orgelbauer Hans Henny Jahnn*, 43–60. Stuttgart: Metzler/Poeschl.

Reiff, Helmut. 1989. "Haut, Körper und Symbol: Zur Rolle des Körperbildes in der psychoanalytischen Psychosomatik." *Jahrbuch der Psychoanalyse* 25:236–255.

Reudenbach, Bruno. 1980. "In mensuram humani corporis." In Christel Meier and Uwe Ruberg, eds., *Text und Bild: Aspekte des Zusammenwirkens zweier Künste in Mittelalter und früher Neuzeit*, 651–688. Wiesbaden: Reichert.

Richter, Paul. 1928. *Geschichte der Dermatologie*. Berlin: Springer.

Riley, Dorothy W., ed. 1993. *My Soul Looks back, 'less I Forget: A Collection of Quotations by People of Color*. New York: HarperCollins.

Rilke, Rainer Maria. 1982. *The Notebooks of Malte Laurids Brigge.* Trans. Stephen Mitchell. New York: Random House.

Roberts, K. B. and J. D. W. Tomlinson. 1992. *The Fabric of the Body: European Tradition of Anatomical Illustration.* Oxford: Oxford University Press, Clarendon.

Robins, Ashley H. 1991. *Biological Perspectives on Human Pigmentation.* New York: Cambridge University Press.

Rogers, Spencer L. 1990. *The Colors of Mankind: The Range and Role of Human Pigmentation.* Springfield, Mass.: Thomas.

Röhrich, Lutz. 1992. *Das große Lexikon der sprichwörtlichen Redensarten.* 3 vols. Freiburg: Herder.

Rost, Georg Alexander. 1956. "Schinden als Todesstrafe." *Der Hautarzt* 7, no. 11: 513–516.

Rousseau, Jean-Jacques. 2000. *Confessions.* Trans. Angela Scholar. Oxford, New York: Oxford University Press.

Rushdy, Ashraf H. A. 1991. "Fraternal Blues: John Edgar Wideman's Homewood Trilogy." *Contemporary Literature* 32, no. 3: 312–345.

Russell, Kathy, Midge Wilson, and Ronald Hall. 1993. *The Color Complex: The Politics of Skin Color Among African Americans.* New York: Doubleday.

Sachs, Hans. 1870. *Hans Sachs.* Ed. Adelbert von Keller. Vol. 5. Hildesheim: Olms.

Sami-Ali, M. 1984. *Le visuel et le tactile.* Paris: Dunod.

Sant, Ann Jessie van. 1993. *Eighteenth-Century Sensibility and the Novel: The Senses in Social Context.* Cambridge: Cambridge University Press.

Sawday, Jonathan. 1990. "The Fate of Marsyas: Dissecting the Renaissance Body." In Lucy Gent and Nigel Llewellyh, eds., *Renaissance Bodies: The Human Figure in English Culture, c. 1540–1660,* 111–135. London: Reaktion.

———. 1995. *The Body Emblazoned: Dissection and the Human Body in Renaissance Culture.* New York: Routledge.

Schechter, Harold. 1994. "Skin Deep: Folk Tales, Face Lifts, and *The Silence of the Lambs.*" *Literature—Interpretation—Theory* 5, no. 1: 19–27.

Scheel, Hans Ludwig. 1961. "Balzac als Physiognomiker." *Archiv für das Studium der neueren Sprachen* 193:227–244.

Schiller, Friedrich. 1958. *Wallenstein: A Historical Drama in Three Parts.* Trans. Charles E. Passage. New York: Ungar.

———. 1967. *On the Aesthetic Education of Man.* Ed. and trans. E. M. Wilkinson and L. A. Willougby. Oxford: Oxford University Press, Clarendon.

Schipperges, Heinrich. 1985. "Die Haut als Universalorgan im Spiegel der Geschichte." *Hautarzt* 36:414–420.

Schmitz, Hermann. 1982a. *Der Leib.* System der Philosophie, vol. 2, part 1. 2d ed. Bonn: Bouvier.

———. 1982b. *Der Rechtsraum.* System der Philosophie, vol. 3, part 2. 2d ed. Bonn: Bouvier.

————. 1992. *Leib und Gefühl: Materialien zu einer philosophischen Therapeutik.* Ed. Hermann Gausebeck and Gerhard Risch. 2d ed. Paderborn: Jungfermann.

Schmölders, Claudia. 1995. *Das Vorurteil im Leibe: Eine Einführung in die Physiognomik.* Berlin: Akademie.

Schnalke, Thomas. 1995. *Diseases in Wax: The History of the Medical Moulage.* Chicago: Quintessence.

Schönfeld, Walter. 1943. "Die Haut als Ausgang der Behandlung, Verhütung und Erkennung fernörtlicher Leiden: Eine geschichtliche Studie." *Südhofs Archiv* 36:43–89.

————. 1954. *Kurze Geschichte der Dermatologie und Venerologie und ihre kulturgeschichtliche Spiegelung.* Hannover: Oppermann.

Schreber, Daniel Paul. 1955. *Memoirs of My Nervous Illness.* Trans. and ed. Ida Macalpine and Richard A. Hunter. London: Dawson.

Schulte-Strathaus, Regine. 1994. "Seelenpein! Zur aktuellen Lage der 2 Millionen Psoriatiker Deutschlands." *TW Dermatologie* 24:6–7.

Séchaud, Evelyne. 1996. "Vom Haut-Ich zur Schmerzhülle." In *Tasten,* 164–184. Kunst- und Ausstellungshalle der BRD, Schriftenreihe Forum 7. Göttingen: Steidl.

Seidler, Günter H. 1988. "Scham: Phänomenologische und psychodynamische Aspekte eines Affekts." Manuscript.

Seitter, Walter. 1979. "Nacktheit als Kleidung." *Tumult* 2:3–24.

Serres, Michel. 1985. *Les cinq sens: Philosophie des corps mêlés.* Paris: Grasset.

Simmel, Georg. 1986. "Zur Psychologie der Scham." In Heinz-Jürgen Dahme and Otthein Rammstedt, eds., *Schriften zur Soziologie: Eine Auswahl,* 149–150. 2d ed. Frankfurt: Suhrkamp.

————. 1989. "Zur Psychologie der Frauen." *Aufsätze, 1887–1890: Über sociale Differenzierung u.a.* Vol. 2 of *Gesamtausgabe.* Ed. Heinz-Jürgen Dahme. Frankfurt: Suhrkamp.

Skrotzi, Dietmar. 1971. *Die Gebärde des Errötens im Werk Heinrich von Kleists.* Munich: Elwert.

Solente, Georges. 1983. "Le Musée de l'Hôpital Saint-Louis." *American Journal of Dermatopathology* 5 (October): 483–489.

Sonntag, Michael. 1989. "Die Zerlegung des Mikrokosmos: Der Körper in der Anatomie des 16. Jahrhunderts." In Dietmar Kamper and Christoph Wulf, eds., *Transfigurationen des Körpers: Spuren der Gewalt in der Geschichte,* 59–96. Berlin: Reimer.

Soons, Alan. 1989. "La piel humana en la narrative corta tradicional." *Revista de Dialecto logia y Tradiciones Populares* 44:73–79.

Spieß, Christian Heinrich. 1976. "Der gläserne Ökonom." In Wolfgang Promies, ed., *Biographien der Wahnsinnigen,* 62–87. Darmstadt: Luchterhand.

Stafford, Barbara Maria. 1993. *Body Criticism: Imagining the Unseen in Enlightenment Art and Medicine.* Cambridge: MIT Press.

———. 1998. *Kunstvolle Wissenschaft: Aufklärung, Unterhaltung und der Niedergang der visuellen Bildung*. Amsterdam, Dresden: Kunst.

Stefan, Verena. 1994. *Häutungen*. Frankfurt: Fischer.

Steinberg, Leo. 1980. "The Line of Fate in Michelangelo's Painting." *Critical Inquiry* (spring): 411–454.

Stelarc. 1984. *Obsolete Body: Suspensions*. Davis, Calif.: JP.

———. 1995. "Von Psycho- zu Cyberstrategien: Prothethik, Robotik und Tele-Existenz." *Die Zukunft des Körpers I, Kunstforum* 132:72–81.

———. 1996. "Fraktale Körper/Ping Body." In *Tasten*, 316–329. Kunst- und Ausstellungshalle der Bundesrepublik Deutschland, Schriftenreihe Forum 7. Göttingen: Steidl.

———. 1997. "Parasite Visions." In *Flesh Factor*. Catalog of the Ars Electronica Festival, 1997. Vienna, New York: Springer.

Stenslie, Stahl. 1995. "Vernetzung des Fleisches." *Die Zukunft des Körpers I, Kunstforum* 132:178–187.

Stephan, Inge. 1988. "Weiblichkeit, Wasser und Tod: Undinen, Melusinen und Wasserfrauen bei Eichendorff und Fouqué." In Hartmut Böhme, ed., *Kulturgeschichte des Wassers*, 234–262. Frankfurt: Suhrkamp.

Stevenson, Anne. 1989. *Bitter Fame: A Life of Sylvia Plath*. Boston: Houghton Mifflin.

Strathern, Andrew. 1977. "Why Is Shame on the Skin?" In John Blacking, ed., *The Anthropology of the Body*, 99–110. London: Academic.

Swift, Jonathan. 1986. *A Tale of a Tub and Other Works*. Ed. Angus Ross and David Woolley. Oxford: Oxford University Press.

Taylor, Mark C. 1995a. "Hautlandschaften/Skinscapes." *Arch+* 129/130 (December): 57–66.

———. 1995b. "Überlegungen zur Haut/Reflections on Skin." *Arch+* 129/130 (December): 113–14.

Tellenbach, Hubert. 1968. *Geschmack und Atmosphäre: Medien menschlichen Elementarkontaktes*. Salzburg: Müller.

Tepl, Johannes von 1947. *Death and the Ploughman*. Trans., ed., and intro. K. W. Maurer. London: Langley and Sons.

Thévoz, Michel. 1984. *The Painted Body*. New York: Skira/Rizzoli.

Theweleit, Klaus. 1993. *Männerphantasien*. 2 vols. Reinbek: Rowohlt.

Thorne, Tony. 1991. *Bloomsbury Dictionary of Contemporary Slang*. London: Bloomsbury.

Tibon-Cornillot, Michel. 1979. "Von der Schminke zu den Prothesen: Elemente einer Theorie zwischen dem Außen und dem Innen des Körpers." *Tumult* 2:25–46.

Tilles, Gérard. 1995. "Histoire des bibliothèques médicales et des musées des hôpitaux de l'assistance publique à Paris: L'example de l'hôpital Saint-Louis." Thesis, Université de Paris XII.

Tilles, Gérard and Daniel Wallach. 1996. *Le musée des moulages de l'hôpital Saint-Louis*. Paris: Doin.

Turner, Terence S. 1993. "The Social Skin." In Catherine B. Burrough and Jeffrey David Ehrenreich, eds., *Reading the Social Body*, 15–39. Iowa City: University of Iowa Press.

D'Urbano, Alba. 1995. "Das Projekt: Hautnah." *Die Zukunft des Körpers I, Kunstforum* 132:90–93.

Valery, Paul. 1960. *Oeuvres*. Ed. Jean Hytier. La Pléiade, 2. Paris: Gallimard.

Venot, Bernard. 1977. *L'écorché*. Catalog of the Musée des Beaux-Arts, Rouen. Rouen, n.p.

Vigarello, Georges. 1988. *Concepts of Cleanliness: Changing Attitudes in France since the Middle Ages*. Trans. Jean Birrell. Cambridge: Cambridge University Press.

Virilio, Paul. 1994. *Die Eroberung des Körpers: Vom Übermenschen zum überreizten Menschen*. Munich: Hanser.

———. 1995. "Von der Perversion zur sexuellen Diversion." *Die Zukunft des Körpers I, Kunstforum* 132:194–196.

Voltaire, François Marie Arouet. 1878. "Essai sur les moeurs et l'esprit des nations." In *Oeuvres complètes de Voltaire*, vol. 12. Ed. L. Moland. Paris: Garnier frères.

de Voraigne, Jacobus. 1993. *The Golden Legend*. Trans. W. G. Ryan. Princeton, N.J.: Princeton University Press.

Wagner, Gustav and Wolfgang J. Mueller. 1970. *Dermatologie in der Kunst*. Biberarch, Riss: Basotherm.

Walker, Alice. 1983. "If the Present Looks Like the Past, What Does the Future Look Like?" In *In Search of Our Mother's Garden: Womanist Prose*, 290–312. San Francisco: Harcourt.

Walther, Elfriede, Susanne Hahn, and Albrecht Scholz. 1993. *Moulagen: Krankheitsbilder in Wachs*. Dresden: DHM.

Weigel, Sigrid. 1991. "Der Körper am Kreuzpunkt von Liebesgeschichte und Rassendiskurs in Heinrich von Kleists Erzählung 'Die Verlobung in St. Domingo.' " In Hans Joachim Kreutzer, ed., *Kleist-Jahrbuch 1991*, 201–217. Stuttgart: Metzler.

Wideman, John Edgar. 1988a. *Damballah*. New York: Random.

———. 1988b. *Sent for You Yesterday*. New York, Vintage.

Wiegman, Robyn. 1995. *American Anatomies: Theorizing Race and Gender*. Durham, N.C.: Duke University Press.

Williamson, Joel. 1980. *New People, Miscegenation, and Mulattos in the United States*. New York: Free.

Wind, Edgar. 1987. "The Flaying of Marsyas." In *Pagan Mysteries in the Renaissance*. New Haven: Yale University Press.

Winnicott, D. W. 1953. "Transitional Objects and Transitional Phenomena: A Study of the First Not-Me Possession." *International Journal of Psycho-Analysis* 34:89–97.

Wollina, Uwe and Karin Wollina. 1990. "Zur Darstellung Hautkranker in der Frührenaissance: Franciscus Petrarca 'Von der Arzney bayder Glück.' " *Hautarzt* 4:519–521.

Woolford, Kirk. 1995. "VRB?" *Die Zukunft des Körpers I, Kunstforum* 132:188–193.

Wulf, Christoph, ed. 1997. *Vom Menschen: Handbuch Historische Anthropologie.* Weinheim: Beltz.

Wurmser, Léon. 1981. *The Mask of Shame.* Baltimore, Md.: Johns Hopkins University Press.

———. 1986. "Die innere Grenze: Das Schamgefühl. Ein Beitrag zur Über-Ich-Analyse." *Jahrbuch der Psychoanalyse* 21:16–41.

———. 1993. *Die Maske der Scham: Die Psychoanalyse von Schamaffekten und Schamkonflikten.* 2d ed. Berlin: Springer.

Wyss, Beat. 1996. *Der Wille zur Kunst: Zur ästhetischen Mentalität der Moderne.* Köln: DuMont.

Zaera, Alejandro. 1995. "Zwischen Gesicht und Landschaft/Between the Face and the Landscape." *Arch+* 129/130 (December): 96–102.

Zanger, Jules. 1983. "Speaking of the Unspeakable: Hawthorne's 'The Birthmark.' " *Modern Philology* 80, no. 4 (May): 364–371.

Zardini, Mirco. 1994. "Pelle, muro, facciata/Skin, Wall, Façade." *Lotus International* 82:38–51.

Zedler, Johann Heinrich. 1961. *Großes vollständiges Universal-Lexikon.* 64 vols. Graz: Akademische Druck- und Verlagsanstalt.

Zingerle, Ignaz. 1989. *Kinder- und Hausmärchen.* Innsbruck, 1852. Reprint, Hildesheim: Olms.

Zizek, Slavoj. 1997. *The Plague of Fantasies.* London: Verso.

Index

Boundary metaphors, skin: body as house, 25–28; clothing, 24; of experience, 19; feelings as, 23; and gender structure, 22; individualization, 18; prison as, 20–21; self-protection, 21–22; shelter as, 20; spirit, 18; of violence, 19
Büchner, Georg, 31, 34
Buffon, Georges-Louis Leclerc du, 145, 147, 150, 171
Burns, facial, 246n. 3. *See also* Facial descriptions

Cage, body as, 126
Calenzuoli, Francesco, 49
Capital punishment, dissection and, 71
Captivity, skin as, 36, 237
Carus, Carl Gustav, 200
Castle of My Skin (Lamming), 170
Cavalieri, Tommaso, 96
Certeau, Michel de, 41
Children, descriptions of skin of, 107
Chris (Aziz and Cucher), 31, *32*
Christian tradition: Adam and Eve in, 90; body as house in, 27, 29; flayings in, 63; sense window in, 28, 29; sinfulness of woman in, 139
Circulation artérielle veineuse et lymphatique de l'intestin (Susini), *50*
Cixous, Hélène, 208
Climate theory, of skin color, 150
Clinic, world's first skin, 57
Clinical medicine, and perception of body, 10. *See also* Anatomy; Medicine
Clinique de l'Hôpital Saint-Louis (Alibert), 54, 55, *56*
Clothes: Franz Kafka on, 250–51n. 1; naked bodies as, 98
"Clothes" (Kafka), 111–13, 250–51n. 1
Color, etymological roots of, 175
Color, skin. *See also* Skin tone: absence of, 168–69; in African American discourse, 163; in African American literature, 15, 183; climate theory of, 150; coding of, 122–23; determination of, 153; and ethnic difference, 15; and history of science, 145–154; interpretation of, 11; in literature, 103, 105, 106, 154–62; "Malphagi membrane," 148; and odor, 159; phenomenon of, vii; phlogiston theory, 151–53; preference for, 177; and racial identification, 143;

social, 164; white-black paradigm for, 145, 253n. 1
"Colored," 147, 148
Coloredness, of African skin, 161
"Color fetish," 180
"Coloring," in African American literature, 183
"Colorism," 169–70
Communication: concept of, 227; dependence on skin of, 11–12; teletactile, 227; touch in, 222, 224
Concealment: dialectic of, 239; skin as agent of, 17, 110
Concentration camps, German, 81
Condillac, Étienne Bonnot de, 195, 197, 198, 200, 240
Conditio humana, skin as, 134
Confessions (Rousseau), 84
Contact. *See also* Communication; Touch: dependence on skin of, 1, 11–12, 236; feelings and, 187
Container: female body as, 89; skin as, 85, 94; skin ego as, 119, 243–44n. 5
Coronation of Richard III, The (Jahnn), 35
Corporeality, phenomenology of, 200–201
Corpse, as spent house, 246n. 9
Cosmetic medicines, 102, 250n.10
Cosmetic practices: cultural history of, 102; surgery, viii
Cover, skin as, 23
Cucher, Sammy, 31
Culture. *See also* African American culture; History, cultural; Western culture: poetics of, 2; role of skin in, 11
Cutaneous sensation, 202
Cutaneous senses, 185, 240; active *vs.* passive, 198; anthropology of, 186; one-dimensional reduction of, 226; in virtual reality, 222
Cyberprojects, 226
Cybersex, 6; computer-directed, 226; installations, 224
Cyber SM-Projekt (Stenslie and Woolford), 224, *225*

Dagognet, François, 7
Damballah (Wideman), 176
Danton's Death (Büchner), 34
"Darkness," in African American literature, 183

EUROPEAN PERSPECTIVES

A Series in Social Thought and Cultural Criticism

Lawrence D. Kritzman, Editor